THE REALIT
REALITY SHOW BUSINESS PLANS

THE REALITY OF REALITY TV
Reality Show Business Plans

- Step-by-Step
- Worksheets
- Sample Plans
- Distribution
- Marketing
- Funding
- Press Releases

- Treatments
- One Pager
- Episodes
- Pitching

Dr. Melissa Caudle

A Publication by On the Lot Productions, LLC
New Orleans, LA

On the Lot the Lot Productions, LLC
Publisher since 2005
www.onthelotproductions.com

™ is registered trademarks of On the Lot Productions, LLC (Logo created by Melanie Bledsoe)

Distributed by Create Space Amazon.com

ISBN – 978-1460916988

Cover Designed by Dr. Melissa Caudle

Graphic Logos for all reality shows in this book created by Dr. Melissa Caudle and are Copyright Protected

Cover Photo by Salvatore Vuono
Author Picture by Robert Zaning of Zaning Portrait Studios
Introduction Photo by Salvatore Vuono
Chapter 1 photo by Bulldogza
Chapter 2 photo by Dr. Melissa Caudle
Chapter 3 photo by Salvatore Vuono
Chapter 4 photo by Salvatore Vuono
Chapter 5 photo by Salvatore Vuono
Chapter 6 photo by Graur Razvan Ionut
Chapter 7 photo by Salvatore Vuono
Chapter 8 photo by Salvatore Vuono
Chapter 9 photo by Salvatore Vuono
Chapter 10 photo by Carlos Porto
Chapter 11 photo by Renjith Krishnan
Chapter 12 photo by Renjith Krishnan
Chapter 13 photo by Renjith Krishnan
Chapter 14 photo by Pixomar
Chapter 15 photo by Dr. Melissa Caudle
Chapter 16 photo by Pixomar
Chapter 17 photo by Simon Howden and Graphic Page Dr. Melissa Caudle
Chapter 18 photo by Simon Howden
Chapter 19 photo by Dr. Melissa Caudle
All other photos taken by Dr. Melissa Caudle

All photos in the book have been used with the permission of their copyright owners and/or www.freedigitalphotos.net

Printed in the United States of America

THE REALITY OF REALITY TV

REALITY SHOW BUSINESS PLANS

BY

DR. MELISSA CAUDLE

TABLE OF CONTENTS

TABLE OF WORKSHEETS

Note: All worksheets are available in an format of 8 X 10 in *The Reality of
Reality TV Workbook* by Dr. Melissa Caudle available from Amazon.com,
CreateSpace e Store, www.onthelotpruductions.com, CreateSpace Direct,
Barnes and Noble and other online and retail outlets.

ACKNOWLEDGEMENT

We are the sum of our parts.

DISCLAIMER

Dr. Melissa Caudle, On the Lot Productions, LLC nor the publisher cannot gauruntee that by following the information in this book will obtain any source of funding for your project.

This book was written for educational purposes only and not as legal, tax, or accounting advice. We cannot be responsible for any documents that you formulate as a result of this book. We cannot take any responsible with what the reader does with the informaiton we provide and any documents the reader produces should be reviewed by a qualified entertainment attorney in the state in which you live. Each state has unique laws.

Likewise, only an attorney can give legal advice and only an accountant can give financial advice.

SPECIAL THANKS

There are many people that I need to thank in their support and encouragement. I'm really afraid that I will miss someone and hurt their feelings. Believe me that is not my intent. So I'll apologize now to anyone that I  may not personally mention because in realty there are so many of you. I am truly grateful and proud to be in your company and listed along side of you on films, television shows and documentary films. Each has in a way guided my path.

I want to express my gratitude to my mentors and to all that have challenged me who include Line Producer Beau Marks and Director/Screenwriter Steve Esteb. Both have a special place in my heart for helping me to develop into the producer I am today.

The next group includes my peers and those that I have worked with on numerous films and reality shows. I would be remiss if I didn't mention by name J.P. Prieto who I met on the reality show *The Girls Next Door* and who I still today value his opinion. Next is my co-producer on *Dark Blue*, Dave C. Kirtland who encourages me to produce quality over quantity and his wife Tracy Davenport who supports me in every way she can.

I have to thank my siblings - Denny, Caylen and Robby who always encourage me to be my best. To Denny, as my brother and as a co-writer, thank you for writing such a funny stage play *The Names Have Been Changed to Protect the Innocent* that made it easy to adapt into the screenplay *Auditing Richard Biggs*. To Caylen who always tries to bring out the best in me as big sisters do. To Robby who always encourages me to be my best and to write. She placed the initial challenge and idea for me to write this book as she did with my very first book I wrote back in 1990.

Auditing Richard Biggs

I have to mention by name my parents. My Mom, Helen Ray, is the most encouraging person I know and I am lucky to have her as a mother. She not only taught me valuable lessons in life but also how to find joy in my life. I'm proud to call her my mom and she is one of my very best friends. Because of her and her unconditional love I was able to have the same kind of relationship with my daughters. So, thank you Mom. Likewise, my Dad, William Ray, without question, if he were alive today

Dr. Mel's Parents and Siblings 1961

would be very proud of me for what I have accomplished. He would have said, "You go girl" and then told me a joke that I wouldn't understand. He gave to me my love for film as we spent many all nighters watching the old black and white classics and all of the musicals we could get a hold of. He passed the love of the arts to me and I now hope to leave my legacy. Thank you Dad and I know you are still at my side. I love you both.

I also want to thank my immediate family who has always supported me no matter what and providing the encouragement that I at times need. First to thank are my three daughters, my three sons-in-law and my three grandchildren. As the saying goes, "Great things come in threes." Each daughter reflects a different part me. Erin represents my educator and writer side and keeps me grounded to help others as she is a third grade teacher. Kelly represents my business side always guiding me in business and marketing matters as she is a business woman. My youngest, Jamie, represents my creative side in the television and film industry as she is an actress in Los Angeles.

To my three sons-in-law that I consider as the sons I never had. Thank you for marrying my daughters and but fathering my three grandchildren. Dimi, Erin's husband, is my consult and guides me in financial matters – he's the moneyman. Roger, Kelly's husband, always has my back on productions and pitches in anywhere he can. He has operated the camera, wrangled extras, and poor baby, suffered through as a production assistant with the three playmates during Mardi Gras on the reality show *The Girls Next Door*. Shear torture from a mother-in-law don't you think? Next, is Hannuard, Jamie's husband, who also supports me, always has words of encouragement for me, and allows me to confide in him. Actually, I can confide in all of my daughters and sons-in-law. I am truly blessed that I have the three girls and their husbands that I consider not only family but friends.

I wish to express my love for my three grandsons, Stamatis, Elias and Roger who are so dear to me. They are without exception the joy of my life and bring such happiness. When all else fails, their little arms reach up to me and their smiles simply melt all my troubles away. Many a page in my books was written with at least one of them at my side.

Dr. Mel with oldest grandson Stamatis hard at work.

Finally yet importantly, to my husband and my best friend, Mike, who always allows me the space and time to fulfill my dream.

PHOTO CREDIT FOR SPECIAL THANKS
Dr. Melissa Caudle's photo taken by Tim Moree'
Dark Blue Poster by On the Lot Producitons, LLC
Poster of Auditing Richard Biggs designed by Zach
Dr. Melissa Caudle with Grandson Stamati taken by his mother

INTRODUCTION

DON'T SKIP READING THIS. YOU NEED TO KNOW

Has someone ever come up to you and said, "You ought to be in a reality show or you should take your act on the road?" Or did they just came right out and asked, "Have you ever thought of doing your own reality show?" Maybe, it was you that said it to your group of friends and family. There was some moment that arrived and made you believe that you could make a reality show or you wouldn't be reading this book. It could have happened anywhere or at anytime. You sat back, pondered the crazy moments in life and then thought, "I'm going to do it. I am going to create my own reality show."

If you feel like I do, you don't want to make a great reality show only to condemn yourself to self-distribution on YOUTUBE or Vimeo. You want it to be on television. You want millions of people to see your show and talk about it the next day at work or at school. Thus, the dilemma arises. How do you take your concept of a reality show and get it funded and get the attention of television networks? Easy, create a great business plan, get funded, go into production and get a distribution deal.

If only creating your show would be that easy everybody would have one. Thank goodness it's not because there wouldn't be any room for your show. The difference is that you are now in the mood not to just think about it, but to do it. You bought this book didn't you? That means you're committed to making your show. That's right. You're reality show created by you for the world to see. Let me be the first to welcome you into the reality show business.

ABOUT THIS BOOK

So, why are you wasting time reading this book? Get out there and get filming. Oh, you can't. You don't have the money, the complete concept, the equipment or a way to get it on television. No worries reality show creator. This book is here to help you make your dreams come true. Read it from cover to cover with due diligence, apply yourself in the practical applications sections, and by the time you have followed the step-by-step guide you will have the necessary foundation and knowledge to create your reality show proposal ready to submit to investors and television executives. Keep in mind that you will be able to create a business plan and two other types of packets. The first is what is called a Reality Show Pitch Packet and the second is an EPK or Electronic Press Kit. They are really one in the same. These packets have everything in them that your business plan will with the exception of budget. That is the only difference.

Think of your reality show business plan in terms of parts. That way it doesn't seem overwhelming and you can take it one step at time. That's what I do. If I had to think of a business plan as a 25-50 page document and look at a white blank monitor screen for hours and have nothing on it, I'd be rather stressed out too. But, when I know the formula and what goes where, it is a lot easier to create them. I do them all the time from the contents to the graphics.   I'm going to share my secret formula with you so you too can write your own business plan and make sure you have all of the components. The reality show business plan includes:

1. The Cover
2. The Confidentiality Agreement
3. Table of Contents
4. The Executive Summary
5. The Logline and Synopsis
6. The Structure of the Show
7. The Cast Members
8. The Production Team
9. Production and Production Schedule
10. The Market
11. Product Placement
12. Distribution
13. Marketing Strategy
14. Investment Opportunity
15. The One-Pager
16. The Budget
17. The Appendix with Resumes, Letters of Intent, Tax Incentives, and News Clippings

NOTE: The packet without The Budget is a Reality Show Pitch Packet or EPK Package. You will need to label your document accordingly.

PURPOSE OF THE BOOK

The purpose of this book is to guide you on a step-by-step journey in developing either your reality show business plan or your reality show pitch package. It is going to be a journey of doing and not just thinking.   It will provide you with the necessary tools to generate your reality show idea in the event you don't already have an idea, give you the tools to write an effective business plan tailored specifically for your reality show concept, guide you in the steps of seeking pre-distribution and how to contact television networks.

Each chapter examines different concepts in formulating your reality show and will assist you later when developing your reality show business plan or pitch package.

GOOD NEWS AND BAD NEWS

How many times in your life has someone started a conversation by saying, "You want the good news or the bad news first?" I'm not going to be any different. I have good news and bad news about this book.

The good news is that I am going to provide you information nobody else in Hollywood wants you to know. It is a must have book for any reality show creator, director or producer. I'll use dozens of statements from real reality show business plans. I even provide a complete example of a reality show business plan in the Appendix. The bad news is that although I am providing this information you have a lot of work ahead of you and there are no easy ways out. Just because I'm providing you with a template and samples of reality show business plans, you can't just copy them and substitute my name and my show titles for yours. You have to develop your plan specifically for your show. The samples I have provided may or may not fit into your genre category for your show; therefore the wording will be different.

Here is a case in point. I'll never forget a friend of mine, I'll call her Natasha to obscure her real identity, came up with a wonderful concept and an idea for a reality show. She told me she had tried to pitch her show to another friend of hers that worked for a major network in the development department. Although they were friends, the friend at the network couldn't help Natasha because she didn't have the "Bible." In Hollywood they often call business plans for pitching ideas "The Bible." Anyway, because Natasha didn't have the document they weren't interested. She asked her friend if she could make a copy of a plan so she could at least see what was in one. By now, you have probably guessed that he wouldn't and couldn't because of confidentiality.

Natasha then searched and searched the internet to find what she needed to do. Nothing was out there in cyberspace. I think you already know this and that's why you purchased this book in the first place. But now it's time for the moral of this story.

Natasha knew that I had produced reality shows and asked if I knew what "Bible" everybody was talking about. "Of course," I said. She replied, "Will you send it to me?" She is a really good friend so I obliged the request. What I didn't know was that she took my plan and literally copied it verbatim. The only things she changed were the title, her name in the place of mine, her company instead of mine and that was it.

The problem with Natasha copying my reality show plan was I had created a reality show based off a documentary for men who had been exonerated from death row called, *Living Out Death Row*. The concept of this show was to follow former death row inmates on re-establishing their lives in the community. Her show is more like *Big Brother*, a surveillance-voyeurism genre reality show where the cameras would never leave from the area where she was filming and she would need to have cameras rolling 24/7. It was to be about a group of rich spoiled teens experiencing the wilderness for the first time by camping out for two weeks with no access to fast food, cell phones, music, television or the internet.

Nothing between our shows matched and nothing made sense. The structure of our shows was different. Our investment needs were different. She was seeking 100% funding and probably needed at least one million dollars to pull this off, while I only needed an additional $75,000. Big difference isn't it? I maintained a different level of return on investments from her. Additionally, I am a producer/director; whereas, she didn't direct and needed to obtain a director.

Natasha's business plan she created which was almost identical to mine didn't work. Oh, she got her network friend to read it but he had to put it in file 13 and wouldn't send it up the ladder for consideration. Why? Because it didn't make sense for what she was planning on doing. That's why I stress that you must complete this book and all the practical applications so your business plan matches your concept and designed specifically for your project. YOU CAN'T JUST COPY MINE. That's the bad news.

Now here is some good news for you again. What you can do is copy my format. It is the same format that Hollywood insiders prefer to read. YEA! You can also copy all of my headings, sub-headings and structure. You can even copy some of my wording if it is considered standard wording. I give you permission to do so since you bought my book and won't charge you extra. I will make it perfectly clear when it is appropriate to do so. To save you time I have developed a Microsoft Word Document Template that you can purchase separately from this book at my website www.onthelotproductions.com. The template will provide you the structure you need and save a great deal of time having to format your document or having to type in standard wording. You won't have to spend hours plugging in the outline and structure into your document. It's all there for you. Believe it or not, I use this template every time I write a reality show business plan.   My philosophy is why invent the wheel when the wheel is already turning.

HOW TO USE THIS BOOK

To get the most out of this book take it one chapter at a time and absorb the contents. After each chapter apply what you learn immediately while writing each section tailored to your show. Don't wait until you finish reading the book to begin writing your reality show business immediately after chapter one.

In each chapter I explain each section of the business plan one topic at a time. I guide you through the process of writing that  section, provide examples from actual reality show business plans and then provide you with a practical application section put what you just learned into action. It is during the practical application section that I get you to start developing your plan one step at a time. I urge you to complete these practical applications and keep them in a notebook binder as you complete them. And, **DO NOT** discard them. You will refer to them often in your journey to complete your reality show business plan.

This all sounds exciting doesn't it? That's because it is. You are now ready to cross the threshold of doing and not just thinking about creating a reality show but become a creator and producer. From here on out, adopt the mantra, "I'm a doer and not just a thinker."

WHY YOU SHOULD BUY THIS BOOK

If you are want to become a creator and producer of a reality show then you have to buy this book. Why? Because it will make achieving your goal of creating your reality show a whole lot easier. It's your guide on how to do it, how to get funding, and most importantly it is the only book of its kind that provides the details for writing a reality show business proposal. It gives you the necessary format that Hollywood Insiders are demanding from you. Why spend hours upon hours trying to figure it out the structure only to discover that you can't find any information on the topic? No one wants to share the information with you. I often feel that it's a very elite club that nobody will invite you into. I've done the research for you. I've laid the groundwork. And as a matter of fact, I follow my own advice and have produced three reality shows and have written dozens of reality television business plans for others following the method and format I present in this book. Learn from a professional in the business of producing reality shows.

You should also buy this book because it is written in layman's terms and is easy to read and easy to follow. It's not filled with rhetoric to simply fill the pages and increase the length. In fact, I tried to limit the number of pages so I wouldn't use up so many trees.

You should also buy this book so you can contact me. That's right. I'd love to hear from you and discuss your plans. Who knows, it could lead to a co-production project like I did with my reality show *Ace Mechanic*. The star of the show contacted me through my company On the Lot Productions, LLC because he wanted to create his own reality show. The problem was that he was a mechanic and not in the business of production. When he found out that in order to present his idea to the television networks, he was lost. He had no idea what they were talking about. He turned to me to write the business plan for him. So I did and during the process fell in love with the concept of the show. Guess what? I produced it. I'm not saying that by buying this book will get me on board with your project, but I am available for consultation. E-mail me at drmelcaudle@gmail.com. Oh, I don't accept unsolicited material or concepts there is a way to send them to me that I address later in this book. So keep reading.

WORKBOOK AND CD THAT GO WITH THIS BOOK

After the three focus groups met to discuss this book one of the biggest feedbacks I received was they wish there was a workbook available for the practical applications. People also wanted me to publish a reality show template for use. I listened and responded to their suggestions and feedback. Thanks to them, both are available for purchase in addition to this book.

The Reality of Reality TV Workbook assists a reality show creator in applying the Practical Application Sections of this book. I recommend that anyone buying this book should also invest in this workbook. It comes in an 8 X 10 format and allows you to fully participate in the Practical Application Section with ease.

The workbook is available from Amazon.com, CreateSpace eStore, www.onthelotpruductions.com, Barnes and Noble, CreateSpace Direct, and other retail outlets (ISBN: 978-1460921593).

The Reality of Reality TV Word Template is a Microsoft Word template that I E-mail to you that is also available for purchase. I recommend that you purchase this template when writing your reality show business plan. There is no need to invent the wheel and it will save you hours of time in formatting your reality show business plan or pitch packet.

The template that accompanies this book is available by emailing me or contacting me through my website at www.onthelotproductions.com.

The Reality of Reality TV DVD Series is in production. This will be a series of videos where I teach you the process of writing reality show business plans. All topics covered in this book will be addressed as well as conversations with me with other reality show creators and producers.

Stay tuned as this series develops as it will be made available from Amazon.com, CreateSpace eStore, CreateSpace Direct, Barnes and Noble, www.onthelotpruductions.com, and other retail outlets.

150 Ways to Fund a Reality Show, by Dr. Melissa Caudle, is a book that provides ways to raise money to produce a reality

show. These methods have been used by the author and shared with others. Also in the book are additional marketing strategies.

Available from Amazon.com, CreateSpace eStore, www.onthelotpruductions.com, Barnes and Noble, CreateSpace Direct and other retail outlets (ISBN 13- 978- 460967133 or ISBN 10- 146096715).

The Reality Show Handbook by Dr. Melissa Caudle is an essential book for reality show producers in that it provides all of the forms necessary to produce and create a reality show. Forms included in this book include developmental arc of a reality show, contracts for creator, cast and crew, safety guidelines, hold harmless agreement, location release, personal releases, product-placement agreements and more. A must have for any reality show producer. This book is available at Amazon.com, www.onthelotproductions.com, Amazon.com CreateSpace eStore, CreateSpace Direct, Barnes and Noble and other retail stores (ISBN-10:1461075319).

CHAPTER 1

THE BIG IDEA

If you're reading this book, chances are you have probably either already examined the notion of creating a reality show or you have even already shot a pilot and you don't know the next step. So now what? You have to package your idea, get financing to produce the series and sell it to the networks.

Making a reality show is fun. And, yes it is very hard work. It's not for those that give up easily. It takes drive, determination, planning and persistence. I am a strong believer that those that fail to plan, plan to fail. It's up to you to decide on which category you want to fall. For me, I'll take planning to succeed on any given day. Producing a reality show is a whole lot different from making a movie or directing a stage play. First, you don't have a script; therefore, you don't know the outcome. Second, they are a lot shorter. Well maybe not when you consider a single season reality show season an average of 13 episodes. Lastly, you don't have to shoot on 35 mm film camera now that pro-consumer high-definition cameras are available to producers at an affordable rate. The Canon XH-A1 is a perfect example of an affordable camera. I have shot three reality shows on this camera and the quality has been exceptional. This camera provides the option to shoot footage at 24 frames per second, just like film. Add a shotgun microphone, a couple of lights, a green screen, and editing software and just about anyone can become a creator and producer of a reality show.

There are numerous advantages to producing a reality show over a television series or feature film. The lower cost is enough for me considering feature films can cost anywhere from $10 to $44 million dollars to produce. Likewise, a high action pack drama or comedy series episode can cost an average of $1.6 million dollars. I don't know about you, but I don't have that kind of money.

Reality shows can be made far less expensive which in terms of economics - more bang for the buck. I helped produce one reality show, eight episodes and a sizzle reel, for $50,000. For

my first reality show I produced four episodes and a sizzle reel for $3,500. It's possible and with a little creativity and the right contacts I think you can do the same. If I believe in you why don't you believe in yourself?

Now let's talk about the script. What script? Exactly. For the most part reality shows are unscripted; thus, you don't have to write a screenplay to start shooting. Do you remember during the writer's strike of 2007 and 2008? All television programming shut down with one exception – reality shows. Even news programs continued to air because they in essence are reality.

So, why not produce a reality show with all of the advantages they have to offer? Come up with an idea and yours could be the next big reality show.

THE BIG IDEA

Topics for your reality show are endless. They are wide-open ranging from following your friends around, finding a celebrity to be the star, demonstrating something spectacular like cooking, highlighting your profession, to hiding and capturing hidden moments. Any topic and any subject are fair game as long as the people in your show agree to participate and sign off on it in a Letter of Intent. That's the easy part. The difficult part is getting your reality show on television. There is a process. So, let's begin.

DECIDING ON THE SUBJECT MATTER

As with any reality show, the first step is deciding on what I call the "BIG 5 Ws" or who, what, when, where, and why. We all

learned these big five "Ws" in elementary school and now after years of wondering why you had to acquire this useless knowledge in the first place you are finally going to get your chance to find out. You needed to learn them in order to create your reality show. At last you know the

answer. You probably would have paid more attention to your fourth grade teacher had she told you that in the beginning. But back when I was in elementary school reality shows didn't really exist. So like you I didn't pay attention either. Now I do. Each time I develop a new reality show I do so based on the "Big 5 W" structure. In no time, I have created an entire concept from start to finish by addressing them. You will too and with a little practice you'll be creating shows instinctively and without hesitation.

Now, let's examine the big five "Ws." I'll begin by taking the time to explain the importance of each and the necessity of learning them now as adults to impact your reality show.

Who?

Without exception all movies, television shows, screenplays and novels are centered on the noun who. Without knowing who the show is about it would be of no interest to audience

Danny Lipford and Dr. Mel

members. One of the very first reality shows to hit the networks was *Today's Homebuilder* starring Danny Lipford. His show detailed how to remodel and repair your home. He started a very small show in Mobile, Alabama and once it was syndicated became a network sensation. Today HGTV has multiple shows around this same concept. Lipford was a trend setter before reality shows became a trend.

Take a minute and think about some of our favorite reality shows. Who is the show about that keeps you coming back? Who is it that captures your attention? Who in it do you love to hate or hate to love whatever the case may be? Who do you like? Who do you want to be like? Who makes you sick at your stomach? Who as a reality star is constantly the target of late night talk show hosts in the form of jokes?

You get the picture. The answers to the above questions center on someone or some group. Take another moment and reflect on these people. In researching for contents of this book I conducted an unofficial and very non-scientific research survey.

I went to my local mall and stopped more than 100 shoppers, male and female and from ages eight to eighty-three. Not one shopper couldn't list or identify at least one reality star. That's fantastic odds when you bat 100 percent.

Dr. Mel with the future reality stars at NATPE

Now it's your turn. What reality stars can you list? Offhand you probably have thought of the sisters in *Keeping up with the Kardashians*; e.g., Kim, Khloe and Kourtney. Maybe, Snookie and The Situation are the first reality star names that popped into your mind from the infamous *Jersey Shore*. Then there are the rock star reality families that dominate the airwaves such *Black Sabbath's* lead vocalist Ozzie along with his wife and kids. Sharon Osborne has gone on to be a judge on the summer sensation *America's Got Talent* while daughter Kelly made her debut on *Dancing with the Stars* and often appears on the series *Fashion Police*. *The Osbornes* may have not been renewed but each have benefitted from their participation. The other family, the famous *Kiss* foursome in *Gene Simmons Family Jewels* still airs today.

Now reflect on the competitive reality shows where normal people compete to win a prize such as *The Amazing Race* or *Survivor*. We can't overlook Tyra Banks and all of those beautiful girls wanting to become models in the reality show *America's Next Top Model*. Both shows created "stars" out of normal people just like you and me. How many reality stars can you list? Two? Four? Eight? Twelve?

Did you identify at least one reality star? Good. These are names that we all know and these shows are based off of people, some famous prior to the show and some made famous because of the show. The point is these reality shows are based on "who" was a part of the show. Without the "who," there would be no show. In other words, no one would be the star.

What?

Simply put, ask "what" the reality show is about. This is a wide-open topic and includes more than star or group of people. It's about what the show is like. The environment you film these cast members is the key; and in relationship to this section we are describing the type of genre your show falls into or the "what."

There is an array of "what" in reality television. In essence, there are a myriad of unique genres. The global explosion came between the years 1999-2000 with the hit reality shows *Big Brother* and *Survivor*. I'll never forget the first airing of *Survivor*. I had my own segment on the CBS morning news affiliate station in New Orleans, LA called *Family Matters with Dr. Mel*. Every morning when I arrived at the station the buzz about *Survivor's* episode the night before was the only thing the producers and floor directors wanted to talk about.

When my show started, which was a live call in segment that began at 6:30 a.m., the callers went crazy over *Survivor*. They too wanted to get my opinion. I had to learn quickly about realty television or I wasn't going to survive. I consider this a funny little twist on life. If you would have told me back then that in 2011 I'd be a reality show creator and producer and write a book on the topic I would have laughed at the thought and told you that you bordered on the verge of insanity.

The genres of reality shows are numerous. Table 1-1 provides an overview.   Familiarize yourself with this table as you will refer to it often throughout this chapter and the rest of the book.

Table 1-1 Reality Show Genres

Documentary *Temptation Island* *Road Rules* *Voices of the Innocent*	**Game Show** *Who Wants to Be a Millionaire* *The Weakest Link*
Life Drama *The Secret Millionaire* *Bad Girls* *16 and Pregnant*	**Dating Shows** *The Bachelor* *Flavor of Love* *For the Love of Money*
Special Environment *Temptation Island* *The Lofters*	**Celebrity** *Dancing with the Stars* *Anna Nicole* *Darren: Sharper Than Ever*
Competition *American Idol* *Project Runway* *So You Think You Can Dance* *Live to Dance*	**Surveillance** *Big Brother* *The 1900 House* *Road Rules* *Wife Swap*
Talk Shows *The Oprah Winfrey Show* *The Tyra Banks Show* *The Jerry Springer Show*	**Professional Activities** *Miami Ink* *The Ace Mechanic* *Face Off*
Paranormal *Ghost Hunters* *Scariest Places on Earth* *Paranormal State* *Celebrity Paranormal State*	**Makeover or Renovation** *Biggest Loser* *The Swan* *Supper Nanny* *Made* *Charm School*

(Note: Not a complete list)

Documentary Genre

The documentary style type reality show follows the day in a life of someone like *The Osbornes*. This sub-genre documents the lifestyle of the cast highlighting the good with the bad. Producers attempt to cultivate the most interesting moments and will often sensationalize them to increase ratings.

One example is on the reality show shot in New Orleans,  *Stephen Seagal: Lawman*. It chronicles Seagal who has been a Jefferson Parish Deputy Sherriff for more than 20 years. Up until his show, he flew under the radar in his capacity as a deputy sheriff and at times even worked with the Jefferson Parish Swat Team. This is the same police department that I used to consult with on gang members when I was a high school

Stephen Seagal filming in New Orleans, Louisiana

principal. Another story I'll have to save for another time. That is how small of world this is. Anyway, the producers capture Seagal responding to police 911 calls as he rides around in a black SUV with the Sherriff of the Jefferson Parish Police force. How unreal is that? The producers sensationalize the smallest violation of the law and have Seagal come to the rescue to protect the citizens of Jefferson Parish. They almost have viewers believe that someone who ran a red-light might be a serial killer. Since I live in Jefferson Parish I guess I should sleep better knowing Seagal is out there on the streets.

Just last week, I found myself having dinner with the Sherriff that Seagal runs with and some fellow political leaders in our community. It was a no-brainer that the concept of reality television surfaced as did the making of my next film *Dark Blue* starring Tracy Miller and Lance Nichols. My company, On the Lot Productions, LLC is co-producing this film and since it is about cops, a rogue morally inept one at that, they found it interesting. You never know when real reality will present itself as real-life drama in your own life.

Game Show Genre

The sub-genre reality game show involves a competition against others for an ultimate prize as in the show *Survivor.* In other shows the contestant can be an individual, as in *Who Wants to be a Millionaire* or team members such as in the *Biggest Loser* or *Shedding for the Wedding.* I better add computer to the list of possible contestants since the appearance of Watson, the IBM computer contestant on *Jeopardy* who competed and won against two humans - Ken Jennings, record holder for most consecutive wins on Jeopardy, and Brad Rutter, record holder for winning the most money on a US syndicated game show. There is slight hope for humanity since Watson missed his final *Jeopardy* question on day one of the competition, "Its largest airport was named for a World War II hero; its second for a World War II battle." Both Jennings and Rutter answered "Chicago," while Watson messed up and guessed "Toronto."

As for all game shows a substantial prize awaits the winner.

Life Drama Genre

In many reality TV programs producers have a cameraman shoot as if they were the fly on the wall to convince viewers that they are stepping into the private life of an individual or group. That is how the terms *docusoap* and *docudrama* were developed. There are also reality shows that follow drama like *America's Most Wanted* or *EMS*. These shows fall into the category of life drama genre.

The Girls Next Door reality show could be considered a Life Drama Genre with a touch of celebrity in that the show captures the lives and events around the three playmates Holly, Bridget and Kendra. For instance, the girls came to New Orleans for

Mardi Gras. The first night in New Orleans, the girls went to the *House of Blues* to attend a charity event at for Brad Pitt's foundation *Make it Right* that benefited the areas of the city hardest hit by Hurricane Katrina 2005. Kendra is pictured to the left with Rockin Dupsie. Later that evening the girls auctioned off a variety of different items, including a tour of the Playboy Mansion. At end of the benefit, the girls presented a $30,000 check to Pitt's foundation.

The next day Bridget and Kendra were extremely sick with the flu, which happened to be Fat Tuesday. I was presented with one of the greatest challenges in producing reality television. I had to find French Onion soup on Mardi Gras day for the girls and get it to them as fast as I could. In New Orleans, everything shuts down on Mardi Gras. Nobody gets in or out of the French  Quarter and all stores with the exception of bars are closed. So this really was a huge challenge. If I couldn't find the soup, we wouldn't be able to finish the episode featuring New Orleans. Fortunately for me I have connections with many of our five star restaurants in the city and *Mr. B's* was able to provide the soup on a moment notice for the girls. The soup did provide the magic cure. Bridget was able to get out of bed, followed by Kendra and then Holly. The three of them partied all night after a quick recovery.

Before leaving New Orleans, the girls took a tour of one of New Orleans oldest cemeteries followed by a visit to the Lower Ninth Ward. They saw all the homes that were completely destroyed during the hurricane. It was extremely emotional for the girls to see all the devastated homes that were not rebuilt and they made the comment that the trip to New Orleans was worth it and very rewarding because they couldn't believe the devastation of the city without seeing it for themselves.

Dating Show Genre

To add to the variety of reality TV programming dating shows surfaced as a popular sub-genre. Although dating shows aren't an original program idea, shows like *The Bachelor* and *The Bachelorette* became a top choice of viewers. I consider *The Bachelor* a spin-off to the seventies show *The Dating Game.*   On *The Bachelor* it became evident that the public loved to tune in to see who was going to be kicked off and who would continue to capture the heart of  the bachelor. Numerous spinoffs from this show resulted such as *Hell's Date, Blind Date*, and *Tough Love* where Drew Barrymore came on as one of the producers.

On the flipside are reality shows such as *Cheaters*.   *The Newlywed Game* was also originated and brought back to life from the seventies and resulted in spin-offs such as The *Millionaire Matchmaker*. I remember at 12 years-old watching my brother and his new bride compete on this show. They didn't win but my introduction to reality shows began at that moment. Things haven't changed in forty years. Somehow audience members love to be matchmakers. This clarifies the popularity of dating style reality shows in today's market. Dating reality shows went global into Canadian and British markets and a big hit with both men and women of all ages.

Special Living Environment Genre

Special living environment reality shows such as *The Colony* are  also popular and attractive to viewers. Although audience viewers know from the beginning that the situation isn't real they watch the show as if they were and are fascinated by them. As an experiment that assisted in my preparation in writing this book I

Photo by Dr. Mel while on the set of *The Colony: Season 2*

signed up to be an extra for *The Colony* season two. It was a quick $80 dollars each day to observe others in the reality show business make a reality show in a different genre than what I produce. I got paid to learn my own craft. I consider that amazing to get on the job training and they pay you. It's really not a bad strategy to follow.

The Colony operated on the premise that an airborne virus is killing off the world's population. It was Armageddon in 2010. The Colonists were instructed to behave accordingly as if they were the last survivors. I played the part of one of 30 marauders who invaded the colonist's compound on several episodes. We raided them, destroyed their compound and on the next to last episode set the colony on fire. It was fascinating watching the main cast in action as I was in the thick of things. I'm used to watching through a monitor in video village. This time, I was upfront and on camera.

The Colonists, as did the Marauders, embraced the reality of the special environment created by the producers. In this case an area of St. Bernard Parish in Louisiana just outside of New

Orleans. The area used for the show was one of the most devastated areas struck by Hurricane Katrina in 2005. Five years after Katrina the area hadn't been touched and it looked like the day after the levees broke. This location was perfect for an apocalyptic reality show. The Marauders had a clear advantage - we were informed by the director beforehand the twist for each episode. All the same, when my friends and family watched the show they really got into it as if the situation of a deadly viral outbreak truly existed.

Surveillance or Voyeurism Genre

One of the most well known genres in reality programming is categorized as surveillance or voyeurism such as *Big Brother* and *The Real World*.   In these shows viewers are attracted to watching life as it happens. It almost has the same effect as when the fictitious audience in the movie *Truman* was so caught up in Jim Carey's character. The same holds true in this genre. Usually cameras will run 24/7 to capture everything that goes on in the house or situation. The audience becomes the fly on the wall so to speak. That is why the show *The Jersey Shore* is so popular.

Celebrity Style Genre

Say what you will about Hollywood, but they are in the money making business and they find ways to make it. One example is tapping into the celebrity world. This  year's cases in point - the new casts for ABC's *Dancing with the Stars* and Donald Trump's *Celebrity Apprentice* on NBC. Kirstie Alley, Sugar Ray Leonard, Ralph Macchio, and my playmate Kendra among others are attached to *Dancing with the Stars*.   Like some before them, they hope that this one show will put new spark in their otherwise crashing careers.

Donald Trump's *Celebrity Apprentice* announced Gary Busey, David Cassidy and LaToya Jackson.   The cast is proving to be a mix of high strung tempers with mediocre talent and skills as they make their way through the challenges that the judges of the dancing show Trump provides. What's interesting about *Dancing with the Stars* and *Celebrity Apprentice* they both have found away to tap into the celebrity reality world without paying the high sums of money often demanded by celebrities.

Stars like Meatloaf and Lisa Rhina, like those on *Dancing with the Stars* are using Trump's reality show platform to kick start their career. I think it is reasonable that some may succeed in their quest for re-stardom. My money is on Ralph Macchio who rose to stardom in the original *Karate Kid*. He already has a background and an attitude for comebacks.

As viewers we watch reality shows because somehow without explanation we are curious to see what these celebrities will do once they are out of their comfort zones. It's important here to note that *Dancing with the Stars* and *Celebrity Apprentice* aren't the same type of a reality show as those that feature a single celebrity. There is a crossover into the competition genre. Shows like *I'm a Celebrity Get me out of Here* and *Dr. Drew* fall into this category. A true celebrity style show features one celebrity such as *Anna Nicole* and *Kendra*. They provide viewers a chance to get into the private lives of those they watch on television or in films.

Why people are attracted to celebrities I'll never understand.  Maybe as an audience we want to identify with them. We consider them friends or somebody we know very well. Hollywood uses these as their weapons. I've worked with some of Hollywood's best including actors Kate Bosworth, James Marsden and James Woods. I celebrated James Marsden's birthday with him along with Kate

Kate Bosworth and Dr. Mel Bosworth while we all were working on the Sony film *Strawdogs*. And just the other night, I called James Woods at midnight to discuss the possibility of him being in my next movie *Dark Blue*. Without exception each eat, sleep and drink just like we do. Nevertheless, audiences love to watch reality shows when it's about a celebrity.

Professional Style Genre

Reality shows can also revolve around professional activities shows such as *Miami Ink* and *Cops*. People love to watch others at work. That is why one of this year's newest reality shows, *Undercover Boss* is such a hit. Other shows such as is *Billy the Exterminator* are following suit. Last night at the wrap party for one of my films, I ran into Wayne Morgan, a colleague in the

Wayne with the Girls

Louisiana Film Industry who founded the H.U.R.D Network and Louisiana Produces, organizations for filmmakers and actors in Louisiana for the purpose to network. Wayne and I have been friends for more than 10 years and he came out to support my film. During our conversation he mentioned to me that *Dog the Bounty Hunter's* producer was looking at him and his friends for a reality show on Security Guards. You see, Wayne is also a security guard for celebrities that come into New Orleans. In fact, I used him and his people to protect Kendra, Bridgette and Holly while we were filming *The Girls Next Door* during Mardi Gras. This only supplants my belief that reality shows around a profession are in high demand.

Leading the race as the top professional genre of reality TV are cooking shows. We all complain about them and we swear up and down that we don't watch them but deep down, they are a guilty pleasure. *The Chopping Block* airs on NBC but came from the land down under. The Australian version of the show was hosted by Matt Moran and Catriona Rowntree. The premise was that two Australian restaurants were reviewed secretly, they would then be given $5000 Australian dollars and 72 hours to revamp their menu

at which point they would be judged by the food from the new selections. NBC picked up the rights to the show and produced an American version hosted by Marco Pierre White. The US version has a different format with multiple contestants competing in an objective based format with a heavy emphasis on competition.

The Emmy award winning reality series *Top Chef* airs on Bravo. Several contestants at the same time complete different food based challenges which are then judged by a panel of well established chefs. This has been by far one of the most successful cooking shows to date.

SyFy Channel is jumping into the cooking genre frying pan this year with their newest reality show starring last year's *Top Chef* Winner. SyFy unveiled the new reality series, *Marcel's Quantum Kitchen*, featuring molecular gastronomist Marcel Vigneron, one of America's most notorious chefs who is on the cutting edge of the culinary field. *Marcel's Quantum Kitchen* follows Vigneron as he begins to explore the potential next phase of his career – to stay at Bar 210 in Los Angeles or break away into a private catering company.

During each episode, a demanding client hires him to pull off extraordinary events and celebrations. Based on the clients' requests, Vigneron dreams up a menu for the event ranging from a dinner party for extreme sports enthusiasts to a "dinner in the sky" themed-party -literally held in mid-air. The new series debuted on March 7, 2011 with minimal ratings and bringing a strong debate with it. Some say the show is not a cooking show because they are not trying to instruct anybody on techniques of cooking or sharing recipes. Rather, If you take the show at face value - a reality show about a very unusual chef and his crew - and bring with it a "how did they do that?" attitude, you will likely find *Quantum Kitchen* entertaining. That is, if you're not put off by the wealthy clients that hire Marcel to make his culinary magic, or by Marcel himself.

Next Food Network Star airs on The Food Network. Winners of this show get as their grand prize their own reality show. Unfortunately for them with one or two exceptions they usually get a lousy time-slot.

Iron Chef America is one of the most popular cooking shows around today. Hosted by Alton Brown this show originated from the Japanese version of *Iron Chef.* The concept of the show is similar to a boxing match straight from the movie *Rocky* - a professional competitor chef who challenges one of the *Iron Chefs* to a cast iron meltdown.

Hell's Kitchen airs on Fox hosted by celebrity chef Gordon Ramsay. Ramsay uses harsh language and is very short tempered. His high strung perfectionist attitude leaves many competitors in tears as they just don't measure up to his expectations.

Competitive Style Genre

Competitive reality shows began to become popular the day after *Fear Factor* aired its first episode. Competitive type shows such as *Project Runway, Survivor* and *America's Next Top Model* provide audiences a chance to get behind certain cast members

 to see them succeed. I believe that as viewers we like to cheer for everyday people and watch them overcome obstacles. In a way we identify with these people. For this type of reality show a big prize awaits the winner as each contestant must go through numerous challenges. Shows in this genre have also created celebrities who have gone on to get their own show and status.

A good example of this is for the show *Tabatha's Salon Takeover*. Tabatha first appeared on the reality show *Shear Genius* hosted by Jaclyn Smith of *Charlie's Angels*. Tabitha didn't win the season she was on but was adored by the viewers. They voted her as "The Audience Favorite" resulting in Bravo green-lighting her own reality show.

Paranormal Style Genre

We can't leave out the paranormal reality shows such as *Ghost Hunters*. In this style of genre supernatural and paranormal activity are followed and the cast of the show attempts to either prove or disprove the existence of each phenomenon. *Paranormal State* airs on channel A&E and follows members of the Paranormal Research Society.

Ghost Lab airs on Discovery Channel. This paranormal show features the crew of everyday paranormal run by Brad and Barry Klinge. They travel the U.S. in a Mobile Lab. *Ghost Adventures* airs on the Travel Channel. Each episode is one hour long. Follow Zak Bagans, Nick Groff and Aaron Goodwin, as they get locked down during each episode and provoke the spirits to interact with them. My favorite episode was done at the Eastern State Penitentiary on death row.

Ghost Hunters International airs on the SyFy channel. Each episode is one hour long. This is a spin-off from the original *Ghost Hunters*. Led by Robb Demarest, this investigative group travels the world to find cases. Investigations have includes

Chillingham Castle and the forgotten underground city of Mary Kings Close.

Makeover or Renovation Style Genre

Makeover shows such as *The Biggest Losers* and *Shedding for the Wedding* attract viewers which bring out a certain element in the programming to see change in people. In this type of show someone or something goes through a transformation. Some shows in this category have failed miserably such as *The Swan* which featured total transformations with cosmetic surgery.

Shows dealing with design or home improvement seem to be the most popular and fall into the category of Renovation. These shows not only demonstrate to viewers how to fix home repair problems but provide advice to spice up living environments. *Design Star* which airs on HGTV is similar in design as the *Next Food Network Star*. The contestant's or designers compete for their own reality design series. *Design on a Dime* also on HGTV shows viewers how to redecorate any space with $1,000 or less.

Extreme Makeover: Home Edition airs on ABC. This show selects a family that needs a new home and coordinates with local contractors to completely overhaul the family's current house. Many other design shows became very popular and have audience appeal. From shows such as *Trading Spaces* and *Design Star* new shows were created and multiple spin-offs. Former

Design Star winner, Emily Henderson, continued to capture audience appeal in her spin-off series. In fact, almost all of these are now in syndication in the domestic and foreign market. It doesn't look as if this genre will die out anytime in the near future.

Closure to Reality Show Genre

Take a moment and look at the following Table 1 -1 on page 17. Pay particular attention to the "what" of each reality show listed in the table and reflect as to why each reality show was placed in a particular genre. Did you identify any crossover into a different category? Sometimes a reality show can.

When?

There are two elements of "when."   The first element is seasonal; whereas the second is time. Several questions should be addressed by a reality show producer. When would it be better to film the show? And, should the show be filmed in the spring, summer, winter, or fall? There is no one correct answer. It depends on the type of show and when it should air to attract the most viewers and have a chance at garnishing high ratings.

For instance, reality shows on the topic of best beaches for a summer vacation, scuba diving or training future Olympic

swimmers, you don't want to film them in the summer, but in the winter, so it can be aired in the summer. Viewers associate swimming as a summer sport. Another example is *Skating with the Stars*. This show is shot during the summer for winter broadcast.   Viewers associate ice skating as a winter sport.   However shows on topics of snowboarding or a show where seven people live together in a ski resort would be filmed during the winter months but would have to air the following year during the winter time. That is why seasonal reality shows aren't such a great hit because the return on the investment is delayed because of the time of year the show can be released for maximum viewing.

In contrast, consider *America's Got Talent*. This is a summer program geared for summer season ratings. For the most part school is out and older audiences want something for entertainment to fill a void in re-run programming that often occurs in the summer. This show is filmed in the winter for summer viewing. For some shows it won't make a difference when they film it as long as you as the creator and producer have at least visited the topic.

The second element of "when" is relevant to the time of day and I'm not talking the time of day a network should air your program. I'm talking when the camera should be turned on. A creator must consider the most effective time to make it believable to the audience. Should it be shot at night or during the day? Should cameras operating 24/7 or only during optimal moments designed by the producer? As in *Survivor*, it  is important to film the competition game portion during the day; whereas, the segment of the tribal council at night when they extinguish the torches. The tribal council segment wouldn't be as effective if shot at high noon. Would it? *Big Brother* has cameras rolling all the time. The producers never know when something air worthy will happen. Timing is critical and elements in *Big Brother* are unpredictable.

More predictable in nature are competitive reality shows such as *American Idol*. Cameras roll at pre-determined segments and not catch what happens in the house where the contestants live. I personally think the producers have missed a great reality show concept by not doing so. However, cameras roll during rehearsals when contestants are mentored by the producers, during live performances and with the feedback session when Ryan Seacrest announces who goes home. All of these moments have been pre-designed by the producers to carry out the developmental arc of the show. This is an important aspect to consider when you design your show.

Where?

Location. Location. Location. And did I mention location. This is the most important element in discussing "where" the reality show should take place. Sit back for the next 30 seconds and think you of favorite reality show. Ask yourself what attracts you to the show in relation to the location. To bring this point home, let's examine the competitive reality show, *Project Runway*. Where, or in this case the location, is this show is

filmed? It takes place in a design studio in New York. This is a very important aspect to the show especially when viewers tend to associate New York City with Fashion Week. This show wouldn't work if it were located in Midland Texas or Baton Rouge Louisiana. Nobody associates these two cities with fashion. I think of cowboys and hayrides when I reflect on Midland and swamps and LSU football for Baton Rouge.

Now consider *Survivor* and *The Amazing Race* and where they are filmed. Wow. Can these shows get any better in the location department? I don't think so. They go all over the world and bring the world into our homes. They are exciting for us as viewers to watch. On the other hand, reality shows such as *Miami Ink*, which are classified as professional reality shows, won't work anywhere but in a tattoo studio. In this case, Miami or the city isn't the key. The show could be filmed in any city the world but only in a tattoo studio. This show would not work if they filmed the show in someone's house or apartment. It just wouldn't be the same nor have the same vibe.

I have filmed several reality shows and films in New Orleans. It is a remarkable city that offers a variety of locations. The key in deciding on the location is to ask, "Is the location suitable and reflect the concept of your reality show?" That is why *Hoops: Life off the Court* was decided that it had to be filmed in Kentucky. That state is known for the love of basketball. My show *The Baker Girls: Sealed with a Kiss* is being shot in New  Orleans but it really doesn't make a difference as to location. It could be shot in any city. In this case, I chose the city that was the most economical for the production. Louisiana offers powerful tax incentives to film in their state and there are plenty of qualified crew and actors available. Besides, with me living in the area there are no transportation or lodging expenses by hiring local.

Why?

Why? Why? Why? The ultimate "W" of the big five Ws is why. You as a producer or creator of a reality show have to ask several questions. Why am I producing this show? Why would people care? Why is the show of importance? Why I tell you;

the reality show will make a difference to someone, somewhere, sometime and for some reason. It could be as simple as saying the show is of importance because it raises the awareness of what tattoo artists go through or why some people choose to get tattoos as in the case of *Miami Ink*.

It could have a personal impact on a young teen girl who may be victim of an online predator and she said "No" after watching an episode on *The America's Most Wanted*. In this case, the "why" of the producers wanted to bring to the attention of the viewers the nature of child predators and help put a stop to this crime. That's a huge why.

In dating type reality shows or surveillance type shows such as *The Bachelor* or *Big Brother* the "why" is shear entertainment. Producing a reality show for entertainment purpose is perfectly fine as long as you as a producer understand "why" the show is being filmed and can relate that to investors in your reality show business plan.

Again, reflect on some of your favorite reality shows listed in Table 1 on page 17. Try to understand the "why" behind each reality show to grasp an understanding of the importance of this "W" and the significance this area holds for your reality show.

YOUR SHOWS 5 "Ws"

Now that I have got you thinking it's time to get really creative and get your thought process working on creating your own reality show. Have you already come up with a concept and title or do you need to do it? If you have, then you are already ahead of the game. If you haven't, gut it up and think of one right now. To accomplish this task do a little brainstorming. Study the reality show genres presented in this chapter and decide which type appeals to you. If you can't decide, put the genres in a hat and randomly select one. By doing so you at least narrowed your genre. And since you purchased this book to learn how to write a business plan for a reality show, you might as well make it count and create a real one. Don't waste valuable time by going through the motion – actually create a reality show. Darren Sharper, five-time Pro NFL and New Orleans Saints Super Bowl champion, manager Darryn Dewalt told me at the beginning of this year that in order to achieve you must stop just thinking about doing things but actually do them. He has been with Sharper for 14 years and given him good advice. Why don't you take the same advice and move forward toward achieving your goal of creating a reality show business plan.

CHAPTER SUMMARY

In this chapter you learned that there are several advantages to creating and producing a reality show rather than a feature film or drama series. Reality shows are cost effective having smaller budgets and crews which equates to more revenue for the television network from advertising. You also learned that there are a many genres in reality television such as: game show, documentary, dating, talk shows, makeover or renovation, paranormal, surveillance and voyeurism, celebrity, professional and competition. Lastly, you learned that all reality show concepts are based on the big five elements of "W" – who, what, when, where and why?

PRACTICAL APPLICATION

The following Practical Applications will assist you as the creator or producer of your reality show to focus on the genre, subject matter and cast of your reality show by applying the big five "Ws." Be sure to start your three inch binder with dividers. You will be starting to prepare your foundation for your reality show.

1. Re-examine Table 1 on page 18. Take time to research at least one show in each category and get an understanding of why that show was placed in the particular category.

2. Using Worksheet 1 add as many reality shows to each genre that hasn't been listed in that genre. The more shows you add, the more you will become familiar with the different genres of reality shows.

3. Use Worksheet 2 to generate your reality show concept.

4. Use Worksheet 3 to answer the questions on the worksheet as it pertains to **YOUR REALITY SHOW CONCEPT**.

Note: The Reality of Reality TV Workbook is available in an 8 X 10 format available from Amazon.com, CreateSpace eStore, www.onthelotpruductions.com, Barnes and Noble, CreateSpace Direct, and other retail outlets. It is the perfect companion to this book and includes all of the worksheets in this book as well as additional forms needed to create a reality show.

PHOTOGRAPHY CREDIT FOR CHAPTER 1
1. Light-bulb for opening chapter by Filomena Scalise/FreeDigitalPhotos.net
2. Keyboard with Question Mark by Filomena Scalise/FreeDigitalPhotos.net
3. Photo of Danny Lipford and Dr. Mel taken by Harold Callaway
4. Photo of Dr. Mel and Madhouse Wrestlers taken by Sonia Pastronelli *Family Matters with Dr. Mel* created by Melanie Bledsoe
5. Photo of Stephen Seagal taken by Dr. Mel Caudle while on set of *Stephen Seagal: Lawman Season 2*
6. Photo of Happy Couple taken by Graphic Artist African
7. Photo of the raid on The Colony compound taken by Dr. Mel Caudle on set of *The Colony: Season 2.*
8. Photo of Kate Bosworth and Dr. Mel Caudle taken by Michelle Tonges, personal assistant to Kate Bosworth.
9. Photo of Wayne Morgan with Playmates taken for Wayne Morgan
10. Photo of Chef in the Kitchen taken by Simon Howden
11. Picture of Jamie Alyson (America's Next Top Model Applicant) taken by Haunard Uribe
12. Photo of Ghost in the Hallway used with permission from freedigitalphoto.net
13. Photo of Renovated Kitchen taken by Dr. Mel Caudle
14. Photo of Scuba diver taken by Healing Dream Photography
15. Photo of Bird and the Sun taken by AKA RAKING DOMS
16. Photo of Sunset taken by AKA RAKING DOMS
17. Photo of the Crescent City Connection in New Orleans taken by Geoffrey Ramsey.
18. Photo of Tattoo Guy taken by Katie Lane

WORKSHEET 1:   REALITY SHOW GENRES

Objective: To identify types of reality show genres.

Review Table 1 and add reality shows currently on television to the appropriate genre.

Documentary	Game Show
Temptation Island	*Who Wants to Be a Millionaire*
Life Drama	**Dating Shows**
The Secret Millionaire	*The Bachelor*
Special Environment	**Celebrity**
Temptation Island	*Dancing with the Stars*
Competition	**Surveillance**
American Idol	*Big Brother*
Talk Shows	**Professional Activities**
The Oprah Winfrey Show	*Miami Ink*
Paranormal	**Makeover or Renovation**
Ghost Hunters	*Biggest Loser*

WORKSHEET 2: CONCEPT DEVELOPMENT

Objective: To identify working concept of your reality show.

Reality Show Project Working Title: _____

REALITY GENRE *(Check the genre that best identifies your reality show)*

☐ Documentary   ☐ Game Show   ☐ Life Drama

☐ Celebrity   ☐ Professional   ☐ Paranormal

☐ Dating Show   ☐ Makeover   ☐ Competition   ☐ Talk Show

POTENTIAL CAST *(Check the DESCRIPTION that best identifies your CAST)*

☐ ONE CELEBRITY   ☐ INDIVIDUAL   ☐ TWO MAIN CHARACTORS

☐ MULTI-CELEBRITIES ☐ MULTI-GROUP   ☐ MORE THAN TEN PEOPLE

LOCATION *(Check the DESCRIPTION that best identifies your CAST)*

☐ **House**   ☐ **Business**   ☐ **Studio**   ☐ **Wilderness**   ☐ **Other**

Describe: _____

PROJECT IMPORTANCE

☐Tells a story   ☐ Teaches Something   ☐ Social Issue

☐ Entertaining   ☐ Someone Wins   ☐To Change a Life

☐ Political   ☐ To Hook up People   ☐Makes a Celebrity

WORSHEET 3: THE BIG 5 Ws

Objective: To identify the Big 5 "W's" for your reality show.

Every good reality show starts with a great concept which includes the Big 5 Ws which includes who, what, when, where, and why. To help generate your own reality show concept, complete the following brainstorming exercise. If you are producing the show yourself generate as many ideas as you can. If you have producing partners, each should complete the exercise and then discuss it and finalize one worksheet that combines the group ideas.

Who is this reality show about?

_____
_____
_____

What will the show be about?

_____
_____
_____

When will the show take place?

_____
_____
_____

Where will the show take place?

_____
_____

Why is this show of interest to others?

_____
_____

NOTES

Write any thoughts or reflections about what you learned in this chapter.

CHAPTER 2

REALITY SHOW BUSINESS PLANS

What the heck is a reality show business plan? It's the document you'll create to get funding and distribution for your reality show is what it is. The problem is Hollywood insiders inform you that in order to be considered for distribution or funding you must have a business plan for your reality show, also called "The Bible," but they won't tell you what goes in one. I'm taking it that since you picked up this book you don't have a clue as to what a reality show business plan or "Bible" is or what one looks like much less what you need to put in it and you're looking for answers. Relax. You've come to the right place.

There are no boilerplate templates for you to use; however there is a standard format with standard contents. Each reality show is uniquely different and range from 20 to 65 pages. The plan must be comprehensive but at the same time succinct. The main goal is to impress investors and network executives enough to green-light your show. It's called green-light in honor of our stop light system. Green is for go!

It took a lot of interviewing Hollywood Insiders before I got to the level where I could write reality show business plans that met their specifications. The biggest frustration came at my expense because nobody in Hollywood would or for that matter could tell me what they wanted included. Go figure that one out. Insiders had the audacity to tell me my plans weren't want they wanted or needed to make a decision; yet, when I asked how I should revise them they couldn't tell me.

Nobody knew what to tell me because at the time I started in this business reality shows were just booming. Television executives didn't understand what they needed either so they couldn't translate it to others. Somewhere stuck between what I was doing and what they wanted wasn't working. I took my clue from the definition of insanity – doing the same thing over and over and getting the same results. In the beginning the results were negative because reality show creators tried to apply the same format they had used for years for feature films and screenplays, but weren't getting any results. Why? Plans formatted in the same structure as plans for feature films don't work for a variety of reasons.

First, business plans for feature films are based from a script. In a reality show there isn't one because they are unscripted. But you still had to present something written from nothing but a concept in order to get funding and distribution.

Second, reality show concepts weren't like TV episodes. TV episodes are scripted unlike reality shows. It wasn't until I sat down with several different network executives that I ascertained what they were looking for. Picture this. There I was sitting at a prominent Hollywood insider's desk. He kept throwing pitch packets one after the other in the trash. It angered him because he was desperately looking for a good quality show idea but couldn't get pass the poor presentation pitch packets.

He couldn't believe the stupidity of people. "How can they submit trash like this?" he asked as he threw another packet into the garbage. I picked up several of the packets out of the trash to review them. Obviously I didn't want to submit a packet in the same format he considered substandard. At least I'd know that much by having examples of what not to do. I challenged him to tell me what was wrong with them. He kept saying the writers weren't giving him enough information on the conceptual design. In order to make a decision to green-light a show he needed more information than a page or two outlining how someone thinks a show should go or a list of 100 ideas of what they think should be included. "None of those matters," he said. "I want specifics, comparisons with other shows, how this show will be structured." That's when the light flashed in my head. It was like a scrolling marquee. He needed comparisons with other shows. He needed to know who was making the show. He ultimately needed structure that business plans for screenplays provide but addressed toward the unscripted format of reality.

Dollar signs flashed before my eyes. I remember the exact moment when I thought, "I can do that." All I needed was that one nudge from one insider. He un-intently provided me the format for reality show business plans that he and others like him were seeking but didn't know or want to tell me. As a result, I went home from that Los Angeles meeting with new clarification and direction. Within one week I wrote my first reality show business plan, called my executive friend and asked him to take a look. Guess what? He loved the format and the red light changed to green. It took about three years before I sat down and wrote this book for others after several of my producing friends were also at a standstill and needed the information.

I still wonder to this day if this deep dark Hollywood insider secret was in fact a secret or was it that nobody wanted to share the information because of the competitive market of reality shows.   I'll probably never know the answer but I don't really care because I figured it out. I felt like a champion fighter winning my first championship. I was Rocky Balboa, little me from New Orleans unraveling one of the deepest secrets in Hollywood history. I took pride in the fact that I knew what nobody would or could tell me. The Hollywood Insider secret now is out of the bag. Now you won't have to spend $7,500 to have me or somebody else that knows the secret to write a plan for you because you can do it yourself. So take a look at the first part of a reality show business plan – The Cover.

The Cover

The Cover of all reality show business plans has five sections. Each item placed on the cover page is placed for a reason. It's not to fill up the space, but to identify to potential partners, co-producers, possible investors, and product placement professionals the following key information:

- Type of business plan.
- Name of the person who prepared the document.
- Name of the show.
- Copyright information.
- Investment opportunity.

Look at Diagraph 2-1 on the next page. It is the front cover to a reality show that I created called *Hoops: Life off the Court*. It's very simplistic in nature but there is a method to my madness. It follows the five aforementioned sections. In fact, it is an example of a standard front cover for all reality show business plans. You can adjust each section for the best presentation and eye appeal. Make it look great and take up the entire page. To format the front cover:

- Type in the type of plan on the top line.

- Space down and identify the creator of the project and who wrote the business plan.
- Center the show's logo in the middle of the page Space down.
- Space down and put the copyright information along with the WGA registration number.
- Space down and put risk statement and confidentially statement.

Diagram2-1 Cover Sheet for Hoops: Life off the Court created by Dr. Melissa Caudle

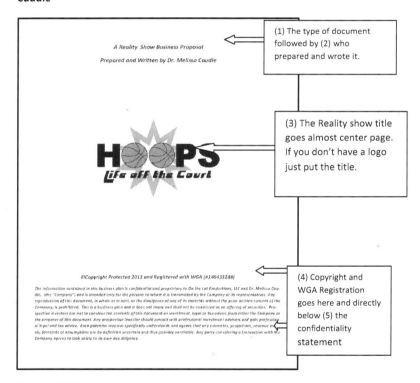

Type of Plan

The first line in diagram 2-1 distinguishes that the document is a reality show business plan. There are different types of business plans an executive or producer can review - a screenplay, a documentary, TV pilot and a reality show. So, tell your readers and distinguish one plan from the other. The only other variance is the Pitch Packet or EPK Package which is shorter to the reality business plan and budget information has been removed. Keep this in mind if you are only going to submit your plan in order to get an option on your project. If so, the networks will decide on the budget and document you generate will be called a reality show proposal not a business plan. By titling your document correctly, it allows the reader to immediately discern that the plan is not for a screenplay, novel, or a treatment, but it is a reality business plan or pitch packet. This section usually is placed on the third line of the document with the standard terminology, "A Reality Show Business Proposal."

I have made the mistake of not distinguishing my document as a reality business proposal and the plan never reached the correct department. Television networks have many different development departments and if your reality show business plan document lands in the creative department for television pilots or film development, they are so busy they are likely to put your reality show business plan in file 13 and not forward it to the right departmental executive. Therefore it is essential to clarify the type of proposal to avoid it ending up in the wrong hands.

The Creator and I Don't Mean God

Once you have clearly identified the type of document you have written, directly under that and centered inform the reader who not only prepared the document but who also is the creator and/or production company. In some cases this could be more than one person. For instance, I could prepare your business plan for you, but you provided the concept and created the project. Then I would be listed as the person who prepared the document and you as the creator. A way to word this is:

A Reality Show Business Plan
Written and Prepared by Dr. Mel Caudle
For
The Sisters, LLC
Created by Erin Alyson Kelly

By wording your title of the page in this format it clearly identifies who wrote the plan as well as who owns the concept of the show and the creator. This information also informs the reader who to contact if they have any questions or desire to enter into negotiation. Questions would be directed toward me as the writer of the plan and ownership questions would be directed at the production company representative. Some people put their phone number beneath their name. However, I find this distracting and place my contact information in two other places in the document. One place is on the One Pager and the next is on the contact sheet for investment opportunity. I will present more on both of these topics later in this book. I also always insert my business card. The best method is while you have the person in front of you put their phone number in your address book of your phone. That way you have it.

The Title

The next section of your cover sheet is the title of the reality show. I never submit a reality show proposal without some sort of graphic or at the minimum using a wild and crazy font for emphasis. Word processing programs nowadays have numerous fonts. Take advantage of them if you don't have the ability to create a graphic logo or to pay a graphics professional.

Additionally, there are many inexpensive graphic arts programs available and logo design programs that I found for less than $30. You can also take advantage of the numerous clip art programs. Since you are not publishing these documents the issue of copyright is not a concern as it is in publishing a book or article. Do a little research and add that spice to your reality show business proposal. Within no time at all you'll be creating graphics for your projects.

Adding the spice in the title is for one reason – it grabs the attention of the reader. Here is a case in point. Below are a variety of fonts and styles for the reality show I created called *Does a Name Make a Difference?*

Does a Name Make a Difference?

DOES A NAME MAKE A DIFFERENCE?

DOES A NAME MAKE A DIFFERENCE?

Does a Name Make a Difference?

Does a Name Make a Difference?

The only difference in the above examples is the style and size of font used. However, in my business plan, the title of my show stands out from the rest of the contents because of the difference in the font style. Now look at the same title but formatted into a graphic logo. It changes the dynamics and the presentation.

Now, examine two front covers for the reality show *Hoops: Life off the Court* in Diagram 2-2 and ask which one is more appealing and grabs your attention? Think about why you like one cover over the other and the merits of each.

Diagram 2-2 Sample Front Covers

Why does one stand out more than the other? It's the graphics and placement. One is more appealing to the eye. Can you determine what this reality show is about by simply looking at the graphics and title? If you guessed it is about a group of basketball players and what they do off the basketball court, you're right. That's the beauty of naming a reality show and having graphics. Keep this in mind as you formulate the title of your reality show. Make sure that both the title and graphics identify to the reader what your show is about. Narrow the title and don't make it too long.

There are many examples of current reality shows with great titles. Simon Fuller, the creator of *American Idol*, used two words as did the creator of *The Bachelor.* In both instances the titled clearly indicates the show's concept. Other shows have been successful using one word such as *Cops* and *Greed*.

On the flip side there are plenty of reality show titles with five words or less. In the end It's not the amount of words chosen for your title; it's whether or not the show clearly identifies what the show is about. Without having to watch many of the current reality shows now airing you can probably guess what they are about just because of their title.

Keep it Legal

The very bottom of the cover sheet references the legal issues of presenting a business plan for your reality show. Distributors, television executives, and producers want to know if you have covered your basis. They do not want to get involved with a project that they can't obtain the rights. They want to know and have assurance that you have the right to present the show to them and who owns the copyright. That is why it will be necessary once you have written your business plan to register it with the Writers Guild of America (WGA). The cost is minimal at $20. By registering your business plan it also protects you as the creator. Likewise, I always register my plan with U.S. Library of Congress. Again, it doesn't cost a great deal of money and you can do it for under $40. The WGA and copyright information goes below the title of the show. There is no definite line because it depends on the size of font and graphics for your title. I try to place mine about three-fourths down the page. The standard format and wording is:

COPYRIGHT © 2011   ALL RIGHTS RESERVED
Registered with WGA (the number)

The Confidentiality Statement and Financial Disclaimer

First and foremost I am not an attorney and I cannot give you legal advice. Only a lawyer can do that. Additionally, I'm not an accountant and can't give you financial advice. What I can tell you is that I was advised by my entertainment attorney to put two statements on my front cover. First my attorney advised me to make sure that I included a statement of confidentiality. Second, he advised me to always state that I am not offering securities and that I am not offering any potential investor advice on investments, taxes or legal advice and they must seek this out on their own. This way, anyone reading the business plan knows up front that they are to proceed at their own due diligence and seek professional advice. However, I did consult with my entertainment attorney and he informed me that there are a variety of statements that can be used to protect us and not break the law when presenting a reality business proposal. What I place in this book is only a guide and you should seek legal advice from an entertainment attorney in your area. However, for your convenience I have included the confidentiality statement that I used for *Hoops: Life off the Court* so you can gain an understanding of what the confidentiality statement looks like.

> The information contained in this business plan is confidential and proprietary of Hoops, LLC (hereafter, THE COMPANY) and is intended only for the persons to whom it is transmitted by the Company or its representatives. Any reproduction of this document, in whole or in part, or the divulgence of any of its contents without the prior written consent of the Company, is prohibited. **This is a reality show business plan.** It does not imply and shall not be construed as an offering of securities. Prospective investors are not to construe the contents of this document as investment, legal or tax advice from either the Company or the preparers of this document. Any prospective investor should consult with professional investment advisors and gain professional legal and tax advice. Each potential investor specifically understands and agrees that any estimates, projections, revenue models, forecasts or assumptions are by definition uncertain and thus possibly unreliable. Any

party considering a transaction with the Company agrees to look solely to its own due diligence.

CHAPTER SUMMARY

In this Chapter we covered the Front Cover of your reality show business proposal which included five main areas: the type of business plan, the preparer, who is the creator, the title of the show and legal ownership section with the confidentiality statement. We also visited why the use of graphics is important for the title of your reality show. Further the title should be target specific to direct the reader of the plan directly to the concept of the show. The chapter ended with the discussion pertaining to the legal issues of a business plan in terms of the confidentiality and risk statements. Formatting guidelines for The Cover Sheet were provided that adhered to the following example.

PRACTICAL APPLICATION

The cover sheet is very important. To start organizing yours complete the following practical applications to reinforce your knowledge.

1. Use Worksheet 4 to generate and finalize your reality show title.

2. Discuss with two other people that you trust, the concept of your reality show and your title. Write down their thoughts and ideas. A lot of times talking with others about your project generates new ideas for you to use.

3. Go to google.com and do a search for images of at least 10 different reality shows. Try to do a search within your own genre. Do you notice any similarities? If so, what? Is there a common theme in graphics? What about the colors they use for their graphics? Do they use one, two or three words in the title? Why do you think that is?

4. Using Worksheet 5 investigate the graphic for the reality show that I created and produced called *The Ace Mechanic*.

5. Now that you have named your reality show, get a little creative with it. There is no time like the present to play with your front cover of your reality show business plan. Use different fonts, colors, and add graphics. Print out your sample graphics and share them with friends and family for feedback.

6. After receiving feedback from friends and family on your logo, make the necessary changes. Print it out and add to your binder.

7. Using the formula and the sample from *Hoops: Life off the Court*, start your reality show business plan in Microsoft

word. Create your front Cover. Print it and add to your binder.

8. To gain further knowledge, research the importance of protecting what you write with the U.S. Library of Congress.

9. Visit www.wga.com and become familiar with them and their website. That way when you are finished with your business plan, you are already familiar with their site, what they do and how to find it.

10. If you come up with a really good title and graphics, copyright it immediately to protect it. Then send it to me. I'd love to take a look at what others have created by reading this book. E-mail me at drmelcaudle@google.com.

PHOTOGRAPHY CREDIT FOR CHAPTER 2

All graphics used in this chapter and logos were designed and created by Dr. Mel Caudle and are trademarks and copyright protected by On the Lot Productions, LLC.

WORKSHEET 4: TITLE OF SHOW

Objective: To create a title for your reality show.

The name of your reality show is important. Review worksheets 1-3 to refresh what your show is about. It is time to brainstorm your reality show's title by completing each section. You will generate a variety of titles ranging from one word to four or more. List as many as you can.

ONE WILL LIKELY BE YOUR TITLE.

ONE WORD TITLES	TWO WORD TITLES	THREE PLUS WORD TITLES

From the list above circle your top five choices.

From the top five circled choices narrow your title to two.

1. _____

2. _____

Now choose your title: _____

WORKSHEET: 5 GRAPHICS

Objective: To learn the importance of branding with graphics.

The graphics for your reality show is extremely important to have in your business plan. It needs to be simple, colorful and relate to what the show is about without anyone needing to read the logline or synopsis.

Review the following graphic for the *Ace Mechanic* reality show and answer the following questions.

What do you think this show is about?

Who do you think it is about?

Where do you think it was filmed; e.g. location?

ANSWER: The show follows a mechanic that is the very best at what he does. There is no automobile problem he can't fix. Other mechanics come to him for training and to solve problems they can't. It was filmed in an automobile repair shop located on HWY 603 in Mississippi.

CHAPTER 3

CONFIDENTIALITY

A Producers' and creators' worse nightmares are that the secret of their show will get out before it is time or their show will be stolen. I have heard numerous tales of these nightmares which were true. This past February I was at a "Pitch Fest" sponsored by La Nuit Comedy Theater in New Orleans. I was one of several expert panelist receiving pitches from hopeful film and reality show producers. During the Q & A session, the question was asked how to protect yourself from having your show stolen out from under you. Even the theater's owner recounted a story in which one of her ideas had been taken. In her case, the concept was the same but the way the show was spelt was changed. There wasn't anything she could do about it.

Unfortunately although you can copyright and register your title and contents of your business plan it is my understanding that you can't copyright a concept. The concept of a cooking show can't be copyright protected, but the specifics and developmental arcs of one show can.

Stealing someone's project doesn't happen often, but it is very important to have a level of trust and maintain confidentiality between you as the creator and the potential investor. There are no guarantees and no assurances. There are plenty of ideas and plenty of producers out there. And, at any given moment you could be coming up with the same concept or idea as someone else. Believe me, it happens. In fact, it happened to me. No kidding. NO! Wait a minute. Nobody stole my idea out from under me, I simply created a show, and before I could finish writing the business plan, there in front of me was the commercial on a network television for the same type of show. I was too late and obliviously it must have been a good idea because there it was. I know I hadn't pitched this project to anyone so it was impossible that my show was stolen. It only proves that somehow we both followed the same path with different results and we walked them side by side. I was just a little slow to the pitch.

Not to say this won't happen again, or a show of mine won't get stolen, as a way to protect myself I maintain a chain of who gets a copy of my business plans. How do I maintain this chain? Easy - every business plan I circulate, the person receiving it must sign a Confidentiality Agreement that I maintain on file. Also, my business plans are controlled copies in that every copy distributed is numbered in sequence.   This controlled numbering system is placed on the second page of the business plan. Diagram 3-1 demonstrates this process.

If there is any comfort at all the president of a large respected production company told me that people in his situation don't want to steal anyone's project. They just want to find good ones to produce.

THE CONFIDENTIALITY STATEMENT PAGE

A confidentiality statement is just that – a statement of confidentiality. It means that the person who signs the agreement agrees not to reveal any content of the business plan, the concept of it and upon request by the owner, in my case, the Limited Liability Company, return the copy immediately. There are several reasons for doing this. First, if for some reason, your show is stolen out from under you, you want to be able to prove who you spoke with about the project and who they were associated with. Next, a potential investor is probably going to ask you who has seen this packet and who you have pitched it too. The right answer should be less than five. Investors and television networks don't want to get involved with what is called an over pitched or cold project.

An over pitched or cold project is a reality show that you have taken just about everywhere and have been turned down. Ask yourself, "Why would anyone want to pick up a project that has been turned down by a dozen other people?" They don't. Even Simon Cowell had difficulties when he pitched *American Idol*. He went to every television station and was turned down with the exception of FOX. He recounted the pitching nightmare one night on the *Tonight Show* with Jay Leno. "I thought it would be easy to sell here in America," Cowell said. "It showed all the signs in Britain of being a success." He had just about given up when he got his green-light for the show on FOX. Cowell also said in an interview that by having pitched in throughout Hollywood to everyone he just about killed the show before it got started. Over pitching is bad and could ruin your chances. Also be wary of telling investors that you have twelve other companies interested in the project. You might think this is a selling point but in reality it puts your project on ice and very cold. It is a turn-off to them.

I am always very careful in what I say to any potential investor or television executive about who is or is not interested in my project. Hollywood insiders have strong egos and they can get their feathers ruffled very easily. They want to feel the importance of being first. Your excitement or your development team's excitement can become your downfall. By placing too much information out for the world to see could ruin your chances. You might think that by posting a trailer on Youtube or Vimeo and grabbing the public's attention would help you but in fact it could ruin your chances in multiple ways. First you just violated confidentiality and non-disclosure by putting a trailer on the internet. Your hot project just became cold. Next, if your show is picked up you could have copyright video of circulating on the web and once on is almost impossible to remove. It's best to keep things low-key with actual video footage. This is not the same as going viral with cast interviews and hype. That's okay. Just don't post actual footage of any potential show.

As for the business plan, it is to your advantage to keep this packet from circulating and get it into the right hands upfront. This will take some time and research on your part to make certain that whomever you decide to pitch your show to produces your type of reality show. Don't waste your or their time by sending them products they have no interest in producing. So, when and if asked, you can show proof by presenting the signed confidentiality agreements. Also, by having a potential investor sign before getting to read your reality show business plan, it shows them upfront that you mean business and that you are a professional.

Now let's dissect the format and structure of the Confidentiality Statement page. The Confidentiality Page has six sections:

- Heading on the first line Confidentiality Agreement.
- Space down and write the risk statement paragraph.
- Space down and write the confidentiality statement paragraph.
- Center the show's graphic logo about three-fourths the way down the page.
- Space down and place the controlled copy portion.

- At the bottom of the page provide the address to return the business plan upon request of copyright owner.

Diagram 3-1 SAMPLE CONFIDENTIALITY AGREEMENT

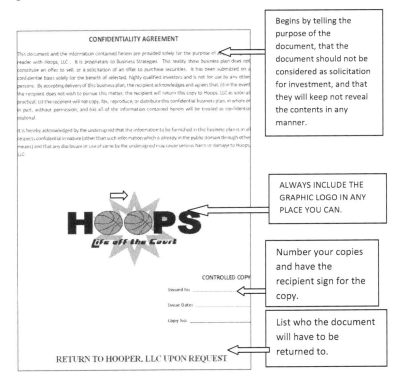

Begins by telling the purpose of the document, that the document should not be considered as solicitation for investment, and that they will keep not reveal the contents in any manner.

ALWAYS INCLUDE THE GRAPHIC LOGO IN ANY PLACE YOU CAN.

Number your copies and have the recipient sign for the copy.

List who the document will have to be returned to.

The Statement Says it All

The Confidentiality Agreement Statement is very similar in nature to the wording on the Front Cover whereby the recipient agrees to maintain confidentiality. Remember my friend that I told you about in the introduction of this book.   Because the network executive had signed a statement of confidentiality it precluded her from sending out or making copies of any plans in her possession. This reason alone is why sample reality show business plans are so hard to come by. The following Confidentiality Statement example is from my reality show

Hoops: Life off the Court and is provided to familiarize you how one is written.

> This document and the information contained herein are provided solely for the purpose of acquainting the reader with Hoops, LLC which is a Limited Liability Company. This reality business plan does not constitute an offer to sell nor is it a solicitation of an offer to purchase securities. It has been submitted on a confidential basis solely for the benefit of selected, highly qualified investors and is not for use by any other persons.

> By accepting delivery of this business plan, the recipient acknowledges and agrees that: (i) in the event the recipient does not wish to pursue this matter, the recipient will return this copy to Hoops, LLC as soon as practical; (ii) the recipient will not copy, fax, reproduce, or distribute this confidential business plan, in whole or in part, without permission; and (iii) all of the information contained herein will be treated as confidential material.

> It is hereby acknowledged by the undersigned that the information to be furnished in this business plan is in all respects confidential in nature (other than such information which is already in the public domain through other means) and that any disclosure or use of same by the undersigned may cause serious harm or damage to Hooper, LLC.

> _____

> Signature of Recipient   Date

After you write the Confidentiality Statement and disclaimer of risk statement for your show read it carefully. Gain an understanding of what it means. To have the ability to offer clarification only adds to your professionalism which separates you from the amateur reality world. Always have your entertainment attorney review any confidentiality statement you include in your plan. They are the only individuals that can provide legal advice.

Logo Placement

The logo of your reality show should be placed larger than life on the Confidentiality Agreement page. Why? How else will anybody know what reality show they are considering? Not really. It should be placed here as a way for quick identification and branding. Please don't confuse this logo for what will appear in the final product once filmed and aired on television. The graphics all change once a network buys your show. This logo is intended to be used for a visual impact for your product and production company and on your marketing materials such as business cards, posters and letterhead.

In my case, I have produced as many as three reality shows at one time and pitched them simultaneously. I maintain a separate file for each reality show with their individual logos. Sometimes I have several documents on my desk I must reference and when an investor calls I can quickly identify the project by the logo. It saves me a great amount of time.

Another reason is for "Branding" your show. Each time the reader of the document sees your logo they immediately identify with it. It brings familiarity to the show before it is aired or in most cases before it is produced. I have included another example in Diagram 3-2 of a Cover Page for you to consider from my reality show *Post Season* currently in development to emphasize branding with a logo.

Although there is not much to the graphic included in the logo, I was able to play with the type of font to create something a little more special. Anyone catch that it is shaped like a cheerleader megaphone? You're now more than likely to remember the name of the reality show since I put a visual in your mind along with the words. Get my point. **BRAND YOUR LOGO**.

Diagram 3-2   Front Cover Example

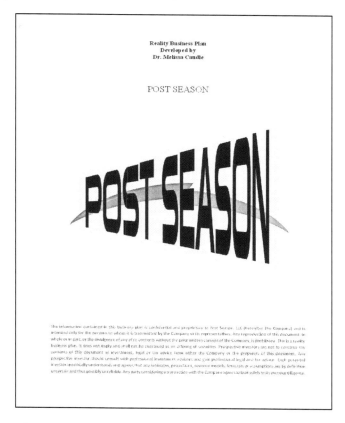

Controlled Copy

It's all about control. If you're a control freak you'll love this part. Otherwise, you will find it a nuisance. But the reality of reality television is that they want a fresh product and not one that has been hammered to death. The only assurance of maintaining any control whatsoever is by using the controlled copy method. By that I mean that each time you print a copy of your business plan, even if it is for yourself, number it. Maintain a log of who receives the copy. Get their name, address, phone number and E-mail address.   Make certain you know how to find these people in the future.

Use the following format to maintain control of your copies by placing this at the bottom of your Confidentiality Agreement page beneath or beside your logo.

CONTROLLED COPY ___ of 5.

Issued to: _____

Issue Date: _____

Copy No: _____

Take a look at Diagram 3-3 on the following page. Pay particular attention to the placement of the logo. I have placed it a little different from the logo from *Hoops: Life off the Court.* There isn't a standard placement for the logo. It is an individual choice and based on what you think looks better in the overall presentation of the page. I tend to place it to add to the overall appearance of the document page.

At this point you might be asking, "Isn't all of this a little redundant?"   It might seem obvious by placing the confidentiality statement and disclaimer on the front page would be enough. The fact is it's not.   Each page serves a distinct purpose. The statement on the front cover informs the reader right away the essence of confidentiality and investment risk of the business plan. It is a way to protect you from the SEC.

The Confidentiality Agreement page serves the purpose to obtain the signature of the recipient and controlled copy number of the business plan. This page will be removed from the document and back into your hands for safe keeping once the signature of the recipient is obtained. If this statement only appeared on the Confidentiality Statement page then it would not be included in the document the recipient maintains when that page is removed. Therefore, it is necessary to have both.

Diagram 3-3   Example Confidentiality Agreement

CONFIDENTIALITY AGREEMENT

This document and the information contained herein are provided solely for the purpose of acquainting the reader with Post Season, LLC and the current television projects it is proprietary to Business Strategies. This business plan does not constitute an offer to sell, or a solicitation of an offer to purchase securities. It has been submitted on a confidential basis solely for the benefit of selected, highly qualified investors and is not for use by any other persons. By accepting delivery of this business plan, the recipient acknowledges and agrees that: (i) in the event the recipient does not wish to pursue this matter, the recipient will return this copy to Post Season, LLC as soon as practical; (ii) the recipient will not copy, fax, reproduce, or distribute this confidential business plan, in whole or in part, without permission; and (iii) all of the information contained herein will be treated as confidential material.

It is hereby acknowledged by the undersigned that the information to be furnished in this business plan is in all respects confidential in nature (other than such information which is already in the public domain through other means) and that any disclosure or use of same by the undersigned may cause serious harm or damage to Post Season, LLC.

CONTROLLED COPY

Issued to: _____

Issue Date: _____

Copy No: _____

RETURN TO POST SEASON, LLC IMMEDIATELY UPON REQUEST TO:
DR. MELISSA CAUDLE
PO BOX xxxxx
ANYWHERE, LA

Return My Copy Please

The last section of the Confidentiality Statement page includes where the document must be returned if the copyright owner requests it. One of the most difficult things to do in the reality show industry is to get a copy back of your reality show business plan. In fact, I really wouldn't count on it if I were you. But you have to make the effort if an investor or distributor wants all copies rescinded to protect their rights. To appease the distributors I make it a point to **NEVER** E-mail a copy of an unproduced reality show to anyone or for any reason if I can help it. It's impossible to rescind an E-mail version. Therefore, I always attempt to send the plan by certified mail with signature receipt required. However, some investors have been very persistent and distance precluded me from hand delivering my plan. I had no other choice but to use the modern method and E-mail it to them.

When and if this scenario crosses your path, don't ever send an unprotected copy – a copy that the receiver can change the contents after opening. Only send a PDF version. This is for two reasons: it protects the copy from being changed and it protects the formatting. Believe me, when you add your graphics and tables, word processing programs are sometimes not compatible and some readers will have a Mac while others will use a PC. Also, reader's computer monitor sizes are all different. Some have a 19 inch while others up to 26 inch monitor screens. The size of the monitor screen changes the format of a document that is not a PDF version to an unreadable mess. Then, prior to sending it, E-mail them a PDF copy of the Confidentiality Agreement page for their signature requesting that they sign it and return it back to you. Also ask them to send you an original signed copy through snail mail. Once you receive the E-mail version go ahead and send the business plan. Make sure you print and keep a hard copy of the Confidentiality Agreement in a file.

The other method is to hand-deliver a copy to the person. I find this method the most effective way to get a business plan into the hands of someone and obtain their original signature. A little bit of advice my entertainment attorney gave me was to have all legal documents signed in blue ink. When I asked him why he informed me that it was easier to determine if the signature was original and not a faxed copy. Once a signature is faxed it usually appears in black. You can take this tip and use it or forget it. The freedom is yours to choose.

RETURN TO SENDER

I can't help but hum the tune Elvis Presley made famous, "Return to sender, address unknown." Now that I got you singing the song, don't fall into the trap and not include the name and address for a recipient to return a controlled copy of the business plan. This is the last part of the Confidentiality Agreement page. I suggest using the following wording.

RETURN TO (NAME OF YOU OR YOUR COMPANY) UPON REQUEST TO:
(LIST YOUR ADDRESS)

I think each part of the Confidentiality Statement page is self explanatory. There are no guarantees that your business plan won't end up in people's hands in which they weren't intended, but at least you have made the effort to prevent it.

LOG FOR CONFIDENTIALITY AGREEMENT

It is very important to always document who you have provided a PDF version or hardcopy of your reality show business plan. In the event you ever have to prove the chain of dissemination you will have a paper trail and files quickly at your disposal. Each time I hand deliver, send by certified mail or E-mail a copy of one of my reality show plans I use the following confidentiality log format. I first make a table with the following six headings:

- Name of the recipient.

- Name of the company.
- Date Sent.
- The method copy was sent.
- The date I received the Confidentiality Agreement.
- Contact Information.

There is full version of this log available in *The Reality of Reality TV Workbook* also for sale from Amazon.com, CreateSpace eStore, www.onthelotpruductions.com, Barnes and Noble, CreateSpace Direct, and other retail outlets (ISBN: 978-1460921593).

Diagram 3-4 Confidentiality Log

CONFIDENTIALITY LOG
REALITY SHOW: _____

Name of Recipient	Name of their Company	Date Sent	Method	Confidentiality Form Received back on	Contact Information
Mark Stanford	BET Ent.	9/1/2011	Hand Delivered	Yes 9/2/2011	1589 XXXXXXX Street Los Angeles, CA XXXXX Email: XXXX@betent@yahoo.com

The more information that you document the easier it will be to prove the chain of ownership. The chain of ownership helps distributors to establish who has rights to the show you created. What this really means is that you must be able to provide the basic data to a distributor when they need it. This will include not only a copy of your registration certificate from the WGA but also any documents that can prove own the literary rights as creator. That is why it is so important for you to document everything that you do. You don't want to be caught up in confusion or a legal battle later. The only other way is to have a literary agent submit all of your reality show business plans.

Also, for each show that you create always use a separate Confidentiality Log. You don't want to mix information between reality shows. For ease in this manner, I also keep a Confidentiality Log Binder at my desk that has dividers in it. Each divider represents the different projects or shows that I am currently pitching. When the phone rings, I grab my binder. In this binder I also keep a telephone log for each show where I can record who just called me, what they said and any follow-up either they must do or they asked me to do. If I check the last column with the arrow it indicates that I need to follow up on this phone call.

Diagram 3-5 Telephone Call Log

CHAPTER SUMMARY

This chapter provided the reader with the necessary information to create the Confidentiality Agreement page for a reality show business plan. The four parts of the page include: type of document, statement that the recipient will not reveal the contents and their signature, controlling the number of copies and who the copies are given to and making certain that the recipient has the necessary information to return the document if requested. Also this chapter discussed various methods to deliver the reality show business plan with the recommendation to always send or give a hard copy and not to send it electronically. Finally, the chain of ownership was presented that eventually you will need as part of a distribution contract. Two forms were provided, the Confidentiality Log form and the Telephone Log form to assist in maintaining communication with investors and television executives.

PRACTICAL APPLICATION

Put what you have learned by completing the following practical application exercises. There are no worksheets for this chapter.

1. Formulate your Confidentiality Agreement for your reality show using a word processing software program. Print it out and add to your binder.

2. Using google.com or bing.com research the history of confidentiality agreements. Find samples on the internet.

3. Give yourself a pat on your back if you completed all of the practical applications in Chapters 1, 2 and 3, you have the first two pages of your reality show business plan. You no longer are staring at a white screen on your computer monitor but have something tangible.

4. Formulate your Confidentiality Log table for your reality show. Print it and add it to your binder. This will make you one step closer to having all of the necessary documents to keep track of your reality show business plan.

5. Complete your next page which is your Table of Contents. Mark that page as the Table of Contents. You can also list all of the following headings

   The Cover
   The Confidentiality Agreement
   Table of Contents
   The Executive Summary
   The Logline and Synopsis
   The Structure of the Show
   The Cast Members
   The Production Team
   Production and Production
   Schedule
   The Market
   Product Placement
   Distribution
   Marketing Strategy
   Investment Opportunity
   The One-Pager
   The Budget
   The Appendix

PHOTOGRAPHY CREDIT FOR CHAPTER 3

Photo for Chapter 3 taken by Salvatore Vuono

CHAPTER 4

THE EXECUTIVE SUMMARY

As a producer and reality show creator I get the question all the time, "What goes into the Executive Summary?" I usually take a deep breath and a good long pause before I answer because I don't want to overwhelm anyone. Then I shake my head and ask the person, "Are you prepared for what's coming?" That's the moment that fright overtakes their face. They know I wouldn't take a long pause for no reason. Once I explain the contents of an Executive Summary they realize they have a lot of work ahead. I always give them the same advice, "Write it last and it will write it's self." And, that's my advice to you with a twist. **WRITE IT LAST** but format it now.

The Executive Summary is just that – a summary of the contents of the business plan. This section is a "work in progress." Consider having all of the pieces to a puzzle lumped into one small area of your business plan. This section got the name Executive Summary because Hollywood insiders wanted to be able to scan a large document in a matter of minutes and to decide if they wanted to continue to read the entire packet. They as executives wanted to read a summary. Thus, the name Executive Summary was forever attached. This reason alone makes the section one of the most important. An investor will more than likely base his decision to either keep reading or to toss the plan while reading this section. That is how important it is. It is a make or break moment. Make certain the information is well written and has impact. Don't embarrass yourself with inaccurate or incomplete information.

In one aspect the Executive Summary is the easiest portion to write and in another way the most difficult. Considering you haven't written the plan yet it will be difficult for you to complete the Executive Summary until such time. That is why it is a work in progress and must be treated as such. So why mention it at all? I have an obligation because sequentially the Executive Summary goes immediately after the Table of Contents. That is why we are addressing it now. But you can't write the entire section at first. What you can do upfront is format the section by adding headings and subtitles in conjunction with "standard" wording. In essence, you will form your outline. By addressing the Executive Summary now you will also become familiar with the other sections of your plan. Once your entire plan is completed you will be able to cut and paste key sentences from those sections into the outline of The Executive Summary you create.

Remember what your English teachers would say, "Tell them what you're going to write, write about it, and tell them again." Treat this section like your old English term papers. The Executive Summary informs the reader in a summary fashion what is in the rest of the plan. To get to the point of being able to write the Executive Summary you need to know what to include and what order it is written. Not all of the sections you write for the reality business plan go into the Executive

Summary. In fact, many of the sections are combined and placed under one of the following eight headings.

- Opening Statement
- Overview of Reality Show
- Cast
- Production Team
- Product Placement Opportunity
- Reality Show Trend
- Distribution and Marketing Strategies
- Investment Projection

While your Executive Summary will have eight headings, your business plan will have more. The reason is the Executive Summary's headings are a combination of several different headings from your business plan.

Table 4-1 compares the headings for your Executive Summary to the headings that comprise your business plan. It also clearly identifies the location to abstract information from your document upon finalization of your reality show plan into your Executive Summary. Pay particular attention to how each section of the Executive Summary is formulated and the various sections that are combined to form the structure. For instance, look at The Opening Statement heading in Table 4-1. This area of your Executive Summary extrapolates information from the production company, logline, structure and more. All combined these elements form the structure for the opening statement.

Likewise, to create the Overview for your reality show it will be necessary to combine the synopsis, logline, target audience and production information. They are not isolated information as in the plan, but merged together. That is why it is important to understand conceptually what differentiates contents of the Executive Summary with contents of the individual sections.

Table: 4-1   Comparison of Headings

Headings for Executive Summary	Headings for Business Plan
Opening Statement (combines production company, logline, structure and More)	The Cover
	The Confidentiality Agreement
	Table of Contents
	The Executive Summary
Overview of Reality Show (combines synopsis, target audience, production information and more)	The Logline and Synopsis
	Structure of Show
	The Cast Members
	The Production Team
Cast (informs who and who isn't attached and production company's desire to secure cast)	Production and Production Schedule
	The Market
	Product Placement
	Distribution Strategy
Production Team (indentifies the production company, producer and director and any other important crew, alliances or consultants)	Marketing Strategy
	Investment Opportunity
	The One Pager
	The Budget
	Appendix
Product Placement Opportunity (summarizes product placement)	
Reality Show Trend (abstracts from the market, product placement)	
Distribution and Marketing Strategy (combines distribution and marketing strategies)	
Investment Projection (abstracts from investment opportunity and budget)	

Opening Statement

Unlike the other headings included in the Executive Summary with portions extracted from different sections of your plan, the Opening Statement is the overview of your company and the project you are going to complete. There are two ways to write your opening statement – as a formed business structure or as a business that will be formed once funding is secured. You will be able to write your opening statement in your business plan document immediately after completing the practical application section for this chapter. Again, you will be working toward filling up your blank white spaces that currently fill your working business plan document as you progress through this book.

Begin your Opening Statement by stating the name and structure of your company, what you are seeking, the genre, when it will be shot, where it will be shot, and why it will be shot. Have you made the connection yet with the five "W's?" Amazing how that works. You have already gotten started on this section by having completed the practical applications of chapters 1 through 3. Here is a practical example from the reality show I created called *Post Season* that is an example of limited liability company.

Example 1

> Post Season, LLC is a Louisiana Limited Liability Company seeking $475,000 for the production of *Post Season* an eight episode reality show with each episode consisting of 45 minutes and product placement endorsements. Post Season will be filmed during the Off-Season of the NFL football league in New Orleans, LA and include five current or former New Orleans Saints Champion football team members who are preparing for "life" after the NFL.

After reading the above opening statement, can you identify who, what, when, why and where? Let's take a closer look as we dissect the parts. Look at the example opening statement below. I have numbered each portion to make it easier for you to identify.

1. Identifies "who." We know that the production company is Post Season, LLC and the cast will consist of current and former New Orleans Saints Super Bowl Champions.

2. Identifies "what" by informing the reader that the company is seeking money. We also know that endorsements for product placement are also being sought.

3. Identifies "when" filming will take place- during the off season.

4. Identifies "where" – in New Orleans, LA.

5. Informs the reader "why" – to prepare NFL football players for careers once they can no longer play.

(1) Post Season, LLC is a Louisiana Limited Liability Company (2) seeking $475,000 for the production of *Post Season* an eight episode reality show with each episode consisting of 45 minutes and product placement endorsements. (3) Post Season will be filmed during the Off-Season of the NFL football (4) league in New Orleans, LA and (1) include five current or former New Orleans Saints Champion football team members (5) who are preparing for "life" after the NFL.

Example 2 is for a company that hasn't been legally formed but the creator and producer plan to do so once funding is secured.

Example 2 *The Baker Girls: Sealed with a Kiss*

> Once funding has been secured from at least one investor, the producer of *The Baker Girls: Sealed with a Kiss* will establish a legal company based on the structure desired by the investor and/or investors so that the structure of said company will be mutually agreed upon for best negotiations and business profit.

The above structure nonetheless contains who, what, when, where and why as before. I have provided the explanation below with each numbered to make it easier for you to identify.

1. Identifies "who." We know that the production company is Baker Girls, LLC.

2. Identifies "what" by informing the reader that the company is seeking money.

3. Identifies "when" filming will take place – once funding has been secured

4. Identifies "where" – in New Orleans, LA.

5. Informs the reader "why."

Same structure I used for *Post Season*, just a little different in the order written.

> **The Opening Statement of your Executive Summary is the only PORTION that will not be re-visited in future chapters.**

---

(1) The producers of The Baker Girls, (4) to be filmed in New Orleans, LA, (3) is seeking $475,000 for the production of the reality show. (3) Once funding has been secured from at least one investor, (1) the producer of *The Baker Girls (2)* will establish a legal company based on the structure desired by the investor and/or investors (5) so that the structure of said company will be mutually agreed upon for best negotiations and business profit.

I frequently get asked "Do I have to put my opening statement in the exact order that you wrote yours?" The answer is "No." Just look at the last two examples. Both contain who, what, when, where and why but the order changed. The point isn't the exact order in which you state it, rather it is whether or not you have included all of the five parts and the sentence makes sense.

The following examples are opening statement variations on the same reality show *Post Season*. Notice how each one contains: who, what, when, where, and why. It becomes a matter of personal preference of the creator or producer and what sounds better to you.

Example 1 *Post Season*

Post Season is a reality show which includes five New Orleans Saints Champion football team members as they prepare for "life" after the NFL. Filmed in New Orleans, LA by Post Season, LLC, a Limited Liability Company, seeks $475,000 for production as well as product-placement.

Example 2 *Post Season*

> Five current and/or former New Orleans Saints Champion football team members prepare for "life" after the NFL during the reality show *Post Season*, produced by Post Season, LLC, a Limited Liability Company seeking $475,000 and product-placement endorsements.

Example 3 *Post Season*

> Post Season, filmed by Post Season, LLC, a Limited Liability Company, features five NFL New Orleans Saints Super Bowl Champions who prepare for "life" after the NFL. *Post Season* is seeking product-placement endorsements as well as $475,000.

Which one do you prefer? What sounds better? The answers reveal a tip for you when you write your opening statement by following one of the above structures.

The Overview of the Reality Show

The Project/Structure section of your Executive Summary purpose is to provide the outline and format of your reality show as well as identify the intended target audience. When I get to Chapters 5 and 6 I will go into much more detail on how to develop the structure of your show. For now you only need to include a standard overview sentence that includes:

- The name of the show, number of episodes.
- Reality show genre.
- Target audience.
- Attributes of the show that makes the show an appealing project.

The following is an example from the reality show *Darren: Sharper than Ever* that includes the aforementioned elements.

Example 1 *Darren: Sharper than Ever*

> *Darren: Sharper than Ever,* is a 13 episode reality show that combines the love of sports with professional football with a target audience ranging from age 9 to 90.   Anyone that loves football and following a professional athlete will love this show.

Notice how the above statement included the genre, target audience and attributes as indicated by the following numbers in Example 2:

1. Title

2. Genre

3. Number of Episodes

4. Target audience

5. Attribute

Example 2 *Darren: Sharper than Ever*

> *(1) Darren: Sharper than Ever, (2) is a 13 episode celebrity reality show* (3) that combines the love of sports with professional football with a *(4) target audience ranging from age 9 to 90.* (5) Anyone that loves football and following a professional athlete will love this show.

Cast

The Cast section of your Executive Summary might be the simplest area to write. It is standard wording once you identify your intent and who you want to be in the show. You either have a cast or you don't. It's that direct. No guess work.

There are four ways in which you can write this section:

1. You have celebrity actors attached.
2. You don't have any celebrity actors attached but you want to.
3. You will use un-known talent and they are attached.
4. You will use un-known talent but they are not attached.

I'm a Celebrity and I'm Attached

If you have actors attached use the following statement:

> The Company has attached well-known actor(s) to our project with the exception of a couple of roles. (Letters of Intent are attached.) It is our desire to hire additional name talent, thereby increasing the show's audience appeal and commercial value.

The statement is quick, succinct and tells your reader that you have well-known actors. You don't have to list them by name in the Executive Summary but you better have the Letters of Intent.

A Letter of Intent is a short and straight forward letter given to a producer or production company and signed by the talent. In this letter, the talent states they have agreed to participate as a cast member in your reality show.

Often actors don't know how to write letters of intent nor do they have the time and will ask you as the producer or creator to write them for their signature. No worries. Always use a formal format for letters that include the sender's return address, date of letter, addressee, reason for the letter, the greeting, the body of the letter and the salutary name. The suggested wording and format for a Letter of Intent follows this structure.

FUTURE ACTORS NAME
ADDRESS

DATE: May 15, 2011

PRODUCER NAME
PRODUCER ADDRESS

RE: LETTER OF INTENT
Dear Producer

I, XXXXX, hereby acknowledge that I will participate in the reality show NAME OF REALITY SHOW, providing that funding is secured. Full fees for my participation will be discussed and negotiated at that time. You may include my name and likeness in any documents you create and disseminate to obtain said funding as well as on your production company's website.

Sincerely,
ACTOR'S NAME

This letter is not a legally binding contract. You will still need to procure those once filming commences.

I'm a Celebrity but I'm not Attached

If you do not have any well-known actors attached to your project tell the truth. Hollywood is basically a very small community. Trust me on this. If an actor is attached they know it. The last thing you want to do is say you have an actor attached and don't. Never state that you have an actor attached unless you have the Letter of Intent from them and then, this letter will be included in the Appendix of your business plan. Word will get around.

If you don't have well known names attached to your project but intend to secure one use the following sentence.

The Company of the reality show desires to hire well known talent for our project.

I'm Un-known but Attached

The third option is if you plan on using un-known talent and you have attached them to your project. Use this statement to identify that this is your intention.

The Company has attached cast members to this project. (Letters of Intent are attached).

I'm Un-known but Want to be a Reality Star

The fourth option is that you do not have any attached cast members and you will have to hold auditions and find them. If this is the case, use the following sentence.

It is The Company's desire to hold open auditions to secure cast members appropriate for our project that have the necessary skills and personality add to audience appeal and commercial value.

The Reality Show Trend

The reality show trend section of your Executive Summary covers two elements: what the industry is doing and what the market is doing. You can't complete this section of your Executive Summary until you conduct basic research. The reality show industry has evolved over the last decade and each year changes. In the U.S. 2010 reality programs are a very popular $25 billion industry. When it began in early 1990 it wasn't more than a $1 billion industry. Each year the amount earned in this industry fluctuates. The amount earned is fluid at best and can either be higher or lower than the year before. You must be accurate in reporting data. You must also put into consideration the type of genre your reality show falls into as well. Some genres are more lucrative with gross profits outweighing the others. That doesn't mean you shouldn't do your show in a particular genre. What this means is that you have to do your research to plug in the numbers for both the trend in the industry and in the market that aligns with your show.

All of this doesn't stop you from being able to write the shell of this section in your Executive Summary. By all means do so. It is more standard than you might otherwise think. What changes is what you find in your research of the market and comparable shows to yours already aired on major networks. A good starting point for this section would be to include the following statement knowing that you will have to revisit and add in the data from research you find later during practical application section in Chapter 11. The standard wording and format for this section is:

> The market for reality shows in XXX genre grossed $X dollars in 2010 in the U.S. and $X worldwide respectively. The success of reality shows similar to (Name of your reality show) is evident as shows like XXXXXXXXX and XXXXXXXX continue to air on XXXX and XXXXX networks. Audience market appeal for this type of programming continues as networks strive to fulfill the demand. (Name of your reality show) offers an opportunity to tap into this market and offers the dimension for high returns with low production cost.

Production Team

The Production Team section in the Executive Summary is easy to write. You state the name of the production company that will produce the reality show, who the producer and director are and if you have a director of photography or other important key crew members attached list them as well. You will not be giving complete biographies and qualifications in this section. One sentence of their experience with reality shows, films or television programs will suffice. The standard format and wording for this section is listed below:

(Name of your production company) will be producing (Name of Show). This is the (state number) time the production company has produced a reality show. (Name of Producer) is the producer for the show and has produced (state number) of reality shows. Additionally, (Name of Director) will be the Director and has directed (state number) of reality shows.

If the Production Company, producer, and/or director have never been associated with another reality show project inform the reader the number of films or television shows they have been involved with instead. The idea is to inform the reader that you have obtained an experienced production company, producer and director.

Lastly, if you have any other important crew members; e.g., director of photography, add the following sentence to your above statement.

(Name of director of photography) will be our director of photography and he has filmed (number of shows or films).

Product-Placement Opportunity

Product-placement is almost never included in a business plan for a feature film; however, it is vital to propelling a business plan forward for a reality show. Product-placement is the locomotive that is driving networks to become more competitive. A great reality show can get derailed quickly if products aren't carefully considered. Also by having products placed in your reality show, it increases the opportunity for funding and increases advertising potential. In fact, many shows have been completely funded by product-placement.

A product properly placed can help shape the brand of your show and likewise increase revenue for the advertiser. Reality show programming is so diverse that advertisers can get in where they fit and not have to compete for the same audience because they have a product that is segment/demo-specific. For the purposes of your Executive Summary section you will not be able to write the entire statement now. You won't be able to until you either secure product endorsements or you generate a list of possible products that are segment/demo specific to your reality show. But like the other portions of your Executive Summary you can get a jump start by placing the following statement with the intentions to revisit and abstract the information after you complete the practical application section in Chapter 12.

A suggested product-placement statement is:

> Many opportunities for segment/demo-specific are available for (Name of reality show.) They include but are not limited to: XXXXXX, XXXXX, XXXXX and XXX. (Name of Company) will actively seek product endorsements to increase market appeal and advertising revenue sources.

Distribution and Marketing Strategy Statement

As reality shows have increased in popularity the more competitive the industry has become. In the Executive Summary section of your plan distribution and marketing strategies are combined in a single heading. However in your actual plan, they are treated as individual sections. It is essential that you as a producer and creator of your show carefully plan all distribution and marketing strategies for potential investors and product-placement companies to review. The decision makers want to know how you intend on getting your show, in essence, their show, distributed and marketed in order to increase the potential profit.

They know that the show will not distribute nor market itself and that the success lies in these strategies. For now, you're not going to write your complete distribution and market plans. However, you are going to put some thought into both.

There are commonalities in all distribution and marketing plans that you can put in your Executive Summary now and then revisit and modify once you have carefully thought them out. You will formulate both during your practical application in Chapter 13.

The standard format for this section of your Executive Summary section is:

> The success of reality shows is directly related to the distribution and marketing strategy. (Name of Company) will not sit idle and intends to pitch (Name of reality show) to the National Association of Television Producers and Executives annual conference as well as appropriate festivals. Likewise (Name of Company) will actively seek to negotiate with appropriate distribution companies known to distribute like genre programming the production. Additionally, all best efforts to market (Name of reality show) will begin during production that includes: establishing a website, Twitter and Facebook Accounts for said reality show and cast members, create an EPK package, and seek publicity in magazines and newspapers. The distribution and marketing strategies are likely to maximize (Name of Company) position for future acquisition by networks and distributors as well as increase future profit (Name of reality show) may earn.

More than likely you will develop more distribution and marketing strategies for your reality show as you develop that section in Chapter 13. In fact, you should. The more creative ways you develop to market and distribute your reality show increases the return of investment and potential profit. If you get stuck and can't brainstorm any ideas you can refer to my book *150 Ways to Fund a Reality Show* (ISBN -146096715) from Amazon.com, Create E Space, Barnes and Noble and other retail outlets that will be available late summer of 2011. This book also has creative marketing ideas.

Investment Projection

All potential investors want to know upfront, "What is the return on my money and how fast will I get it back?" In this industry it is called return on investment (ROI). With that said, this section of the Executive Summary will probably be looked at first and foremost by investors after they finish the Executive Summary section. So make it simple and easy to understand. Also, make it accurate and **DON'T** promise anything. In fact, tell them upfront that this is a risky business and that there is no guarantee that their money will even be returned.

Reality show production is a highly competitive business. Be honest always and make no promises because it is impossible to predict the return on investment. This will also keep you out of trouble with the Securities and Exchange Commission (SEC). During the practical applications section in Chapter 14 you will do the necessary research and then revisit your statement to update it. For now, you can include the following standard wording in your plan.

> (Name of Company) seeks $X to fund the reality show (Name of reality show). (Name of Company) desires to obtain all funding from private investors. Investing in any reality is risky and there is no guarantee that there will be a return on investment. **This is a reality show business plan.** It does not imply and shall not be construed as an offering of securities. Prospective investors are not to construe the contents of this document as investment, legal or tax advice from either the Company or the preparers of this document. Any prospective investor should consult with professional investment advisors and gain professional legal and tax advice. Each potential investor specifically understands and agrees that any estimates, projections, revenue models, forecasts or assumptions are by definition uncertain and impossible to obtain from reality show programming. Any party considering a transaction with the Company agrees to look solely to its own due diligence.

CHAPTER SUMMARY

The Executive Summary section identified the eight headings to for this section: Opening Statement; Overview of Reality Show; Cast; Production Team; Product Placement Opportunity; Reality Show Trend; Distribution and Marketing Strategies; and Investment Projection Return and provided standard statements for each. Although it is impossible to write the entire Executive Summary at the beginning stages of development of your reality show business plan, a creator can outline the contents and include standard wording. All sections created early in the creation process must be re-visited once the entire plan is completed. That is why in the beginning stage an Executive Summary is a work in progress. The author advises that the Executive Summary section should be written and complete last. Sample formatting and standard acceptable wording for each section of the Executive Summary were provided as a guide.

PRACTICAL APPLICATION

1. Use Worksheet 6 to formulate your Opening Statement for the Executive Summary Section. Once complete add your statement to your business plan document.

2. Use Worksheet 7 to formulate your overview of your reality show.

3. Use Worksheet 8 to formulate your Reality Show Trend Statement.

4. Use Worksheet 9 to create your cast members.

5. Use Worksheet 10 to generate your production team statement.

6. Use Worksheet 11 to generate product placement opportunities.

7. Use Worksheet 12 to generate distribution and marketing strategies.

8. Use Worksheet 13 to create your investment opportunity statement.

PHOTOGRAPHY CREDIT FOR CHAPTER 4
Chapter 4 photo taken by Salvatore Vuano

WORKSHEET 6: OPENING STATEMENT

Objective: To create an Opening Statement for the Executive Summary Section of your reality show business plan.

Applying the five "Ws" you will create your opening statement following the below format:

> Post Season, LLC is a Louisiana Limited Liability Company seeking $475,000 for the production of *Post Season* an eight (8) episode reality show with each episode consisting of 45 minutes and product placement endorsements. Post Season will be filmed during the Off-Season of the NFL football league in New Orleans, LA and include five (5) current or former New Orleans Saints Champion football team members who are preparing for "life" after the NFL.

1.   Fill in the blanks with your information specific to your reality show.

What is the name of your company? _____

How much funding are you seeking? _____

What is the name of your reality show? _____

How many episodes are you planning on filming? _____

How long is each episode?   ____ If it is only a pilot indicate: ___Yes

When will you film your show? _____

What city and state will you film your show? _____

Who are your cast members: _____

2. Following the above sample put together your opening statement three different ways. Then choose the one you prefer.

3. Transfer your opening statement into your reality show business document that you have been creating. Always print a hardcopy and add to your binder.

WORKSHEET 7: OVEVIEW OF PROJECT

Objective: Create the overview for the Executive Summary Statement for your reality show business plan.

Using the following statement as a template, identify your target audience.

> *Darren: Sharper than Ever,* is a 13 episode reality show that combines the love of sports with professional football with a target audience ranging from age 9 to 90.   Anyone that loves football and following a professional athlete will love this show.

1. Identify your target age range audience for your show. Why?

2. What type of person is likely to watch your show? Why?

3. What are the attributes for your show? Why?

4. What will viewers find appealing? Why?

5. What about your show is unique and different from any other currently produced show?

6. Look at your answers above. Circle the age of your audience, the type of audience, the key attributes etc.

7. Using the information you circled formulate two or three opening statements using the above template.

8. Choose the best opening statement from step 7 and type it into your reality show business document. Print a hardcopy and add to your binder

WORKSHEET 8: TREND STATEMENT

Objective: To create the Marketing Trend Statement for your reality show proposal.

1. Using the format below type in the standard wording into your reality show document.

> The market for reality shows grossed *$X dollars in 2010 in the U.S. and $X worldwide respectively. The success of reality shows similar to* **(Name of your reality show)** *is evident as shows like* **XXXXXXXXX** *and* **XXXXXXXX** *continue to air on* **XXXX** *and* **XXXXX** *networks. Audience market appeal for this type of programming continues as networks strive to fulfill the demand.* **(Name of your reality show)** *offers an opportunity to tap into this market* and offers the dimension *for high returns with low production cost.*

2. Look up the definition to gross and net income to gain an understanding of the terms.

3. Begin researching gross income for 10 reality shows that fit into your genre of reality show programming. How much has each earned? Keep this information handy and in your binder so that when it comes to creating the section in your reality show business plan you will have the information for quick reference.

4. Write your Marketing Trend statement into your document. Print a hardcopy and put it into your binder.

WORKSHEET 9: CAST MEMBERS

Objective: To identify the cast to be attached to your show.

1.   What type of cast do you have for your show? Check all that apply.

☐ Attached Celebrity Cast

☐ Want Celebrities but don't have them attached

☐ Unknown individuals already attached

☐ Unknown individuals needs to be attached

2. Generate a list of possible celebrities that could be included.

3. Generate a list of people that you know that would make great cast members.

4. List any and all people that have agreed to be in your show.

5. Generate 2 to 3 sample statements that identifies your type of cast and who is and is not attached by following the samples in this chapter under the heading cast.

6. Choose the best one and type it into your reality show business document. Print a hardcopy and put it into your binder.

WORKSHEET 10: PRODUCTION TEAM

Objective: To generate the Production Team Statement for the Executive Summary.

1. What is the name of your production company?

2. What type of company is it? Check the one that applies.
☐ LLC   ☐ Partnership   ☐ Sole Proprietor   ☐ Other

3. List all producers and experience with reality shows.

4. Who is the director of this project? Is the director attached to the show? ☐ Yes ☐ No

5. What is the director's experience with reality shows?

6.   Who is the producer of this project?   Is the producer attached to the show? ☐ Yes ☐ No

7. What is the producer's experience with reality shows?

8.   Generate your Executive Summary Statements using this format and then type it into your reality show business plan. Print a hardcopy once finished and place in your binder.

(Name of your production company) will be producing (Name of Show).   This is the (state number) time the production company has produced a reality show. (Name of Producer) is the producer for the show and has produced (state number) of reality shows.   Additionally, (Name of Director) will be the Director and has directed (state number) of reality shows.

WORKSHEET 11: PRODUCT-PLACEMENT

Objective: Use Worksheet 10 to generate product-placement opportunities specifically for your reality show.

1. Generate a list of at least 10 products that can be used by your cast members.

1. _____   6._____
2. _____   7._____
3. _____   8._____
4. _____   9._____
5. _____   10._____

2. Generate a list a vendors that your company currently does business with.

3.   Using the sample format provided in this chapter choose two to three of the products from the above list that hold the most potential to increase advertising dollars.

> *Many opportunities for segment/demo-specific are available for (Name of reality show.) They include but are not limited to: XXXXXX, XXXXX, XXXXX and blank. (Name of Company) will actively seek product endorsements to increase market appeal and advertising revenue sources.*

4. Formulate your product-placement statement following the format provided in this chapter and type it into your reality show business plan document. Print a hardcopy and put into your binder.

WORKSHEET 12: DISTRIBUTION AND MARKETING

Objective: To generate distribution and marketing strategies.

1. Generate at least 10 distribution strategies.

2.   Generate as many marketing strategies that you can identify.

3.   Use the format provided in this chapter create your Distribution and Marketing Strategy statement for your Executive Summary by replacing the bold type in your plan.

> *The success of reality shows is directly related to the distribution and marketing strategy.* ***(Name of Company)*** *will not sit idle and intends to pitch* ***(Name of reality show)*** *to the National Association of Television Producers and Executives annual conference as well as appropriate festivals. Likewise* ***(Name of Company)*** *will actively seek to negotiate with appropriate distribution companies known to distribute like genre programming the production. Additionally, all best efforts to market* ***(Name of reality show)*** *will begin during production that includes:* ***(list your ways you identified above)*** *for said reality show and cast members, create an EPK package, and seek publicity in magazines and newspapers. The distribution and marketing strategies are likely to maximize* ***(Name of Company)*** *position for future acquisition by networks and distributors as well as increase future profit* ***(Name of reality show)*** *may earn.*

4. Type your Distribution and Marketing Strategy statement into your reality show business plan. Print a hardcopy and place into your binder.

WORKSHEET 13: INVESTMENT STATEMENT

Objective: To create the Investment Opportunity Statement format for your reality show business proposal.

1. Although your numbers will be left blank for now, using the sample in this chapter type in the shell of your Investment Opportunity Statement into your reality show business plan by replacing the bold type print below. Print a hardcopy upon completion and put into your binder.

> *(Name of Company) seeks $X to fund the reality show (Name of reality show). (Name of Company) desires to obtain all funding from private investors. Investing in any reality is risky and there is no guarantee that there will be a return on investment. **This is a reality show business plan.** It does not imply and shall not be construed as an offering of securities. Prospective investors are not to construe the contents of this document as investment, legal or tax advice from either the Company or the preparers of this document. Any prospective investor should consult with professional investment advisors and gain professional legal and tax advice. Each potential investor specifically understands and agrees that any estimates, projections, revenue models, forecasts or assumptions are by definition uncertain and thus possibly unreliable. Any party considering a transaction with the Company agrees to look solely to its own due diligence. (Name of Company) projects gross revenue of approximately $X with a net producer/investor profit of $X for (Name of Reality Show).*

2. Continue to research investment risk statements on the internet.

CHAPTER 5

LOGLINE AND SYNOPSIS

Some people reading this book will already know what a logline and synopsis are while others may think I'm speaking Greek to them. I'm not rest assured. But just to make certain that everybody is on the same page I will discuss them both. You will learn how to write your logline and synopsis in the chapter's Practical Application section. If per chance you have already developed either your logline or synopsis, continue reading anyway because you will more than likely be able to hone them after you read the information provided.

Both loglines and synopsis are very important and key elements to your reality show. A logline could make the difference as to whether your reality show gets picked up or not. It serves as your calling card and a way into the door of decision makers. It's my experience that a poorly written logline usually reflects a poorly developed concept which is reflected in a synopsis. A network executive can spot a poorly written logline and synopsis a mile away.

WHAT IS A LOGLINE?

A logline describes your reality show. It is that one sentence summarization of that show's programming. It's that short blurb in the TV Guide which clues you into what the program is about. Its sole purpose is to grab your attention and make you watch that program. That's a logline in the simplest form of an explanation.

A logline does the same thing for a reality show. It's written to grab the attention of investors and to summarize in one key sentence your show. That way when you're asked, "What is your show about?" you don't have to manufacture something quickly. At all times you should be able to answer that question when friends, family and investors ask it. When I was an industry panelist at a "Pitch Fest" I was surprised by the number of people who didn't have a logline or synopsis for their show. These people paid a lot of money to have the opportunity to pitch their show to seven different industry executives. On this panel were agents, producers, managers, and development executives. Likewise, I have creators contact me all the time and cannot express to me their logline for their show.

The "Pitch Fest" was set up like speed dating. Each person would have five minutes to pitch one-on-one with each panel member. I saw over 75 people that day. It baffled me when I asked them for the logline. Most of them didn't know what I was talking about. My attention level was at the bottom. Why should I listen if they couldn't tell me in one sentence their show? It was obvious that they didn't put a great amount of thought into their project they were in love with. They came across as if they had this wonderful idea that they wanted someone else to run with. It doesn't work that way. You as a creator and producer have to be in love with your project and present it as such. If as a creator you don't have a logline that grabs the attention of those reading your plan you may lose your opportunity to get funding and/or product-placement.

I'm not the only one that feels this way. I know for a fact program development executives at major networks don't read a business plan if the logline doesn't impress them. I remember a meeting with one of the producer's of a reality show for BET. He told me his show was turned down five times because he couldn't narrow his project to one sentence. When he finally constructed his one sentence logline, he got funding and that reality show is one of the top ten watched today.

Creating a Logline

A logline for a reality show and screenplay are written identically and follow the same structure and format. So, if you already know how to write one for screenplays you are a step ahead of the game. Just revisit it and make sure it grabs the attention of the reader.

Creating a logline is easier said than done. In fact, many screenplay writers tell me it's harder to write the logline than it was to write the 125 page screenplay for their feature film. Without a written script, it is harder to hone your concept into a logline sentence as is the case for reality shows. You don't have a script or a screenplay that drives your logline. Instead, you have a single concept. This should not detour you in developing your logline. In a way, it should make it easier because you are not confined and have freedom of expression on your side.

A logline can be broken down into four elements:

- A subject
- A verb
- An action
- An outcome

Take a look at the following loglines.

Example 1 Hoops*: Life off the Court*

> A group of college basketball players engage in life of the court as they develop team dynamics.

Example 2 The *Ace Mechanic*

> A certified auto mechanic pays it forward to wayward travelers and discovers he gets more out of it than his customers.

Example 3 The *Baker Girls: Sealed with a Kiss*

> Five retail shoe salesgirls embark on life after work as they develop friendships within their circle.

The three examples all contain the four different elements – a subject, verb, action, and outcome. Review the same loglines from above but this time I numbered each according to the four elements required:

(1) Subject

(2) Verbs

(3) Action

(4) Outcome

Example 1 *Hoops: Life off the Court*

> (1) A group of six college basketball players with nothing in common (2) engage (3) in life of the court (4) as they develop team dynamics.

Example 2 *The Ace Mechanic*

> (1) A certified auto mechanic in a rural Mississippi town (2) pays (3) it forward to wayward travelers and (4) discovers he gets more out of it than his customers.

Example 3 *The Baker Girls*

> (1) Five retail shoe salesgirl at a Baker's in a mall (2) embark (3) on life after work (4) as they develop friendships within the circle.

Loglines do not have to be written in the same order as the examples. You could start by stating the outcome first. The point is to have a logline that sounds great and is easy for you to recite. The final logline in Example 4 is from *The Baker Girls*. This time I restructured it to emphasize that the elements can be re-arranged for impact. In this example I started with the outcome followed by the subject, verb and action.

Example 4 *The Baker Girls: Sealed with a Kiss*

> As they develop friendships within the circle, five retail shoe salesgirls at a Baker's store in a mall embark on life after work.

The Subject of the Logline

All reality shows are about somebody or a group of people. These are the subjects. In essence, you already know the subject of your reality show because you have completed all of the prior practical application sections. Review each completed Worksheets of 2, 6 and 9. To further develop your subject of your reality show logline ask, "Who is my character or characters?" Your subject can be either an individual or a group. In the aforementioned examples the subjects of the three reality shows are: *a group of college basketball players*, *certified auto mechanic*, and *shoe salesgirls*. Have you clearly identified yours? You will need to be able to identify your subject in order to create your logline.

The Verb of the Logline

In order to identify the verb for your logline ask, "What is my subject doing?" Another question to ask is, "What journey is my subject taking?"   The answer to either question will pinpoint the verb for your logline. In the three previous examples the action words *pays*, *embark* and *engage* implies that something is happening. In most loglines the verb is usually only one word. A good dictionary will come in handy to assist in the identification of creative verbs for your logline. It also helps to visualize your subjects and what they are doing. Also, there is nothing wrong with using a Thesaurus to identify creative verbs.

The Action of the Logline

The action of your logline is best defined by asking, "What is my subject doing?" Identify where the action takes them after you wrote the initial verb. The three logline examples the actions include where they take place; e.g., *life after work*, *dealings with wayward travelers*, and *life off the basketball court*. Again, it helps to visualize your subjects doing something and then narrow that action to words.

The Outcome of the Logline

As with any good screenplay it is also necessary for your subject of your reality show to have a goal or a major transformation commonly known as a character arc. That's how you identify your outcome for your reality show logline. Ask, "What did my subject get out this?" Also, ponder the question, "Did your subject undergo a transformation or did somebody else as a result of what your subject did?" Transformations can either be physical, emotional or refer to a new skill or relationship between others. No matter the type of transformation, it will identify the outcome for your logline as in the outcomes for my three examples: *the basketball players develop team dynamics, the ace mechanic discovers he gets more out of it than his costumers* and *the shoe salesgirls form friendships that will last a lifetime.*

The Do's and Don'ts of Logline Writing

I get asked numerous of times what are the Do's and Don'ts of writing a logline for a reality show because they are a little different from screenplays. So I have listed them for you.

Do

Take time to develop your logline, but develop it first before your concept. Then hone it and polish it throughout the writing of your business plan. Up to the last moment, consider it a work in progress.

Write at least 12 different loglines for your show. Manipulate them in different order using different verbs. One of them you will fall in love with.

Ask your friends and relatives which of the 12 Loglines you created sticks with them. To accomplish this task, read out loud your loglines, watch their reactions, and then ask them which one they remember the most.

Be open to suggestions from others if they come up with one.

Keep your logline to one sentence.

Practice writing loglines by reversing the order of the four elements. They don't always have to appear in the same order.

For added spice to your Logline feel free to add what type of reality genre your show falls into.

Be brief.

Don't

Don't include the entire concept of your show by telling what the entire show is about.

Never use analogies such as, "It's the Osbournes meeting Donald Trump." It's the mark of an amateur and analogies are only used in loglines for screenplays.

Never use clichés.

Never say anything close that your reality is absolutely the best on the market unless you created an Emmy Award winning show and the Emmy is on your fireplace mantle.

Don't complicate your logline by using words nobody understands but you. Keep them simple, but use enticing words.

Never go over more than 25 words.

WHAT IS A SYNOPSIS?

 A synopsis is a paragraph, usually 5 to 9 sentences in length that describes your show. It is a summary of what happens during a particular season or a very condensed version of your show.

A synopsis should not be confused with a treatment which goes into greater detail and includes a summary of each episode. A treatment can be anywhere in length from one to five pages and expands on the three acts like those for a screenplay. Seeing that a reality show is unscripted you can't write a treatment unless you have completed filming your project. If that is the case, your reality show treatment would be an overview of what transpired over the duration of the show highlighting significant events of each show. It is also appropriate to include quotes made by cast members.

Creating a synopsis for a reality show is difficult because you have no idea what's going to happen. It's unscripted. This is a big contrast when writing the synopsis for a screenplay which is scripted. So what do you do?

The answer is complicated if you haven't filmed any portion of your show. However, you can state the conceptual basis of the show and the format that it will follow. By doing so, it creates a natural flow for your readers. It also directs you on the right path as a creator.

Another direction is to include all major characters and the obstacles or conflict they may face. These obstacles can be a planned event you designed for the show although you don't know the outcome.

What goes into a Synopsis?

Take a look at this example. It is a sample from a reality show I haven't produced and don't plan on producing, not because it isn't good, but it is totally made up to demonstrate that you can write a synopsis for something that hasn't been created.

Title: *The Man Behind #9*

The Man Behind #9 is a celebrity style reality show with eight episodes created by Dr. Melissa Caudle following Drew Brees, a Super Bowl Champion Quarterback, a father of two and a community advocate. *Sports Illustrated,* "Man of the Year" has a direct way of getting things done on the field - with some of the best statistics in the NFL. His sharpness and razor edge skill as a top quarterback translates to his off-the-field life in his community. He makes a difference to a city once devastated by Hurricane Katrina. For the past six years Drew Brees has brought hope to New Orleans, the city he now calls home. While off the field, Drew Brees raises awareness for the homeless, produces fund raising events for charities, brings laughter and joy to children stricken with terminal diseases, and more. On the Lot Productions, LLC, under the direction of Dr. Melissa Caudle, presents a bold new reality series which steps into the life of a Super Bowl Champion Drew Brees. Throughout this 13 part series Drew Brees is joined by his closest friends in the NFL and community leaders. We get to know the man behind #9.

In the aforementioned sample did you get a clear concept of what my make believe show is going to be about? Do you know who the subject of the show is? Do you have a good idea what he will be doing in the show? Do you know the type of man he is? Do you know who the creator of the show is? Do you know who is producing the show and who will be directing it? I sure hope so.

The Man Behind #9 synopsis demonstrates the key elements. Let's break a synopsis into the different elements to reveal how to write not just a good synopsis for a reality show, but a great one with meaning and structure.

The following table lists the parts of a well constructed synopsis for any reality show.

Table 5-1   Parts of a Reality Show Synopsis

(1) Title of the Show
(2) Genre
(3) Number of Episodes
(4) Creator
(5) Subject
(6) What makes the subject special
(7) What the subject will be involved in
(8) The Production Team
(9) An outcome
(10) The reason for the show

Using my make belief sample synopsis *The Man Behind #9,* I have isolated the 10 elements according to the associating numbers used in Table 5-1.

> *(1) The Man Behind #9* (2) is a celebrity style reality show (3) with eight Episodes (4) created by Dr. Melissa Caudle (5) that follows Drew Brees, a Super Bowl Champion Quarterback, a father of two and a community advocate. *Sports Illustrated, "* Man of the Year"(6) has a direct way of getting things done on the field - with some of the best statics in the NFL. His sharpness and razor edge skill as a top quarterback translates to his off-the-field life in his community. He makes a difference to a city that was once devastated by Hurricane Katrina. For the past 6 years Drew Brees has brought hope to New Orleans, the city he now calls home. (7) While off the field, Drew Brees raises awareness for the homeless, produces fund raising events for charities, brings laughter and joy to children stricken with terminal diseases, and more. (8) On the Lot Productions, LLC, under the direction of Dr. Melissa Caudle (9) presents a bold new reality series which steps into the life of a Super Bowl Champion Drew Brees as he impacts the New Orleans and Surrounding communities with his generosity. (5) Throughout this 13 part series Drew Brees is joined by his closest friends in the NFL and community leaders. (10) We get to know the man behind #9.

The Title

I almost always start my synopsis with the title of my show. This drills the name of the show from the beginning. If I put a lot of effort into the name of the show, the readers should already have a general concept of what the show is about. That's the cleverness of a creative title that represents the show.

Genre

By identifying to the reader the type of genre your reality show falls into, it sets a tone or a pace for the rest of the synopsis. It's more subliminal that anything but it carries an impact. The reader can identify immediately if it is a game show or if a celebrity is involved. The genre often impacts the way the synopsis is written as well as the outcome of the show. For a review of genres refer to Table 1:1 in Chapter One.

Creator

Always include the name of the creator of the show. The creator is the person or group of individuals that came up with the show's concept and if they were smart registered with the Writer's Guild of America (WGA) and/or U.S. Copyright Service. Network executives want to know who owns the copyright and rights to the show and you will have to eventually prove the chain of control. Save yourselves a big headache for the future by registering you concept for the $20 dollars it takes for the WGA. For more information on registering your concepts visit www.wga.com.

Subject

By listing the subject by name it takes out the guess work for the reader if it is a celebrity. If your show is capitalizing on un-known talent you don't have to list every cast member, you just define the type of group. You may mention your subject as often as you like.

Special Attributes

In order to identify the special attributes start by asking, "What makes this person or group special?" By identifying key characteristics and key attributes of your subject matter it allows the reader to know the type of personalities the show will feature. This section is often difficult to write but can write itself if you ask your subject matter to tell you what others think of them. Also ask their friends and families. There is always something unique and special about a future realty star or you wouldn't be interested in having them as a part of your show.

The Production Team

Clearly identify the production company by name, as well as the producer and the director. Often, a television executive already knows the reputation of the company and/or the producer and director of the show and has a relationship with them. It is happened to me on several occasions where a television executive saw my name and picked up the phone and called me to pitch the show to them instead of them reading having to read about it. It comes in handy once you establish a reputation in the industry.

The Outcome

Briefly state the outcome of the show which is the end result. Each genre of reality show has different outcomes. So make certain that your outcome matches your show.

The Reason for the Show

Television executives want to know why the show is important or why anyone would want to watch the show. I always try to have my final reason to be a play on words of the title. It's catchy and creative and holds the most potential to stick in executives minds. In essence, it is a small marketing tool or tagline that you can use.

The Do's and Don'ts of Writing a Reality Show Synopsis

Here is some practical advice when writing your synopsis. Always be creative but don't be too lengthy by providing too much information.

Do's

Keep the synopsis to no more than nine sentences. Eight is even better.

Always check you spelling and grammar of the completed synopsis.

Always try to capture the essence of the show by revealing the concept.

Do not include your subplots and every detail. If you do, it becomes more of a treatment for your show rather than a synopsis. Treatments are for screenplays or completed reality show series.

Always state something interesting about the main character or group of your show.

Always state the genre category of your show.

Always write several different synopses for you project and choose the best.

Don't

Don't overwrite it by making it three pages.

Don't include everything and every detail.

Don't use cliché sentences like, "You will love this show or it will be the best show on television."

CHAPTER SUMMARY

In this chapter loglines and synopsis were defined as well as how to create them. The four key elements to include in a logline are: subject, verb, action and outcome. There are 10 key elements in a synopsis: title of the show; number of episodes; genre; creator; subject ; what makes the subject special; what the subject will be involved with; the production team; outcome; and reason for the show. A good logline is a predictor to the quality of reality show created.

PRACTICAL APPLICATION

1. Conduct a Google search on developing loglines.

2. Go to your television and begin reading all of the one line sentences for your favorite television programs. Read as many loglines as you can. Write down the ones that really grab your attention. You may want to refer to the structure of them for future reference.

3. Locate written loglines in a TV guide, newspaper, and websites. Do they differ from the ones that appear for your favorite shows? If so, ask yourself why?

4. Using Worksheet 14, create your logline. Share your logline with friends and family to identify the best logline. If you are not satisfied with the outcome, re-write and add until you have developed a logline that is enticing. Prior to completing your business plan you will get to re-visit this area and change it. A logline should be a work in progress.

5. Type in your working logline into your reality show business proposal. Print a hardcopy and put into your binder.

6. Using Worksheet 15, create your synopsis and then put in plan. Print a hardcopy and put into your binder.

PHOTOGRAPHY CREDIT FOR CHAPTER 5
Chapter 5 photo taken by Salvatore Vuono

WORKSHEET 14: LOGLINE

Objective: To create the logline for your reality show.

Using the format presented in Chapter 5 and using the sample below as a guide, generate 10 loglines for your reality show by filling in the blanks.

Subject	Verb	Action	Outcome

(A group of college basketball players) (engage) (in life of the court) (as they develop team dynamics)

1. _____ _____ _____ _____.
   Subject   Verb   Action   Outcome

2. _____ _____ _____ _____.
   Subject   Verb   Action   Outcome

3. _____ _____ _____ _____.
   Subject   Verb   Action   Outcome

4. _____ _____ _____ _____.
   Subject   Verb   Action   Outcome

5. _____ _____ _____ _____.
   Subject   Verb   Action   Outcome

6. _____ _____ _____ _____.
   Subject   Verb   Action   Outcome

7. _____ _____ _____ _____.
   Subject   Verb   Action   Outcome

8. _____ _____ _____ _____.
   Subject   Verb   Action   Outcome

9. _____ _____ _____ _____.
   Subject   Verb   Action   Outcome

10. _____ _____ _____ _____.
    Subject   Verb   Action   Outcome

Share the 10 loglines with friends and family.

WORKSHEET 15: SYNOPSIS

Objective: To create the synopsis for your reality show.

1. Fill in the blanks as it pertains to your reality show. The 10 elements for a synopsis include: title of the show; number of episodes; genre; creator; subject ; what makes the subject special; what the subject will be involved with; the production team; outcome; and reason for the show.

Synopsis Template

_____, _____ of episodes, a _____ style reality show created
(Title of Show)   (#)   (Genre)

By _____ that follows _____. _____ is
   (Creator)   (Subject)   (Subject)

_____ and _____as he/she or they do _____
(Attribute)   (Attribute)   (What the subject does)

_____.
(What the subject does)

_____ will be produced by _____, and directed
(Title of Show)   (Name of Company)

by _____. Join _____ as the _____
(Director's Name)   (Subject)   (Outcome)

is achieved. _____.
            (Sentence to bring in Title of Show in a creative manner.)

2. Repeat above activity until you develop a synopsis the hones into your reality show.

Synopsis 1

Synopsis 2

Synopsis 3

3. Type your final logline and synopsis into your plan. Print a hardcopy and put it into your binder.

CHAPTER 6

REALITY SHOW FORMAT

Plato said "Wise men talk because they have something important to say, fools talk because they have to say something." Plato, one of the world's philosophers of all time was wise beyond his years. Little did he know at the time he scribed that quote that reality shows would be the craze in the 21st Century. His words ring true today as shows are structured around what is or is not said. This never held more true to me than when I watched *The Bachelor* the other night. Yes, I hate to admit it, but I do watch this show as well as many more reality shows. I consider it research. And besides it was Valentine's Day.

What I realized during this brief moment of my insanity was the bachelor changed the structure of the show that had always been set in stone. It really wasn't what he said. It all revolved in what he didn't say. He had made up his mind on whom he was sending home and he didn't want to go through the social cocktail party and spend one-on-one time with each girl for their last ditch effort to stay. "I don't want to put you girls through this," he said. "I'm going to keep my promise."

Promise to what? For a moment I thought he had lost his mind and for just an instant I got pulled into the possibility that all of it was for real. He was going to find love or he had found it for the second time. How exciting is that? Right here on national television true love at last for the second time. Remember this season's bachelor is a repeat. He eventually broke up with his first true love and here is his second opportunity. I did come to my senses as he sent home a very beautiful young lady that I thought he should have kept. I reminded myself that this was all part of the reality of a reality show. None of it is really real.

Are Reality Shows Really Real?

It is an oxymoron to say that a reality show is real because they become non real the moment that a camera starts rolling. It is part of the Chaos Theory I was well schooled in graduate school. A butterfly flies somewhere in Japan and affects me in New

Orleans because the little wings fluttered and moved the air. So when a camera rolls, it changes everything. The reality you think you are seeing has been impacted by the butterfly in Japan. You have to remember, who in life goes around with a camera capturing their everyday life? No one - that is unless you are on a reality TV show. That's why they aren't real. The camera changes people and ultimately their behavior. The reality we witness isn't true reality at all. It's all part of a well thought out plan that I call "The Producer Effect." Much like the butterfly in Japan that causes changes, the producer and camera does as well.

The Producer Effect

In reality shows there is an episode producer or creator that designs what is going to happen. They define the developmental arcs. A trick is to put an ear-piece in a cast member's ear and a field-director speaks to this person and guides them in what to say and often gives them movement directives. How do I know? I know because I've either worn the earpiece myself in a show as a cast member or was the field-producer who directed the event. These field producers provide a false reality that the cast lives out.

A perfect example is the reality show *The Colony* that airs on The Discovery Channel. If you haven't watched this one, you

Dr. Mel as a Marauder

should. There is a lot you can learn from it from a creator's point of view. Earlier in this book I told you that I joined up as an extra on *The Colony: Season Two*. I participated as one of the Marauders on four different episodes. Without exception, at least two extras at all times wore ear-pieces as the field-producer spoke and directed us when to attack the colonists, when to explode the fire bombs, when to invade the house, and even what to steal or to destroy in the compound. In the picture on the left, that's me as one of the Marauders. We were filming at a remote house that could only be accessed by boat. That's me on the deck waiting. About 30 of us waited in hiding as the Colonists would arrive soon by boat to take over our camp. We were instructed to defend our home. The only thing real was the unscripted dialogue and that is why it's called reality.

The structure and format of each episode remained the same. Each day when we arrived to base camp the director had a diagram on a white erase board with objectives and targets for the day. We were briefed by him on the specific outcome he wanted the show to take. As cast members we were instructed to make certain that our task was accomplished according to the guidelines presented by the director. That was our job. I'm not sure what would have happened if we didn't follow the orders as we never strayed.

I learned a lot by participating on *The Colony* as an extra, or as I've been corrected, a professional background actor. For one, it slammed the fact that all shows had to have a structure and format. It also proved that reality shows weren't real and just about any topic or subject could be a potential show.

All reality shows do have structure and format. Without both there would be nothing but chaos and no direction.   I like to think of the reality show format as a map or blueprint. You wouldn't start out driving from Chicago headed for a great week in New Orleans to experience Mardi gras without a plan would you? You would have to know how you were going to get there, where you would while getting there, do some budgeting to know how much you could spend, how many days it will take to get there, how many days you are going to stay, and where you would lay your head at night.

There is a lot of planning to the trip as is for planning your reality show. It is here and now that a creator and producer of the show you must think out these details and be able to put into writing. It will serve two purposes: to guide you in developing your concept and to identify to investors how the show will proceed.

To take this step requires you to have a background in reality shows. This means, you need to watch them and watch them often. That's why I watch so many. Believe me, I'd rather watch a good movie, but since I create reality shows for a living I better know my competition. I encourage you to develop the same habit. Watch as many as you can as often as you can to learn from them and not to be entertained by them. Try to watch at least one show every day while you are developing your own. Learn their format, structure and developmental arcs. Don't become a coach potato. Actively become involved watching reality shows with pen and paper in hand. The more you know the better you will be as a creator. You need to become a scholar of sorts to the reality show world. Why? This is the only way to become familiar with reality show formats and their structure.

I guarantee that every reality show has three elements: beginning, middle and end. There are no ifs ands or buts about it. I call them the development arcs. Basically in one format or another, all reality shows, no matter the genre follow a structural base containing the following six developmental arcs:

- Opening and introduction of cast.
- Challenge presentation.
- Working on the challenge.
- Obstacle to challenge.
- Reconciliation.
- Closure with an outcome to the challenge.

What this all means to you as a creator of a reality show is by applying these six developmental arcs you can design your reality show blueprint.   Your blueprint will distinguish your show from that of an amateur rank to that of a professional level creator. Watch several different reality shows and you'll get a general idea. Watch with intent and purpose. Start identifying the developmental arcs within the beginning, middle and end of each show.

THE BEGINNING

To open any show there is always a beginning which identifies the first developmental arc. A beginning provides as an overview of what happened last week and who is in the show whether they are judges, contestants, groups, or a celebrity. It establishes for the viewer what type of genre the show falls. A viewer knows upfront during the opening minutes exactly what type of show they are about to view. Consider a show that introduces judges, rules and contestants. There is no doubt that it is some sort of game show or competition show with a winner receiving a prize at the end. Likewise if a family is introduced such as in *Keeping up with the Kardashians* or *Gene Simmons Family Jewels,* the viewer knows it is about a celebrity family. The time allotted for the opening usually is no more than four minutes so make it count.

THE MIDDLE

Once a show style and cast has been introduced the middle of the show takes place. This section includes several developmental arcs:

- Presentation of the challenge.
- Working on challenge.
- The obstacle to achievement.

This formula applies to any genre or reality programming and not just game shows. Within each celebrity style genre the celebrity faces a task or experiences something that they have to achieve. They face obstacles, fighting with someone, getting a speeding ticket, late somewhere etc. The same holds true in shows such as *The Bachelor* and *Hoarders.* The middle section usually last about 15 minutes for a 22 minute show and 32 minutes for a 44 minute show.

THE END

Once the show reaches a certain point the cast members are faced with the remaining three developmental arcs:

- Significant challenge.
- Resolution.
- Closure with outcome achieved.

It is here that your cast overcomes all challenges he or she just faced or is interviewed about the experience and brings resolution and closure to the show. This section is typically about 3 to 4 minutes long.

BLUEPRINT OF *PROJECT RUNWAY*

Let's start by examining the blueprint and developmental arcs to one of the most popular reality shows on television - *Project Runway*. I chose this show for two reasons - it's not a celebrity style genre reality show and most importantly in has a dynamic development arc and structure. It is my opinion that the creator of the show did a fantastic job in developing the show's developmental arcs for the best success.

The Beginning of Project Runway

The show opens and the first couple minutes inform viewers what happened last week. Heidi, the host of the show, walks out onto a runway while the contestants of the show sit in rows looking up to her on the runway. She announces a hint of the challenge the contestants are about to face. She sends the group of off to meet Tim Gunn. Thus, the first developmental arc of introduction of the cast is met.

The Middle of Project Runway

This moves us to the next developmental arc – the challenge. It goes something like this. Several contestants stand somewhere in a majestic setting with an eye-popping backdrop waiting to hear the explanation of the challenge by Tim Gunn. They're not disappointed because as scripted by a field-producer Tim arrives and delivers the pending challenge. Within minutes, Tim sends all of the contestants to obtain their supplies; which begins developmental arc three – working on the challenge. The contestants either go to *Moods*, a fabric store, or some other wild place like a scrap yard to gather materials to complete the challenge. The blueprint is it is always the same. They become the hunters and gatherers.

Once the contestant's supplies have been secured they go to the workroom where frustration always set in. I haven't seen a show where it hasn't happened this way. We are still on developmental arc three but it becomes more pronounced as they continue to work on the challenge before them. But before too much frustration can develop, in walks Tim Gunn to assess the situation and give his advice. He ends this segment by stating, "Make it work." As predicted, some contestants are relieved after the "Make it work moment," while some contestants' emotions heighten. The stakes rise and once again the contestants are left to work. This brings us directly to developmental arc four - they face obstacles to their challenge.

As soon as they get into the groove of things, in walks Tim Gunn again and announces, "I'm sending in your models." There is always a problem where some model doesn't show up or some piece of clothing doesn't fit. Nothing is perfect in the reality world. The contestants do what they can to make it work before Tim Gunn sends them to their New York lofts for the night.

The next morning back into the workroom, another obstacle occurs. This brings us to developmental arc five - reconciliation. Some problem always happens that might prevent one of the contestants from finishing on time, but somehow they manage. In the history of *Project Runway* they have never sent a model down the runway naked. They fit their models and then send the models off to hair and make-up. Finally, Tim Gunn arrives and announces, "It's off to the runway" and off to the runway for the final showdown and developmental arc five – the reconciliation.

Once at the runway, the judges, Nina Garcia, Michael Kors and a special guest are introduced by Heidi Klum. The runway show begins as the models first strike a pose to form a silhouette prior to walking the runway. Each contestant looks and admires their work as Nina, Michael and Heidi diligently writes notes. After all designs have been presented, the judges send the contestants backstage so they can have a "little chat" to discuss what they liked and disliked about each of the contestants' garments.

The End of Project Runway

Once the judges have completed their chat, they bring the contestants back onto the runway to meet their fate -they are either in the bottom or in the top in the scoring. As expected, developmental arc six in action commences – the closure. Heidi always announces the runner-up first followed by the winner. Then the bottom group is left and one meets their fate, a kiss on the cheek by Heidi and off to the workroom to pack up and say goodbye with the final part of developmental arc six – closure complete.   And that is the format, structure and developmental arcs of *Project Runway*.

No matter the reality show, these six developmental arcs can be identified. I challenge you to start watching reality shows with a new set of skills. Watch in order to identify their blueprints and developmental arcs. This activity will only enhance your own ability to create your show. The more you know the better creator you will become.

DEFINING YOUR BLUEPRINT

How does all of this apply to you and your show? Easy, you too will have to design a structure and format that includes the beginning, middle and end while applying the six developmental arcs - of the opening and introduction of cast; challenge presentation, working on the challenge, obstacle to challenge, reconciliation and closure with an outcome to the challenge. Always maintain this focus when designing your show.

22 Minutes VS 44 Minutes

To begin defining your blueprint you must consider the length of your episodes.   The time allotted will have a direct impact. Although all six of the developmental arcs will still be present, you will have to adjust each episode to fit within either 22 minutes or 44 minutes. That's right. You don't create a 30 minute program or a 60 minute program because each episode must contain eight minutes of advertising per 30 minutes. You should be relieved because now your production cost just went down by eight minutes of film per 30 minutes of programming.

To decide on the length of the program it is best to take into consideration what you are trying to accomplish for the show. Shows like *The Bachelor* and *Rock of Love* can't be accomplished in a 22 minute timeframe each week when you look at the blueprint of the show. They have to have time to get to know the girls, go on dates, spend one-on-one quality time and say goodbye to somebody. The same is true of *America's Next Top Model* and shows such as *American Idol* and *So you Think you can Dance*. Time wise these shows aren't conducive to accomplish the six developmental arcs in 22 minutes.

However, by maximizing 44 minutes the creators created workable shows for programs such as *American Idol* and *The Bachelor*. It's the exact opposite for some of the celebrity reality shows where we get a glimpse into one event that happens to a celebrity during one show. In these shows, they can accomplish the six developmental arcs within a 22 minute time constraint. For instance, Kendra's birthday party in *The Girl's Next* Door or one of the shows that I worked on as project coordinator when the girls visited New Orleans during Mardi gras is a perfect example. Not to bring in politics, but *Sarah Palin's Alaska* might have been better accomplished within a 22 minute framework.

Format and Structure

Now that you have decided either on a 22 minute or 44 how will you allot the time to develop the six arcs? What will your subjects or subject be doing week-end and week-out? Although activities for each episode will be different, that doesn't mean your framework will.

I hope I've provided enough evidence for you to know that you must adhere to the six developmental arcs in planning your show. Equate your decision to that of a contractor who is building a bunch of condos in one structure. All have the same framework; blueprints; either one, two, or three bedrooms etc.; but when the condo owners come on board the type of flooring, the style of cabinets, wall color choice and how it will be furnished changes by the decisions each owner makes. The same concept applies for the structure and format of your reality show. You will follow the same blueprint for each episode, but the contents and topics will be modified each time.

There are certain tips to keep in mind when designing your blueprint. Examine the amount of time you need in each arc to make certain that it is fully developed. Some arcs need more than others. To emphasize, to give contestants an opening challenge may only take one to two minutes, but for them to complete the challenge might take eight minutes in a game type reality show. For a celebrity style show it might only take two minutes to layout the challenge but it 12 minutes to complete.

DEVELOPING YOUR SHOW

An auto mechanic came to me because he wanted his own reality show. He thought it would not only be easy to accomplish but also fun to do. He quickly learned that he couldn't just point a camera at his shop and hope for something to happen, but careful planning and consideration had to be put into it. We first had to decide how long we wanted each episode. After careful consideration we decided that each episode should be 22 minutes. One reason was financial. I felt that we could get more than one episode filmed during a single day because of the number of customers that came into his shop. The second reason we felt that we had a better chance of holding an audience's attention within the 22 minutes. We reviewed several other reality shows in this genre and decided that this length seemed to be the most successful for this type of programming.

The following is the development chart I use for the creation of each reality show. Diagram 6-1 is the chart for *The Ace Mechanic*. The important elements are all incorporated and laid out in a manner that shares the blueprint of the show.

Diagram 6-1 Blueprint Arc for *Ace Mechanic*

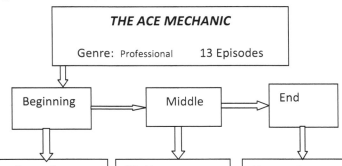

THE ACE MECHANIC

Genre: Professional   13 Episodes

Beginning	Middle	End

How will your show open? Introduce each cast member. Also, secretary always reads each horoscope.

The Challenge: Each episode begins by The Ace Mechanic passing out today's work orders. A wayward traveler is stranded and ACE needs to tow them in.

Working on Challenge:

Traveler always has a personal issue to resolve; e.g. needs new car, has to get somewhere quick, has ran out of money but has to get to a funeral etc.

The Obstacle: Can't find car part, car, mechanic can't figure out or fix car

Almost reaching obstacle: Think car or problem is fixed but it's not.

Overcoming Obstacle: The Ace Mechanic steps in to save the day, he solves problem, pays it forward with kindness to strangers by giving money, coming down on price, fixing it for free.

Reconciliation: Travelers head on into the sunset happy. Ace gives testimony of how that traveler impacted him.

Closure: Summary

Diagram 6-1 highlights exactly what is going to happen in each episode of *The Ace Mechanic*. Therefore, while filming each episode, although we do not have a script, we do have a format to follow and know what footage we need. Each of the developmental arcs is allotted a certain amount of time within the 22 minute frame.

In essence, we plan the footage according to the blueprint. This by all means doesn't mean that we don't capture random moments that have impact. We do. What it does mean is that we are not capturing footage we do not need with 300 hours of raw footage we don't plan on using in the first place. In the editing room that creates an undue burden. My philosophy is that I always shoot to edit. I advise you the same once you get to that point.

FORMAT AND STRUCTURE BREAKDOWN PAGE

I have spent this entire chapter to get to this point. How does this apply to your reality show business plan? The reason was so that you would have enough information and put in enough time and thought into developing your episode breakdowns. You will need to provide this information to investors and television executives. It is not good enough to simply put into your business plan what you want to shoot but you also need to include a well thought out list of possible episodes.

When placing this information in your business plan, you will not be using a diagram like Diagram 6-1. Instead, you will state the format of the show and list the episodes. The format outlines the six developmental arcs; whereas, each episodes identifies the topics. Diagram 6-2 is a sample taken from the reality show *Hoops: Life off Court*. Notice how it is formatted in the business plan document.

Diagram 6-2   Format and Show Structure

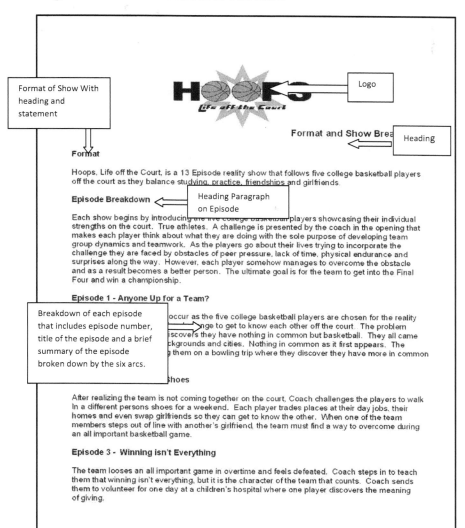

Format of Show With heading and statement

Logo

Format and Show Brea

Heading

Format

Hoops, Life off the Court, is a 13 Episode reality show that follows five college basketball players off the court as they balance studying, practice, friendships and girlfriends.

Episode Breakdown

Heading Paragraph on Episode

Each show begins by introducing the five college basketball players showcasing their individual strengths on the court. True athletes. A challenge is presented by the coach in the opening that makes each player think about what they are doing with the sole purpose of developing team group dynamics and teamwork. As the players go about their lives trying to incorporate the challenge they are faced by obstacles of peer pressure, lack of time, physical endurance and surprises along the way. However, each player somehow manages to overcome the obstacle and as a result becomes a better person. The ultimate goal is for the team to get into the Final Four and win a championship.

Episode 1 - Anyone Up for a Team?

Breakdown of each episode that includes episode number, title of the episode and a brief summary of the episode broken down by the six arcs.

occur as the five college basketball players are chosen for the reality nge to get to know each other off the court. The problem iscovers they have nothing in common but basketball. They all came ckgrounds and cities. Nothing in common as it first appears. The g them on a bowling trip where they discover they have more in common

hoes

After realizing the team is not coming together on the court, Coach challenges the players to walk In a different persons shoes for a weekend. Each player trades places at their day jobs, their homes and even swap girlfriends so they can get to know the other. When one of the team members steps out of line with another's girlfriend, the team must find a way to overcome during an all important basketball game.

Episode 3 - Winning isn't Everything

The team looses an all important game in overtime and feels defeated. Coach steps in to teach them that winning isn't everything, but it is the character of the team that counts. Coach sends them to volunteer for one day at a children's hospital where one player discovers the meaning of giving.

The above section is easy to format and will be placed on a heading page by itself with the correct subheadings. The format of this page is:

- Place your logo centered at the top of the page.
- Space down and put the heading Format and Show Breakdown in a bold font and size 14.
- Double space again and put the subheading Format in bold and size 12 font.
- Space down and write the one sentence format structure.

As an option you can also add a paragraph in this section of your plan that defines the allotted framework such as:

TIME STRUCTURE FOR ACE MECHANIC

4 MINUTES: Opening and introduction of cast.

2 MINUTES: Challenge presentation.

8 MINUTES: Working on the challenge.

5 MINUTES: Obstacle to challenge.

2 MINUTES: Reconciliation.

1 MINUTE: Closure with an outcome to the challenge.

This section wasn't included in the previous example but is in the sample business plan in the Appendix. You would put this section immediately before you begin to describe the episode breakdowns.

The next subheading is the Episode Breakdown. These paragraphs follow the six developmental arcs: opening, challenge, working on the challenge, the obstacle and the reconciliation with the outcome. Individual topics for each episode should be carefully designed to make each episode fit the blueprint and at the same time be original in concept.

The following example provides an opening paragraph for your section of Episode Breakdown.

Example *Hoops: Life off the Court*

> *Hoops: Life off the Court* is a 13 Episode reality show that follows six college basketball players off the court as they balance studying, practice, friendships and girlfriends.

Notice the example is very similar to the original logline for that show. The only exception is the number of episodes stated. The original logline for Hoops: *Life off the Court is*:

> A group of college basketball players engage in life of the court as they develop team dynamics.

The difference between the two statements is the expansion of the types of activities the cast are involved while off the court. More specific details are provided in the paragraph that describes the episode breakdowns. Is one way better than another? Not really, it depends on personal preference. In a pinch you can always use your original logline.

Episode Breakdowns

When creating episode breakdowns, be certain to follow the six developmental arcs. Be creative and visualize where you want  your cast members filmed or what they will do during the specified time allotted. Ask, "What activity or event would best make for interesting viewing?" For *Hoops: Life off the Court*, I knew where I wanted to film. I considered the facts. I knew I had six players that had nothing in common that were coming together to try to get to the Final Four. That was the ultimate goal so the entire show was directed toward achieving this task for the final outcome of the show. For this goal to be achieved I also knew that team dynamics would come into play so I would have to create the environment to provide different opportunities. I gave them the butterfly in Japan to make things happen while filming. That's where each challenge became important for each episode. Look at the following example of the Breakdown Paragraph for *Hoops: Life off the Court.*

> Each show begins by introducing six college basketball players showcasing their individual Strengths on the court. They are true athletes in every sense. A challenge is presented by the coach who makes each player think about what they are doing with the sole purpose of developing group dynamics and teamwork. Their Coach offers advice and solutions to help each succeed in their effort. As the players go about their lives trying to incorporate the challenge they are faced by obstacles of peer pressure, lack of time, physical endurance and surprises along the way. However, each player somehow manages to overcome the obstacle and as a result becomes a better person. The ultimate goal is for the team to get into the Final Four and win a championship.

In the above example can you identify the six developmental arcs? To aide in your identification, I will distinguish each area by numbering and highlighting every other one in grey so they are easier to identify.

1. The opening/introduction.

2. The challenge.

3. Working on the challenge.

4. The obstacles.

5. The reconciliation.

6. The overall outcome with closure.

(1) Each episode of *Hoops: Life off the Court* begins by introducing six college basketball players showcasing their individual Strengths on the court. True athletes. (2) A challenge is presented by the coach that makes each player think about what they are doing with the sole purpose of developing group dynamics and teamwork. (3) Their Coach offers advice and solutions to help each succeed in their effort. (4) As the players go about their lives trying to incorporate the challenge they are faced by obstacles of peer pressure, lack of time, physical endurance and surprises along the way. (5) However, each player somehow manages to overcome the obstacle and as a result becomes a better person. (6) The ultimate goal is for the team to get into the Final Four and win a championship.

Now that an opening blueprint paragraph has been formed you can now develop the blueprint specifics for each episode within the reality show series. These paragraphs differ from the above breakdown paragraph because each provides specific activities. Remember that big condo complex we were building earlier in this chapter. The breakdown paragraph is equivalent to the condo's framework and shell. It's now time to decorate and make each unit distinctive.

Not all of the six arcs have to be addressed in the exposition of each episode. Rather, the important factor is to provide succinct information that allows the reader to gain an understanding and direction of each episode. Ask, "How does each episode fit in with the rest of them?" Will each episode end in a cliffhanger or stand independent? How will each episode be similar or how will they be different.

EXAMPLE 1 *Hoops: Life off the Court*

Episode 1 - *Anyone Up for a Team?*

This episode begins by introducing all cast members - the six players and their coach. The show is hosted by Lebron X, a professional NBA player. Team basketball tryouts for a college occur as the six college basketball players are chosen for the reality show. The six team members are given the challenge to get to know each other off the court. Problems surface when the group discovers they have nothing in common but basketball. They all came from different lifestyles, backgrounds and cities.   The Coach intervenes by taking them on a bowling trip where they discover they have more in common than originally thought. They bring their new friendship to the court during practice.

EXAMPLE 2 *Hoops: Life off the Court*

Episode 2 - *Walk in my Shoes*

After realizing the team is not coming together on the court, Coach challenges the players to "walk in a different persons shoes" for a weekend. Each player trades places at their day jobs, their home and even swap girlfriends so they can get to know the other. When one of the team member steps out of line with another's girlfriend, the team must find a way to overcome the tension during an all important basketball game. After the game, the team discusses what they learned by walking in another players shoes.

EXAMPLE 3 *Hoops: Life off the* Court

Episode 3 - *Winning isn't Everything*

The team loses an all important game in overtime and feels defeated. Coach steps in to teach the six basketball players the concept - winning isn't everything, but it is the character of the team that counts. Coach sends the team to volunteer for one day at a children's hospital where one player discovers the meaning of giving to others. The team comes together on the court and when one player is injured the game is on the line. The team applies what they learned from one of the children at the hospital.

As a creator of your show, you can apply the six developmental arcs to your show within the structure of a complete beginning, middle and end.

CHAPTER SUMMARY

In this chapter the reader was presented with the concept of developing the format and structure of a reality show and why the blueprint is important. The concept that all reality shows have a beginning, middle and end was discussed. Further, within the confines of the three basic elements six developmental arcs were presented that must be included in a reality show format and structure: opening and introduction of cast; challenge presentation, working on the challenge, obstacle to challenge, reconciliation and closure with an outcome to the challenge. Moreover, examples were provided and instruction given to create an episode outline. Samples were provided.

PRACTICAL APPLICATION

Note: You will need 10 or more copies of Worksheet 16 for the following practical applications.

1. Using the Worksheet 16 transfer the information on the reality show *Project Runway* from the blueprint description provided in this Chapter.

2. You will need to make one copy of Worksheet 16 for every reality show you watch. Use Worksheet 16 to take your notes on as many reality shows as you can. The more reality shows you watch the more proficient you will become and the easier it will be for you to create your blueprint.

3. Using Worksheet 16 develop the blueprint for your reality show project which will become your format. Add this to your reality show business plan. Print a hardcopy for your binder.

4. Use Worksheet 16 to develop individual concept topics for each episode for your reality show.

5. Format the page in your business plan document. Refer to the following diagram as a reference. Place your logo centered at the top, followed by the heading and subheadings.

5. Extract the information from Worksheet 16 that you developed for your reality show and write a paragraph describing how your show will work following the six arcs of cast, challenge, working on the challenge, obstacle to challenge, reconciliation and closure. When finished with your breakdown paragraph type it into your business plan document under the subheading Format.

6. Generate your episode breakdowns. Give each episode a catchy title. Use the six arcs to develop each area. Once complete, place your episodes into your business plan document. Print a hardcopy and put into your binder.

PHOTOGRAPHY CREDIT FOR CHAPTER 6
Chapter 6 photo taken by Graur Razvan Ionut
Dr. Mel on set on *The Colony Season 2* taken by Miranda Stipen
Basketball going through hoop taken by xedosy4/freedigitalphoto.net

WORKSHEET 16: DEVELOPING BLUEPRINT

Objective 1: To identify blueprints to other reality shows.

Objective 2: Develop your blueprint and episodes for your reality show.

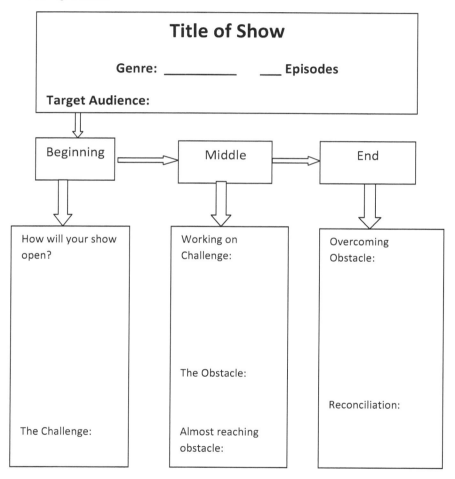

Develop each of your episode breakdowns for your reality show.

Episode 1

Episode 2

Episode 3

Episode 4

Episode 5

Episode 6

Episode 7

Episode 8

Episode 9

Episode 10

Episode 11

Episode 12

Episode 13

Write down your reflection on this activity. How will it guide you to further develop your reality show?

CHAPTER 7

CAST

In the late sixties Andy Warhol stated that "In the future, everyone will be world-famous for 15 minutes." How could he have known that he would be the predictor of reality television and that a whole new kind of celebrity would be created? Historian and social theorist Daniel J. Boorstin defined the celebrity as "a person who is known for his well-knownness." This about sums it up for the cast of your reality show – they either will already be famous or one that will have their 15 minutes of fame. I like to call them "Realebrities" instead of celebrities.

Who can forget "Realebrities" Jessica Simpson and her husband Nick Lachey. They had their show, which by the way was cancelled in 2003. Does this make Jessica a star celebrity or a "Realebrity?" I'm not picking on Jessica. I like her. In fact, I have met her and worked with her on the movie *Dukes of Hazzard*. That's the only reason I know a film that she has acted in. Can you name any? If you ask her today what her career is

she'll tell you that she is a singer. For the life of me I can't think
of any songs she sang
either. So, what's up with
her? Is she on the famous
list track all because of a
reality show?

I can say the same thing
about her former hubby
Nick Lachey. What has he
been in other than his own
reality show?   Can you
name   anything   at   all?

Dr. Mel with Dukes of Hazzard Car known as
The General Lee.

Believe it or not he is trying. He, unlike Jessica, does claim to be
an actor. Just the other night I was watching *Hawaii Five-O* and
to my amazement Nick was playing the villain. He didn't do too
badly, but his guest appearance doesn't put him in the ranks of
a Brad Pitt or Tom Cruise.

There are plenty more "Realebrities." Do the names Snookie
and The Situation come to mind? Some people have never
watched one episode of *The Jersey Shore* but know who they
are and what show they are in. Even *Saturday Night Live* does
spoofs on them. They are in every sense of the term true
"Realebrities." As a creator and producer of a reality show it is
your responsibility to bring to the audience more "Realebrities."
Yes, the public demands it. So make certain that your cast holds
this same Snookie or The Situation potential. They are
marketable. Cast somebody the paparazzi are going to want to
chase and exploit. It'll make your job of selling your show
easier. Give the audience people we either love or love to hate.

PICKING YOUR CAST

Sometimes your cast just falls into your lap while others you
really have to go and hold auditions in order to find. There's
nothing wrong with either way. Just know what you are looking
for and make them fit your reality show concept. If I'm doing a

show on a group of college age basketball players I'd better make sure they can play. Likewise, if I'm doing a show on a NFL player he'd better not have a dull life and being a lady's magnet would hurt either. A show centered on life in a dorm better have some group dynamics and a variety of personalities and hidden conflicts and agendas. If everybody was the same nobody will want to watch them. Audiences would become board and lose interest if everybody was just alike.

I have a casting tip for you. Make sure your cast members can handle being in front of a camera. This may sound silly to you but not everyone is comfortable in front of a camera. In fact this area has been my biggest frustration. People get in front of the camera and think they have to talk into it and not to the other cast members. They try to pose in front of the camera instead of pretending that it isn't there. I have also seen people start to stutter and although are a very outgoing person once the camera was rolling became very shy and was so nervous they quit. That's why a camera test is a good idea.

Tips for Finding Your Cast

Finding the right cast for your show isn't as easy as it may seem. You need to put time and effort into it. Not everyone will make a great cast member but more than likely just about everybody wants to have their own reality show. Everyday somebody comes up to me when they find out what I do for a living and pitches their reality show idea. The conversation always goes like this. "I'd make a great reality star because I'm outgoing, good looking and funny." I have discovered that more than likely they aren't right for the job. The only advantage is having so many people pitch their ideas to me when I hear and see a good one I know it instantly. It is up to you to develop this same instinct to find and develop your talent that is just right for your reality show. Here are some tips to help you along the way.

Go with who you know. It's easier and faster.

Decide on if your cast is going to include both male and females.

Vary the cast member's age. Start at the youngest possible for the show and cast a cast member at the other end of the spectrum. It makes for more interesting viewing and dynamics for the show.

Hold open auditions. Find out who is out there that might be the next Snookie.

Don't take people's word that they can act. Being in a reality show really isn't about acting it is about being able to act yourself.

Encourage people to submit taped auditions. At least this way you can see for yourself how they come across on camera.

Don't give in for convenience. Keep looking until you find the cast member you need.

Attend actor showcases in your city to get a good idea of the local talent pool.

Audit as many acting classes taught by different instructors as you can to identify potential talent for your show.

Attend film festivals in your city to screen for talent.

Attend an open "mic" comedy night in your community.

THE CASTING HEADING IN YOUR BUSINESS PLAN

The Casting heading for your business plan is a separate section. More than likely, if your cast is comprised of people that don't have credits to their name you will more than likely have to list their attributes and what makes them perfect for you project. If possible give all a nickname. They stick in the mind of viewers.

The layout for the Cast section is simple.

- The title of the reality show is placed on the first line.
- Space down one and use a size 14 bold font for the heading Cast followed by name of show.
- Space down one and place opening paragraph of two to three sentences.

Diagram 7-1 is an example of the Cast page section of a reality show business plan.   It does not include pictures of cast members but feel free to do so in yours. If I had included it, I would have put them to the left of each of their names as I do in the sample business plan in the last chapter of this book.

Diagram 7-1   Cast Section of Business Plan

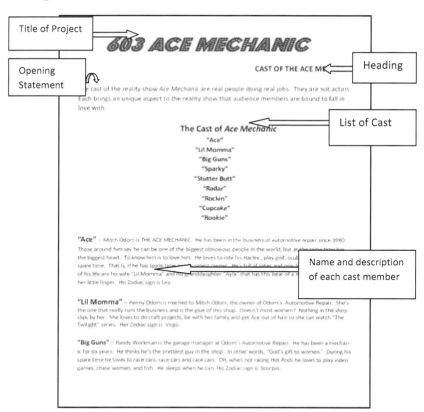

I always begin my Cast page with an opening statement that describes the type of cast that will be in the show. The examples below demonstrate opening paragraphs for three different reality shows.

Example 1: *Ace Mechanic*

> The cast of the reality show *Ace Mechanic* are real people doing real jobs. They are not actors. Each brings unique aspects to the reality show that audience members are bound to fall in love with.

Example 2: *The Baker Girls: Sealed with a Kiss*

> The cast of The Baker Girls are salesgirls who work at a national shoe store. The girls range in ages from 16 to 30 and bring a variety to the show. Some of the girls are single where others are married with children.

Example 3: *Darren: Sharper than Ever*

> Super Bowl Champion and five-time NFL Hall of Fame football player Darren Sharper is NFL's GQ man and stars in *Darren: Sharper than Ever*. He is surrounded by family and friends as witness his life behind the scenes.

The next portion of this section identifies the cast members by name that is attached to the project which is usually centered on the page for easy identification. I also like to use a bold font. In the following example, I chose to use the cast member's nicknames because these are the names that we wanted them to be known by. When I write the biographies for each that is when I include their birth names.

Example 1 – *Ace Mechanic*

THE CAST
"Ace"
"Lil Momma"
"Big Guns"
"Sparky"
"Stutter Butt"
"Radar"
"Rockyn"
"Cupcake"
"Rookie"

Once I list each cast member I then provide a description of each person that includes key attributes and experience. The cast member descriptions always contain five items:

1. The cast member's name.
2. What that cast member does.
3. Identify key attributes about the cast member.
4. Highlights their experience.
5. Details of attachment to the project.

Example 2 is the formatting I used for *Ace Mechanic* cast members. I inserted a picture to demonstrate where one would be placed if you choose to go this route. Notice within five sentences I provide enough information about her to allow the reader of my plan to know who she is, what she does as well as her attributes. I do not provide a complete biography stating when or where she born, who are parents are, nor where she went to school. None of these have relevance to the show.

Example 2 – Biography from the reality show *Ace Mechanic*.

"**Rockyn**" – Robbyn XXXX is the Customer Service Specialist with a constant smile at XXXX Automotive. She's full of laughter and absolutely loves people. Having worked as an inspector during major disasters she finds this job a little more upbeat. During her spare time she loves being with her kids and this single mom is looking for love on an online dating site. She knows the right man is out there, she just believes he lives on another planet – maybe Mars. She has film experience as an extra on more than a dozen films. Her Zodiac sign is Pieces. "Rockyn" is attached to this project.

Example 3 – Cast Biography from the reality *show Hoops: Life off the Court*

"Lil Jumper" - Jeremy L. XXX, known as "Lil Jumper," is the team captain and there is nothing little about him. Measuring a 6' 11", Jeremy is the tallest of the team members. He is studying to be an attorney and thinks his size will be an asset in the courtroom. He was an All-Star high school basketball player and dreams of moving on to the NBA upon graduation. His enjoys playing video games and listening to rap music during his spare time. He most admires Michael Jordon and what he has done for the game of basketball. He is attached to this project.

Example 4 – Cast Biography from the reality show *The Baker Girls: Sealed with a Kiss*

Jamie – Jamie is the little sister to the manager of the shoe store. Her personal life often gets in the way of her day job which makes it difficult for her older sister who might have to fire her. The only thing Jamie cares about is living her dream and wants to move to Hollywood to become an actress. Her hobbies include photography, hiking, and fashion. Jamie is married to a guy from Columbia. She is the former lead actress in the web-series *Britney Meetup* and has the leading role in the film *Demented Half*. She was also in the music video with the Tick Tock singer Keisha. Jamie is attached to this project.

Example 5 – Cast Biography from *Here Comes the Bride*

Erin G. planned all of her life for a fairy-tale wedding. Every detail from her wedding gown, flowers and bridesmaids were considered and carefully orchestrated. What she didn't count on was that she was marrying into a Greek family full of traditions and customs setting in motion a different wedding than she dreamed of as a little girl. Erin takes everything seriously as she has a type A personality. Nothing is left to chance. Erin earned a Master's degree from Loyola University in World Religion and is a teacher in the public school system.

Example 6- Cast Biography from *The Baker Girls: Sealed with a Kiss*

Kelly M. is the tough business manager from a local retail outlet shoe store. Having earned her degree in business, she applies her knowledge and skill to run one of the highest selling stores for chain of stores. Kelly assembled a young and talented sales crew, who form a unique bond with each other. Kelly is married and has a son who she claims has changed her life.

CHAPTER SUMMARY

This chapter explained how to write the section of a reality business plan for the cast members. Also provided were key features and personalities a producer should look for when identifying cast members such as age, skills and attributes of each cast member and then how to narrow those for the case biographies. A sample was provided that identified the structure of each cast members biography that includes: name, what they do, attributes, experience and whether they are attached to the project.

PRACTICAL APPLICATION

1. In your reality show business document format the structure of your Cast Section following the guideline presented in this chapter.

2. Using Worksheet 17 Generate a list of potential cast members as they relate to your project. List as many as you can. If you have already identified your cast, don't skip this area; however make a list of potential substitutes. You never know when someone becomes unavailable or changes their mind.

3. Using Worksheet 18 Generate biography information based off cast members attributes and work experience. Make enough copies of Worksheet 18 so that you complete the information for each of your cast members.

4. Using Worksheet 19 construct your cast member's biographies by extracting the information from Worksheet 18. You will need to make enough copies of Worksheet 19 that equals the same number of your cast members.

5. Transfer each cast member's biography from Worksheets 19 into the correct section in your reality show business plan document. Print a hardcopy and put into your binder.

6. If you so choose, place a picture of each cast member into your reality show business plan in the appropriate area.

Photography Credit for Chapter 7
Picture of Dr. Mel with the *Dukes of Hazzard* car *The General Lee* was taken by her daughter.
Robbyn's picture provided by her and used with Robbyn's permission.
Jeremy L's picture provided by cast member
Jamie C, Kelly M. and Erin G photos taken by Mel Caudle

WORKSHEET 17: YOUR CAST

Objective: Generate a list of potential cast members for your project that follows their name, what they do, attributes, experience and whether they are attached to the project.

1. List the cast members you have already attached to your show.

1. _____

2. _____

3. _____

4. _____

5. _____

6. _____

2. List three potential cast members below that you think would be perfect for your show that could be possible substitutes.

1. _____

2. _____

3. _____

3. Review your list above. Is there a variance in age, sex and ethnicity? If not, you might want to revisit the list. The more range the more likely there will be more appeal to potential audiences.

WORKSEET 18: CAST INFORMATION

Objective: To identify key attributes of each cast member.

Make enough copies of this worksheet that correlates to the number of your cast members.

Cast Member

Name: _____

Nickname: _____

Age: _____   M/F: _____

Ethnicity: _____   Profession: _____

What makes this person interesting?

What skill does this person have that makes them a good choice for your show?

What about this person that makes them interesting?

What experience do they bring to your project?

Is this person attached to the project?

WORKSHEET 19: CAST BIOS

Objective: Generate cast member's biographies for inclusion into your reality show plan. You will need to make enough copies of this worksheet that equals the number of your cast.

1. Use the following template to generate your cast member's biographies.

The below bio statement includes all of the five elements and can serve as a guide post for describing each of your cast.

1. The cast member
2. Indicates what that cast member does.
3. Identifies key attributes about the cast member
4. Highlights her experience.
5. Details whether or not the cast member is attached to the project.

 (1) "Rockyn" – Robbyn Stroud (2) is the Customer Service Specialist with a smile at Odom's Automotive. (3) She's full of laughter and absolutely loves people. Having worked as an inspector during major disasters she finds this job a little more upbeat. During her spare time she loves being with her kids and online dating. She knows the right man is out there, she just believes he lives on another planet – maybe Mars. (4)She has film experience as an extra on more than a dozen films. (3)Her Zodiac sign is Pieces. (5) "Rockyn" is attached to this project.

_____ **is a** _____**at** _____.
(Name of Cast)   *(Profession)*   *(Where they are employed)*

He/She is known for _____,_____, **and** _____.
                         (List attribute) (List attribute) (List attribute)

He/She also believes _____.
(list something they believe are does in their spare time)

He/She has ____ **experience in** _____. _____ **is/is not**
  (# yrs if Experience)   (in film and/or television)   (Name of Cast Member)

attached to this project.

2. Manipulate the wording of each cast member until you get a paragraph that is appealing. Hint: I often allow individual cast members to review and/or make deletions and changes. Sometimes what they provide is better than mine.

3. After formulating each cast member's biography, put into your reality show business plan. Print a hardcopy and put in your binder.

CHAPTER 8

PRODUCTION TEAM

The Production Team section of your reality show business plan requires you to put all of the pieces to a puzzle together. Every member of your production team serves a different role. Your reality show business plan has three mandatory subheadings or categories with a possible fourth if you have attached additional key crew members and/or consultants to your project. The Production Team section outlines who will be running the show in all aspects and who is in charge. Investors want to know who will be making the decisions of how, when and why their money is being spent and whether or not those making those decisions are qualified to do so in the first place. They will ultimately want to know:

- What type of company are they dealing with?

- Who will lead the team?
- Is the person leading the team qualified and experienced?
- Has the leader surrounded themselves with others that are experienced and qualified?
- Who are the other producers involved and have they done it before?
- Is the director experienced and qualified?
- What type of company structure will be put into place and who will have control?

By addressing the aforementioned questions in your reality show plan now, rather than later, increases more faith in investors in the overall plan. It is an indicator for them to determine you know what you are doing. Successful individuals attached to your project breeds confidence in your investors. They want to believe that you can, but sometimes you have to prove it by presenting your team players. Your team should be loosely comprised of the following individuals:

- The Executive Producer
- The Producer(s)
- The Director
- Essential Crew
- Essential Affiliates and Consultants

To format the Production Team page of your business plan follow these guidelines:

- Place the title of your project centered on the first line.
- Space down and flush the text to the right, place the heading in all caps, font size 14.
- Space down again, flush left, put your subheading in font size 12.
- Space down and begin your text for each production. team member beginning with the producer followed by the director and the rest of the team members.

Diagram 8-1   Production Team Page

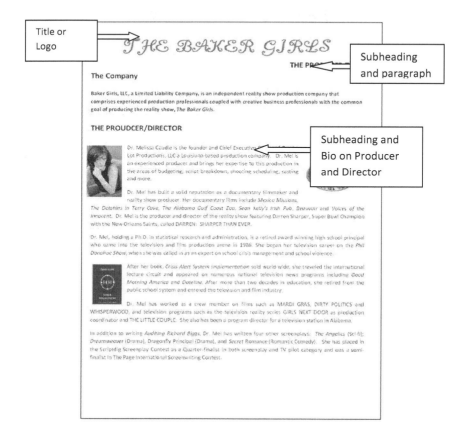

All necessary components are identified as well as my picture and graphics on the Production Team page. If there is more than one producer add their picture and biography information as well. A word of advice - this isn't the time to be lazy by cutting and pasting a producer's information from IMDB or putting their resume here. Those items belong in an Appendix if you choose to include them.

THE PRODUCTION COMPANY

One might think this would be a simple statement by stating the name of your company. Sorry, it's not that easy. A great deal of thought and planning has to go into this area. One of which is deciding the type of company you are going to present. When making this decision, make certain you always consult with either a corporate attorney that specializes in corporations or your entertainment attorney. I am not either therefore cannot provide you legal advice.

To Thyself be True

There are many types of companies that you can form for a reality show. And, any type of company you mention in your reality show business plan can be easily verified through an internet search or through information from *Daily Variety* and *Hollywood Reporter* by a potential investor. If you are not a limited liability company don't state that you are. Instead state that you plan on incorporating. What do you think a future investor will believe about your honesty and integrity if you say one thing that isn't true? Do you honestly think they would want to do business with you and give you money? I wouldn't.

When it all boils down to it investors make their final decision on the type of person or people they will be dealing with and their relationship. In the end no matter how well written your reality show business plan is or how well you presented it; it will ultimately come down to the integrity you have maintained. I like to set the example in all of my business dealings that not only do I mean what I say but I say what I mean. That way anyone that deals with me knows that my "Yes" means "Yes" and that my "No" means "No." In this business you don't want to position yourself into a difficult situation with lack of integrity.

Types of Companies

Investors want to know if you are legitimate and mean business. They will be asking, "Who will manage the money, keep the accounting, protect them legally and keep them out of trouble with both the SEC and the IRS?" The only way is to form a legal business of some sort separate from their and your individual money accounts. I have worked with several Sony films over the last couple of years and even they form smaller corporate entities for each movie or television show they produce. I follow the same path for each of my own projects. The last thing I want is for someone to make a claim that they own a part of my production company On the Lot Productions, LLC. Instead, they only can lay claim to the project in which they have invested.

There are seven types of businesses currently operating in the United States.

- A nonprofit company – a company formed for non-commercial purposes only.
- A joint venture – when two businesses join together.
- A corporation – operates as a sole individual and their assets are liable and not the people running them. A corporation can incur debt, sue and be sued.
- A limited liability company – combines a partnership and a corporation. Gains and losses bypass the LLC and go directly to the owners without being taxed.
- A limited partnership – two partners comprise this type of business and they provide the financial backing.
- A general partnership – two or more partners make up the business and which has to be registered in the city of operation by law. The partners cannot lose more money than what they put into it.
- A sole proprietorship – only one individual operates the company and no protection is provided from being debt, being sued or tax burdens.

Each business type has certain advantages. It will be your responsibility to research each, consult your entertainment or business attorney, and make the necessary decision. This is not the function of this book. However, most production companies choose a limited liability company (LLC) because of the tax benefits it offers as well as the protection. That is the reason I choose to form a LLC for all of my projects whether they are a reality show, documentary or feature film.

The Production Company's Opening Paragraph

Under the subheading The Company you will identify the name of the company, what type of company it is and who formed the company. Below is the example from *The Baker Girls*.

Example 1 The *Baker Girls: Sealed with a Kiss*

> The Company
>
> Baker Girls, LLC, a Limited Liability Company, is an independent reality show production company that comprises experienced production professionals coupled with creative business professionals with the common goal of producing the reality show, *The Baker Girls: Sealed with a Kiss.*

The statement is short and succinct. A no frills statement to say the least. However, four important elements are present:

1. The Company.

2. The type of company formed.

3. The participants in The Company.

4. Why The Company was formed.

The example below identifies the four key elements in *The Baker Girls: Sealed with a Kiss* company statement and are shaded to match for easy identification.

Example 2 The Company Statement – *The Baker Girls*

The Company

(1) Baker Girls, LLC, (2) a Limited Liability Company, (3 is an independent reality show production company that comprises experienced production professionals coupled with creative business (4) professionals with the common goal of producing the reality show, *The Baker Girls*.

THE PRODUCER

Finally, we get to you as the producer. It is here that investors will be asking:

- Who is the producer?
- What qualifies him/her to be a producer?
- What experience does the producer bring to the table?

It is your responsibility to tell investors the truth. Don't fabricate items to enhance your resume. They can easily find all the information they want on you by doing an internet search. Try my name for example. There is tons of information on the

internet about me from the books, screenplays, reality shows and articles I have written to the different movies I have helped produced. You can even find out what I look like and what movies I have acted in. Some information on the internet about me is inaccurate but it does prove that an investor can find out about me and what I have done. An investor always researches my name and often tells me stuff I didn't know about myself that was on the internet. In a way it's scary. Anything you ever wanted to know about a person can be found on the internet and then some. Times have changed.

So what do you do if you don't have experience as a producer? No worries. Tell them that, but always add skills that you bring to the table. When I started in production I had zero experience as a producer; however, investors were impressed that I had a PhD and that I was a prior high school principal and adjunct professor. Those experiences had no connection to film and television production. But instead, my experience told investors that I had leadership and decision making skills which both are essential skills in the production world. You too will have skills and experience to bring to the table.

I won't waste space here in giving you an example of my bio. You can read that at the end of this book in the section About the Author. This is what I use in all of my business plans. Suffice it to say, when writing your bio, state your name, education, training, and experience. Also include the experience you have which make qualifies you to be a producer.

THE DIRECTOR

The next subheading of the Production Team page lists the director for the project. If the producer and director are one in the same, as in my case, they are combined and you need not repeat the information. However, if the director is someone other than the producer, place their information according to the producer's format that follows: the director's name, education, training, and experience. Also include, what is it that makes your director qualified to direct your reality show and whether he/she is attached to the project.

What do you do if you do not have a director attached? You say that in your plan. However, you will include the following statement.

> It is The Company's desire to attach a qualified and experienced director to our project. Our wish list includes: _____ or _____.

A word of caution – don't just start adding names of directors. This could back fire on you. First, make certain that the director does direct the type of reality show you are producing. Then make careful consideration as to whether or not it will even be financially feasible. You don't want to make a suggestion for a specific director and get investor's hopes up only to discover they have to settle for second best. It would be better not to include your wish list at all if this is the case. If it is any consolation for your consideration, I have never put a wish list in my reality show business plans. I have only done so for a feature film.

AFFILIATIONS AND CONSULTANTS

President Truman stated, "The mark of a genius is to know where to find the answers." How right Truman was. I don't know a single producer that hasn't had a mentor, advisor or someone they turn too to answer questions when needed. I learned early in my career as an educator that a person that I could bounce information off of or gain from their experience was beneficial to me. The same holds true in producing a reality show. I have certain industry professionals that I frequently call upon to bounce ideas. I also am one of those people who receive frequent calls from a variety of individuals as a mentor.

It has been a couple of years since I worked on the reality show *The Girls Next Door*, but I am still in communication with at least seven crew members including the production supervisor who now works for the BET reality series *Tiny and Toya*. When they were filming in New Orleans I was one of the first people he contacted for suggestions and guidance. Because of our past working relationship I was able to suggest crew, locations and guidance with our state's tax incentives. Likewise he was able to set up a meeting for me with the executive producer for this show. Network alliances such as these are critical and investors want to know if you are going to be going it alone. The more affiliations and consultants you have the better. It doesn't mean that you are incapable; it means you are smart.

Therefore include your mentors and consultants; that is if you have any that makes sense.

You must contact any individual you place as an affiliation or consultant for your project for permission prior to inclusion. Don't put yourself in the situation that you have an individual to rely on only to find out that the investor knows this person as well. Imagine that the investor calls up the person you listed as a consultant and that person responds by saying they know nothing about the project. It doesn't look good for you.

Once you have finished identifying individuals as mentors or consultants, there will be certain business and organizations that you will be affiliated with and want to include. You won't have to seek permission to include them because of the type of business they are. For example, your state's and city's film commission offer valuable resources as does AFTRA, WGA and the U.S. Library of Congress.

CHAPTER SUMMARY

In this chapter the heading for the Production Team in your reality show business plan was discussed followed by the four subheadings for inclusion that consists of: the production company, producer(s), director, and any affiliations or consultants. The reader was advised to seek permission of any consultant to be listed as such prior to the inclusion.

PRACTICAL APPLICATION

1. Using Worksheet 20, formulate your company's opening paragraph. Once Worksheet 20 is completed, transfer the statement into your reality show business plan document. Print a hardcopy and put it in your binder.

2. Using Worksheet 21, formulate the biography for the producer of your reality show. Be sure to include the name and what experience and skills the producer brings to the project. Once complete, transfer the information to your reality show

business plan document. Print a hardcopy and put it in your binder.

3. Using Worksheet 22, formulate the bio for the director of your reality show. Be sure to include the name and what experience and skills the director brings to the project. Once complete, transfer the information to your reality show business plan document. Print a hardcopy and put it in your binder.

4. Using Worksheet 23, formulate a list of affiliations and contacts that you can use as a resource. Once finalized, transfer the information to your reality show business plan document. Print a hardcopy and put it in your binder.

PHOTOGRAPHY CREDIT FOR CHAPTER 8

Chapter 8 photo taken by Salvatore Vuono
Photo of Dr. Mel with the General Lee taken by Bill Ray
Photo of Robyn taken by Dr. Mel
Photo of Jeremy provided by Jeremy Lyles
Photo of Jamie Alyson taken by Dr. Mel
Photo of Dr. Mel taken by Harold Callaway

WORKSHEET 20: COMPANY STATEMENT

Objective: To formulate the Production Team opening statement.

1.   Using the four import elements: company name, type of company, participants, and why the company was formed complete your opening statement.

Key:
1. Name of the company
2. Type of company formed
2. Participants in the company
4. Why the company was formed.

The Company

(1) Baker Girls, LLC, (2) a Limited Liability Company, (3) is an independent reality show production company that comprises experienced production professionals coupled with creative business (4) professionals with the common goal of producing the reality show, *The Baker Girls: Sealed with a Kiss.*

1. Answer the following questions.

1. What is the name of your company?

2. What type of company have you formed?

3. What individuals formed this company?

4. Why was the company formed?

2.   Using your answers from above, formulate your opening statement.

3.   Transfer your opening statement to your reality show business document. Print a hardcopy and put into your binder.

WORKSHEET 21: PRODUCER'S BIO

Objective: To formulate the producer's bio for your reality show business plan.

Answer the following questions.

1. Who is your producer?

2. What has your producer ever produced?

3.   What business skills does the producer bring to your project?

4. What experience in production does your producer have?

5. What experience, other than production, makes this producer uniquely qualified?

6. Use the information above to generate a paragraph for your producer.

7. Print a hardcopy and put into your binder.

WORKSHEET 22: DIRECTOR'S BIO

Objective: To formulate the director's bio for your reality show business plan.

Answer the following questions.

1. Who is your director?

2. Has your director directed or produced any reality shows, television or films? If so, what?

3. What business skills does the director bring to your project?

4. What experience in production does your director have?

5. What experience, other than directing, makes this director uniquely qualified?

6. Is your director attached to the project?

7. Use the information created during this exercise and generate a paragraph for your producer.

8. Print a hardcopy and put into your binder.

WORKSHEET 23: CONSULTANTS

Objective: To identify affiliations and consultants.

1. Make a list of the people in the following table that you know and can rely on that will make your job as a creator and/or producer of a reality show easier.

Name of Contact	Area of Expertise	Contact Information

2. Contact each person from the list created and see if they are willing to be listed as a resource. (You cannot include them in your business plan unless they agree to do so.)

3. Make a list of business associations in the following table that you can refer to that will make your job as a creator and/or producer of a reality show.

Name of Business/Organization	Area of Expertise	Contact Information

4. Circle the contacts of individuals and Organizations above that have agreed to be listed in your plan. Print a hardcopy of each list and put into your binder.

CHAPTER 9

PRODUCTION

The art of producing a reality show is all encompassing and very complex in nature. Those that fail to plan, plan to fail. As a producer and creator of a reality show you will have to be involved in every aspect. When it comes to including The Production section in your business plan you can break it down into three areas:

- Pre-production
- Production or principal photography
- Post-production

As an experienced filmmaker you might already know the stages of production. Regardless, take my advice and treat this area as new territory or as if you are going to have to introduce the production concept to someone that has no experience. There are two kinds of investors – those that have invested in a production and those that have not. A potential investor may or may not have any knowledge of the process of production. A television executive on the other hand will. But this does not preclude you from having to include the basic concepts and definitions of the three areas in your reality show business plan.

PRE-PRODUCTION

Pre-production is exactly as the word indicates. It is everything that you do to plan for the principal photography of your reality show.   It covers finding a crew, cast, development of the episode breakdown, shooting schedule, designing sets, finding locations, and more. It takes time to do all of the above and investors are going to want to know how long it will take from the time they fund your show until it can get on the air.

Does this mean that you are going to have to develop a production shooting schedule? No, you will not. What you will provide is three to six sentences of what goes into pre-production. Suggested wording follows:

> There are three stages to producing a reality show: pre-production, production and post-production.   During the pre-production stage all decisions regarding the production itself will be identified, cast members will be secured, crew will be attached, all locations for shooting will be identified, vendors will be identified with appropriate contracts and product placement will be considered. Pre-production will take X weeks.

PRODUCTION

Once you have clearly identified the nature of pre-production you will follow the above statement or one you develop with several more sentences that outlines the steps involved during the production process. Suggested wording follows:

Once pre-production is completed, The Company will move into the production phase or principal photography for XXX reality show. During this time X episodes will be filmed. One episode will be filmed each week until the story is completely developed. Principal photography will last X weeks.

POST-PRODUCTION

The final couple of sentences pertain to completing the project and obtaining distribution. Suggested wording follows:

The Company upon completion of principal photography will immediately transition into post-production. All titling, music and sound will be inserted as well as clearly defined episodes that meet the story development arc. While in post-production, The Company will seek a distributor for the project. Post-production will last X weeks.

The Production Section of your reality show is formatted by:

- Place the logo graphic centered and at the top of the page.
- Space down with the heading title Production in all caps, size 14 bold font.
- Space down and insert the three paragraphs that outline the process of pre-production, production and post-production.

Below each of the three paragraphs I usually place a small summary of the production timeline that looks like this:

Example 1

Production Timeline

Preproduction   6 Weeks
Production   13 Weeks
Post Production   12 Weeks

Putting it All Together

The Production Section of your reality show business plan should not be more that a single page. Diagram 9-1 is an example of the production page.

Diagram 9-1 Production Page

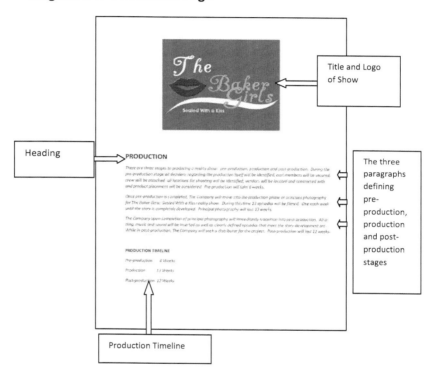

Of course the individual amount of time for pre-production, production and post-production will vary according to each project and what has been agreed upon by the investors and/or network executives. Once all three paragraphs are included in your plan you can provide a production schedule outline if you have one. In most cases, you won't have this information because you have not received funding. The individual parts to this section are identified by the title of the show, dates for pre-production, production and post-production. I always provide a statement of key activities that will take place. It also serves as a guideline for established meetings. Diagram 9-2 is an example Production Schedule Timeline.

Diagram 9-2　Production Schedule

CHAPTER SUMMARY

In this chapter three parts of production were defined which included: pre-production, production and post-production. Sample wording was provided for each section as well as an example of a production schedule timeline. In addition, an example of The Production page was provided.

PRACTICAL APPLICATION

1. Using Worksheet 24 develop the Production section of your reality show business plan.

PHOTOGRAPHY CREDIT FOR CHAPTER 9
Photo for Chapter 9 taken by Salvatore Vuono

WORKSHEET 24 : PRODUCTION SECTION

Objective: Write the Production Section of your reality show business plan.

1. Are you developing a sizzle reel or a production outline for one or more episodes? Check the appropriate box.

☐ Sizzle Reel   ☐ 1 Pilot Episode   ☐ 4 – 7 Episodes   ☐ 8 -13 Episodes

2. How many weeks do you think it will take for pre-production? Check the appropriate box.

☐ 1 Day   ☐ 3 Days   ☐ 6 Days

☐ 2 Weeks   ☐ 4-6 Weeks   ☐ More than 6 Weeks

Why do you think it will take this long?

3. How many days of shooting will it take to complete each episode?

☐ 1 Day   ☐ 3 Days   ☐ 5 Days   ☐ Other

4. How long will it take for the complete principal photography? _____ Weeks

5. How long do you think post-production or editing will take? _____ Weeks

6. Use the information above to complete the Production Section following the following format:

> *There are three stages to producing a reality show: pre-production, production and post-production. During the pre-production stage all decisions regarding the production itself will be identified, cast members will be secured, crew will be attached, all locations for shooting will be identified, vendors will be located and contracted with and product placement will be considered. Pre-production **will take** ____ **weeks**. Once pre-production is completed, The Company will move into the production phase or principal photography **for** ____ **reality** show. During this **time** ___ **episodes** will be filmed. One each week until the story is completely developed. Principal photography will **last** ___ **weeks**. The Company upon completion of principal photography will immediately transition into post-production. All titling, music and sound will be inserted as well as clearly defined episodes that meet the story development arc. While in post-production, The Company will seek a distributor for the project. Post-production will **last** ____ **weeks**.*

7. Type the above statement into your reality show business plan. Print a hardcopy and put it into your binder.

8. Review the production schedule in this book. If you have gotten that far in your production formulate a production schedule.

DATE	ACTIVITY	ASSIGNED TO
3/17/2011	PRE-DUCTION MEETING	ALL TEAM MEMBERS

CHAPTER 10

REALITY SHOW STATISTICS

Having earned my PhD in statistical research I have to admit this section of any reality show plan is my favorite. For others it is their worst nightmare or fear. But for me, this is where I get to research how well reality television shows, both similar and different to mine, fair on television. It's not only about the numbers but also it is about trends in a very competitive market. Trends and numbers in the reality show industry are always fluctuating. Consider these facts and figures like a moving river into a large ocean. In fact, it's about the constant moving market and industry trends of reality TV. You want your show to move and not become a stagnant pond.

In general reality TV shows emerge onto the market at an alarming rate according to Neilson ratings. Along with the emergence of information about who is watching these shows, which in essence provides producers and creators of reality shows guidance when developing new shows. Also gleaned from the ratings are how popular shows are in certain markets and which shows get more ratings such as finales, pilots and season premiers. All of this information is taken into account by network and advertising executives. There is little room for creativity because the facts deal with actuality. A show either got a certain percent of viewership or it didn't. Likewise, a show was either in the top five viewer's choice or not. The information that you put in this section should only contain the facts and not projections.

Criss Angel filming in New Orleans

Statistically speaking reality shows have done amazingly well in ratings and it doesn't look like this is going to change in the near future. That is one reason why reality TV is so popular. People love them. The viewing public can't get enough of them. Since 2000 the reality TV has become more real than ever. Larry Namar, co-founder of E! Entertainment says,

"Reality television is television, it's not a fad." I have to agree with him at this point as reality show ratings soar each season. According to the ratings the top 10 reality shows of all-time are:

- *American Idol*
- *Survivor*
- *Amazing Race*
- *Big Brother*
- *America's Next Top Model*
- *Real World*
- *Project Runway*
- *The Biggest Loser*
- *So you Think You can Dance*
- *Criss Angel: Mindfreak*

Did your favorite make the list? There has to be a reason for your answer. *American Idol* attracts over 50% of the market share meaning that over 50% of television viewers in America watch this show. No other show can say that. *American Idol* even beats out popular shows such as *Friends* and *CSI* in overall ratings. Some reports indicate 3 out of 4 boys and girls not only watch television but their favorite shows are reality TV shows. Higher ratings means higher revenues and advertising dollars spent. That's good news for reality show creators.

The popularity of reality shows doesn't stop in America but spreads to across the pond in the United Kingdom. Statistics for the UK state that 70% of the population have watched reality TV and continue to watch on a continued basis.   Maybe this answers why some of our favorite reality shows originated from overseas.

No one can answer whether or not these trends will continue in the future. But for now, it doesn't seem to be slowing down. The good news is that all of this wonderful information goes into your business plan in the heading The Market.   This information helps investors in generating a conceptual idea of the market availability for reality shows. Hopefully, it will be your reality show. It's a matter of supply and demand. The audience demands the continuation of their favorite reality shows as well as new ones and programming executives supply them.

The Market

Meeting the supply and demand are what you as a creator and producer of a reality show provide. However, before you can meet the demand you have to know how and where your show fits in relationship to currently aired shows. You will be asked:

- Are there similar reality shows currently on television?
- How is your show the same?

- How does your show provide something new and original?
- Will your show be competing with an existing show?
- What television stations currently air your type of show?
- What advertisers come on board?

Provide the answers in the heading The Market. In order to do so, you will have to do research. To start, brainstorm a list of current and past reality shows that could be considered similar to yours. Identify what television stations run them. Finally, develop a list of advertisers for these shows. All of this information identifies your reality show market comparison.

The market section can range from a single paragraph to three pages depending on the style of your reality show. If you have a celebrity style reality show you wouldn't address the market trends as they relate to the show *American Idol*. That doesn't make sense. You would want to include statistics about shows such *Anna Nicole*, *The Osbournes*, or *Gene Simmons Family Jewels*. In other words match your show. Compare apples to apples and bananas to bananas.

Look at the following market trend statement from my reality show *The Baker Girls: Sealed with a Kiss*. In this case, I had to compare current reality shows similar in design and nature to mine.

> *The Baker Girls: Sealed with a Kiss* offers the viewing audience a glance inside the private lives of five beautiful girls who sell shoes for living. Conflict arises in the store as a power struggle emerges. Once Saturday night is in full swing, the girls hit the clubs for a night of partying. There is no other show currently on television that follows a group of everyday girls. They do not live together, but work and party together. In the show, *The Girls Next Door*, they all live within a single house with a millionaire playboy. After the show was

discontinued, the girls each received some sort of spin-off series which became popular - *Kendra, Holly's World*, and *Bridgette's Sexiest Beaches*. The closest show would be the spinoff show with the Kardashians, *Kourtney and Khloe Take Miami* and now *Kourtney and Khloe Take New York* which has not only become popular but continues to air with high ratings for the network. TV audiences watch reality shows that feature young beautiful girls. *The Baker Girls: Sealed with a Kiss* provides this type of programming without crossing the line. It's *Jersey Shore* without the boys and the house. Audience members of both sexes and all age ranges will be attracted to *The Baker Girls: Sealed with a Kiss*.

With one of my shows I created with Darren DeWalt of The Dewalt Experience, *Darren: Sharper than Ever* I had some sort of basis and similarity in which to compare this show. Three other NFL players had their own show. Chad Ochocinco and Tyrell Owens were making NFL history with their shows and another with Michael Vick had failed. Why would there be an interest in a fourth show about an NFL player? The answer came in the structure and nature of the proposed show. I remember sitting at a long table top for 10 discussing the concept of the show with producer and creator of reality shows James Dubos. Dubos is known in the reality show genre for shows such as The *Michael Vick Project, Toya and Tiny, Hell Date* and *Monica Still Standing*. He asked me point blank, "How would the show with Darren be any different from Chad's and Tyrell's? Luckily I had the answer. Both shows had a different goal and outcome. One was to find the love of his life while the other showcases his life. Darren's show would bring in the element of community involvement and making a difference in the community while showcasing the importance of health issues. The other three shows would be my market comparison.

Unlike a business proposal for a feature film, the market section in a reality television business plan does not need all of the charts on how much money a show has made at the box office in domestic and foreign film markets. Instead, go for the ratings and the popularity. Include in your market paragraph(s) the following:

- Title of show.
- Compare at least three similar shows.
- State why this show would appeal to the audience.
- State how the show is different from current programming.
- List at least one show that your show would closely be like.
- State who is the intended audience.

Because of the overwhelming and ever changing data a standardized and formatted statement cannot be constructed. Rather, use the bullet points as a guideline and the example I provided with *The Baker Girls*.

The Industry

Advertising Age magazine, reported early in 2010 that the *American Idol* franchise is "conservatively valued at $2.5 billion" and climbing. This makes *American Idol* possibly the most lucrative multimedia property of all time. The franchise can generate more than 8.1 million in each half hour according to *Adweek Magazine*. That's why the *American Idol* franchise could afford to offer Simon Cowell, past judge, an $80 million contract his last year which he ultimately turned down. That's also why they can charge more for advertising placement during their finale than the NFL does during a Super Bowl Championship game. That's a lot of money and a whole lot of facts.

The subheading The Industry covers exactly that – the facts. It reveals the industry of reality television and the potential to make money. In The Industry section of your reality show business plan include all facts and figures from research about the latest trends of reality shows.   You will want to unveil the following:

- The current trend of reality shows at the time you write your business plan.
- The number of television stations airing reality television programs.
- The most watched reality show.
- The future of reality television.
- Advertising projections

To ascertain these areas you will need to conduct research on the internet and in entertainment magazines such as *Advertising Age Magazine*, *Adweek Magazine*, *Forbes*, *Hollywood Reporter* and *Variety*.   For example, I looked up on *Variety's* magazine's website on February 4, 2011 and discovered the number one television show that was viewed the night before.   The answer was *American Idol* with 21.7 million viewers.   I also easily identified the rest of the top 10 watched shows that night.   I furthered discovered that Bravo renewed *Top Chef* for another season, that Spike ordered a reality show featuring the trapped miners, USA picked up a series called *WWE Tough Enough*, and lots more.   These are all facts that I can include in my Industry Trend statement.

When I went to *Forbes* online magazine I was able to identify that out of the top ten all time moneymaking television shows, four of them have been reality television shows.   Up there on the list in addition to *American Idol* was *Survivor*, *Dancing with the Stars* and *America's Got Talent*.   I can go to multiple websites everyday and start charting statistics in reality programming.   While sitting at my desk I can determine the highest ranking show, type of audience that watches it, how much advertising was spent, and number of viewers.   All of this information accounts for the industry trend and demonstrates that reality television programming isn't slowing down; which by the way is great news for you. Therefore, don't be shy and tell others in your business plan that this program genre is for real and is here to stay.

To write the industry section that is exactly what you do – tell others about the mainstay of reality TV. Maintain data for about two weeks to identify trends. What networks are picking up shows? What shows are being renewed? What shows failed? All of these hold a key into the industry of reality television that can't be ignored.

Like the section on the market there is no standardized statement for the industry section. Rather you must abstract from the facts. Research is the key to writing a fantastic section for the industry section of your plan for reality TV. Always include the following information in the Industry section:

- Figures for the past five years (state how much the industry increased over the years).
- State the number of shows set to be aired or produced this year or next.
- Identify and list the reality shows that have had DVD sales and distribution.
- Identify shows that have been picked up by cable or pay-for-view.
- Inform the reader the amount of revenue reality shows have brought to television over the last five years.

Unlike feature film business plans it is not necessary to place charts or graphs unless you are inclined to do so. Simple statement of facts is the preferred choice by reality television executives. Below is an example for the industry section of excerpted from *Hoops: Life off the Court*.

Example 1   Industry Statement

According to News Corp. an increase of $121 million in its 2010 fiscal year's second quarter has been reported.

Much of that revenue comes from successful reality television programs such as *American Idol*. Top executives at Fox Broadcasting Company are elated too also report that second quarter contributions increased more than 50% from the same period last year. This growth reflects stronger advertising market, particularly to reality shows.

Other networks including but not limited to CBS, NBC, TLC, Fox and BET also have reported in 2010 increased advertising revenue that is coupled with the reality show market trend. They attributed the results to increased advertising revenue by the National Football League and interest of the American public to watch sports. Other networks such as A&E, TLC, The Discovery Channel, and BET also report an increase in fiscal year 2010 in relationship to advertising dollars when it comes to reality shows.

According to *Forbes* Magazine, the trend of increased spending in advertising began about 6 years ago and continues to spiral upward as the popularity of reality television remains in high demand throughout 2011. Nielsen Company found that the reality television industry continues to gain in popularity with more than 70% of viewers in 2010 say that they watch reality television programming. According to the *Daily Variety* and *Hollywood Reporter more* than 122 new reality show programs are slated to be produced in 2011, an increase each year since 2006. A recent 2009 study by Nielsen Company ratings reported that when age is a factor, people 18 and younger report that 3 out 4 individuals prefer reality television programming; an industry that is worth an estimated 2.1 billion dollars in the United States as reported by *Advertising Ad Magazine*.

Word of caution – remember that the above is an example and not a boilerplate statement. Facts and figures constantly fluctuate up and down like the tide of an ocean as new fiscal years and quarters emerge. Your data should adjust accordingly. Therefore, depending on when you write your reality show proposal the latest information should be obtained.

CHAPTER SUMMARY

It shouldn't be a surprise to anybody that reality TV is popular TV. In this chapter the headings The Market and The Industry were discussed and the necessity of researching each for inclusion in a reality television show business plan for the most up-to-date statistics. Information on the latest data can be found by researching on the internet as well as researching leading magazines such as *Forbes*, *Daily Variety*, and the *Hollywood Reporter*. Data fluctuates and should always be up to date and researched for each reality show. The objective is to supply programming data that meets the demand of the viewing audience.

PRACTICAL APPLICATION

1. Do an internet search on the top 10 reality shows. Is there a trend in the style of programming? Does it include all genres?

2. Using Worksheet 25, review the market trend in accordance with your reality show.

3. Using Worksheet 26, gather data that will help to identify the current trend in realty show programming.

PHOTOGRAPHY CREDIT FOR CHAPTER 10
Chapter 10 photo taken by Carlos Porto
Criss Angel photo taken by Dr. Melissa Caudle

WORKSHEET 25: MARKET TREND

Objective: To identify the Reality Show Market Trend as it relates to your reality show project.

1. Answer the following questions?

List three similar reality shows currently airing on television?

How is your show the like the above shows?

How is show your different?

What show would your show most likely be competing against?

What television networks currently air your type of show?

What advertisers come on board?

2. Formulate your marketing paragraph for your business plan from the information you identified from above. Print a hardcopy and put in your binder.

WORKSHEET 26: INDUSTRY TREND

Objective: To write a paragraph on current reality show industry trend for placement in your reality show business plan.

1. For the next seven days research and identify the ratings for current reality shows.

Show Title	Network	Rating

2. What type of reality show seems to be the most popular? Why do you think so?

3.   Conduct an internet search and identify any new reality shows that are being picked up? Is there a trend? Look for network similarity, genres, producers etc.

4. Search on the internet the following bouillon key words:

Reality Show and Trends

Reality Top 10 Shows

Highest Rated Reality Show

Longest Running Reality Show

Reality Shows and Target Audiences

Networks and Reality Shows

Highest Gross and Reality Show

Networks Buying Reality Shows

Production Companies and Reality Shows

5. What key elements did you discover?

6. Find any facts and figures on how much reality shows have brought in during the last five years from a variety of sources online and in magazines?

7. Write a paragraph on the current trend for reality shows and include it in the proper section for your reality show business plan. Print a hardcopy and put into your binder.

8. Identify magazines that advertise reality shows.

9. Research the websites from *Daily Variety* and *Hollywood Reporter* to identify current statistics.

10. Start to develop a list of websites that you can go to that publish information on reality shows, how well they are doing and new reality shows in the making.

CHAPTER 11

PRODUCT-PLACEMENT

Product-placement is not a new concept. In fact it has been around for more than nine decades. Among the most famous were the early accounts in silent films in the Academy Award winning film for Best Picture film *Wings* (1927) in which a plug for Hershey's chocolate was made. Other examples include the 1932 film, *Horse Feathers* in which the main character played by Thelma Todd falls from a canoe into a river. When she calls for a life saver, Groucho Marx pulls out *Life Savers* candy and tosses it to her. Then a prominent copy of the magazine National Geographic was placed in the film *It's a Wonderful Life* (1946) which was directed by Frank Capra.

The use of product-placement may have begun in silent films, but they became even more popular during the early years of

Soap Operas. That's how Soap Operas got their genre. These shows were sponsored by Proctor and Gamble and their detergents. What worked backed in the early years still holds true today. In fact, product-placement can make or break a reality show.

Product-placement is a form of advertising; however it's not an in-your-face commercial. Rather, product-placement is a way to embed a company's product into a show by having the actors either use the product or talk about it in a natural way. The idea is not to stop the flow of the show by mentioning the product but to evoke a stronger connection with the product to the audience and to dovetail content by targeting a specific target group. One of the best examples in a reality show I can think of is in *Jersey Shore* when they play a specific song that connects what one of the cast members are going through. While the song is playing, the producer's superimpose the name of the song and where you can go and download it. The philosophy is that if it's in *Jersey Shore*, it must be a good song. They generate millions of dollars this way. According to PQMEDIA, a consulting firm that tracks the product-placement market, product-placement revenue is estimated at to $5.6 billion in 2010. Something producers and creators of reality programming should be aware and take note.

Product-placement can be considered the life sustaining element of reality television. Shows like *Big Brother*, *American Idol, The Real World, Project Runway*, and *Extreme Makeover* have set the standards. During the show *Big Brother,* cast members say, "Have you checked out the latest product by X Company?" While another says, "I have to go and get me one of those," which is a perfect example of product-placement. *American Idol* judges sit behind their judging table drinking in a cup marked Coca Cola and the final Idol contestants participate in a music video that includes Ford vehicles. This year, some of the Idol contestants arrived at the audition in a caravan of Ford cars which indicates a strategic product-placement move.

Participants in *Extreme Makeover* also dash out in a Ford vehicle to Sears in every episode to buy Kenmore appliances.

Product-placement isn't by chance but by design. Advertisers know that the general audience nowadays watch shows on their computers, Netflix or record them on their DVR for replay to avoid commercials. We as a public are tired of in your face commercials unless it is Super Bowl Sunday. Nonetheless, advertisers want their products to be advertised and by utilizing product-placement, viewers can't avoid product information embedded into shows. It's a win win situation for a producer of a reality show. So, take advantage of it. Identify as many products that you can that would be considered a natural placement in the show.

Identifying Potential Product-Placement

When identifying potential products for product-placement it is important to review your intended episodes for the show as well as identifying current products that your cast members use. For example, in the reality show *Darren: Sharper than Ever*, NFL pro football player Darren Sharper is a natural for product-placement. Look at all the gear he uses on and off the field. He exercises. So, he needs clothing to exercise in that fits his needs. He wears tennis shoes. He sleeps in a hyperbaric chamber to enhance his health. He watches sports on a big screen television. He plans on using an on-line dating service. As a producer I need only to write down everything that Darren uses in his real-life and start making contact with the companies. He's a high profile celebrity so endorsements come a little easier.

However, product-placement generation for my shows such as *The Baker Girls: Sealed with a Kiss* and the *Ace Mechanic* is just as easy. They just may not be as easy to secure. This does not preclude me from listing them in my realty show business plan. I list them. Then secure a product-placement specialist or company to pursue endorsements once the plan has been completed. Example products for *The Baker Girls: Sealed with a Kiss* includes the shoes they wear from Bakers; the make-up they use; the clothing they buy; where they shop; the cell phones they use; and the places the eat and drink. The list is endless when it comes to these girls. The same holds true for the *Ace Mechanic*. During the television show the mechanics use certain tools, parts, have supply houses, go fishing on charter boats and visit certain restaurants. Table 10-1 identifies sample product-placement items and the respective companies for *The Baker Girls* and the *Ace Mechanic*.

Table10-1 Product-Placement Ideas

THE BAKER GIRLS	THE ACE MECHANIC
Make-up	**Auto Parts**
Maybelline	Every Auto Part from Chevy to Ford
Cover Girl	**Tools**
Revlon	Snap-on-Tools
Shoes	Sears
Bakers Shoes	**Auto Supplies**
Restaurants	Advanced Auto
Olive Garden	NAPA
Pizza Hut	**Tires**
Subway	Hasselbien Tire
Arby's	Goodyear Tires
McDonald's	Michelin Tires
Night Clubs	**Alarm Systems**
The Hide-a-way	Dictograph Alarms
The Cat's Meow	**Printing**
Theaters	M&M Printing
Pinnacle	**Computers**
Soft Drinks	Dell
Coca-Cola	Apple
Pepsi	Toshiba
Dr. Pepper	**Office Supplies**
Barq's Root beer	Office Depot
Gatorade	Staples
Water	**Towing Trucks**
Kentwood	Chevy
Aquafina	Ford
Alcohol	**Cell Phone**
Abita Beer	ATT
Kettle One Vodka	T-Mobile

Another thing that I try to incorporate into my business plan is a level of participation by companies. Some companies want to "buy-in" at 100% and have their product included in every show, while others choose to have their product in only one or two episodes. You don't want exclude a potential funding source with an all or nothing product-placement program.

To emphasize, the level of involvement for the *Ace Mechanic* had three levels: Red, Blue and White. These levels were based from the colors from the *Ace Mechanic* logo. Whereas, *The Baker Girls* levels for product-placement were identified by *Pumps, Boots, Sandals* and *Flats*. For the reality show *Darren: Sharper than Ever,* I plan on only providing two levels: Super Bowl Level and Championship Level. The higher the level or the more times that a product is used in the show the more the buy in cost to the advertising company.

The idea is to generate money in your pocket and a source of funding that networks will be able to sell advertising slots for. After all that's how networks and production companies make money. The best approach is not to mention the "Buy-in" dollar amount or what it will cost to have their products into the show. I leave that up to the branding placement specialists and the network executives once production begins. The only exception to listing the "Buy-in" dollar amount is if you plan on self-distribution by going straight to DVD or to the internet.

ABOUT PRODUCT-PLACEMENT

Your reality show business plan must address product placement unlike a proposal for a feature film. Rarely if ever would you address this in a feature film proposal. The wording isn't that complex. The complexity lies in identifying the products and listing them for inclusion into your reality show. Again, this isn't an in-your-face placement but must come across in a natural and unobtrusive manner. So, how do you include it into your plan?

First, provide a brief introduction of the concept of product-placement for your readers followed by listing the perfect type of products and how each product would be used in their natural environment by cast members. Review the following examples.

Example 1: *The Baker Girls: Sealed with a Kiss*

> Product-placement is a well known tool for advertisers to increase revenue for their products and the reality show, *The Baker Girls: Sealed with a Kiss* provides the maximum exposure for a variety of products. The Baker Girls are beautiful from head to toe. Not a hair is out of place and their make-up applied to perfection. But to get this way, they rely on several products from Goody Brushes, clips and headbands to the Revlon long lasting make-up. And to keep their bubbling personalities while at work they drink Abita Root Beer. All products are a natural inclusion into the show as well as many others.

Example 2: *Ace Mechanic*

> Increasing revenue for advertisers should always be a goal for a reality show and The *Ace Mechanic* is perfect for product-placement. Throughout the show, each mechanic must rely on tools and auto parts to complete their work. What better way to highlight a product than by naturally using it and having ace mechanics comment on why they insist on using Snap-on Tools when changing out a motor or while racing dragsters. Also what better way than for an ace mechanic to speak of the quality of Pennzoil Oil or tires from Goodyear?

Using these products isn't a through it your face advertisement but rather a natural progression of how and why a certain product or tool is used. The *Ace Mechanic* holds unlimited potential for product placement.

CHAPTER SUMMARY

In this chapter product placement as it relates to your reality show and business plan was discussed. The importance of attracting products and getting the endorsements was developed as well as how to identify potential product endorsements. Levels of product placement campaigns were discussed.

PRACTICAL APPLICATION

1. Watch three reality shows with the intent on identifying the products that were intentionally placed in the show. List them. How were they used by the participants and/or actors?

2. Using Worksheet 27, generate a list of products that could potentially be endorsed or placed in your reality show.

3. Using Worksheet 28, generate a complete Table of products by categories that can be used by your cast. Transfer Table into the appropriate section of your reality show business plan. Print a hardcopy and place in your binder.

PHOTOGRAPHY CREDIT FOR CHAPTER 11
Chapter 11 photo taken by Renjith Krishnan
Photo "Money in Your Pocket" taken by Apikhomboonwaroot and used with permission.

WORKSHEET 27: PRODUCT-PLACEMENT ITEMS

Objective: To identify future products for product-placement into your reality show.

1. Generate 15 products that either your current cast uses in everyday life.

1_____   2. _____   3. _____

4_____   5. _____   6. _____

1_____   2. _____   3. _____

7_____   8. _____   9. _____

10_____   11. _____   12. _____

13_____   14. _____   15. _____

2. Are there any specialty items that a specific cast member is known for? If so list cast member and item.

3. Does any cast member currently have a commercial or endorse products?

4. If the cast is being filmed at a work environment, list products which are natural to the environment?

5.   What national company's product would lend itself for possible product-placement?

6. In the appropriate section of your reality show business plan, outline the product-placement products following the format below or one you created.

> Increasing revenue for advertisers should always be a goal for a reality show and (NAME OF YOUR SHOW) is perfect for product-placement. Throughout the show, each cast member uses (LIST A COMMON PRODUCT). What better way to highlight (NAME A PRODUCT) than by naturally using it and having (NAME A CAST MEMBER) comment on why HE/SHE insists on using (NAME A ITEM) to (HOW IT IS USED). Also, what better way than for cast members to speak of the quality of (NAME A PRODUCT) and (NAME ANOTHER PRODUCT). This isn't a through it your face advertisement but rather a natural progression of how and why (NAME A PRODUCT) is used. The *(NAME OF REALITY SHOW)* holds unlimited potential for product placement to increase advertising revenue.

7.   Add completed product-placement statement into your reality show plan. Print a hardcopy and put into your binder.

WORKSHEET 28: PRODUCT-PLACEMENT TABLE

Objective: To generate a Table that can be placed in your reality show business plan.

1. Fill in products and companies for product-placement for your reality show.

Product-Placement Category:	Product-Placement Category:
Product-Placement Category :	Product-Placement Category:
Product-Placement Category:	Product-Placement Category:
Product-Placement Category:	Product-Placement Category:
Product-Placement Category:	Product-Placement Category:

1. Begin researching products from other shows similar to yours in design and genre.

CHAPTER 12

DISTRIBUTION

Once production of a reality show is complete, producers usually seek distribution which is independent of the production process. Distribution covers all aspects of duplicating the show, promoting it, selling it in domestic and foreign television, cable and DVD markets. Many factors must be considered; e.g., the genre of the reality show, how people will find out about the show, and how will you decide on the best distributor for the project—all these factor into the success of the show.   There are lots of things that must be well thought out.   Will it go to cable TV? Will it DVD after it is aired? Will it go to *Hula* or *Netflix*?

When shopping a reality show the goal is to get it into as many markets as you can. In fact, there are about 50 top markets internationally.   If you're lucky, you will get CBS Television Distribution (CTD) to cut you a deal. President of Sales for CTD Joe DiSalvo is known for getting shows into the major markets world-wide.   CTD is the pre-eminent company in television syndication with a library of more than 70,000 titles.   With offices in six major cities including Los Angeles, New York, Atlanta and Chicago, they are a force to contend with.   Just this past January of 2011, DeSalvo successfully got the new reality show *Excused* sold and cleared for 46 of the 50 to world-wide markets.   I think this is unprecedented.   Talk about *Excused* was rampant at the 2011 NATPE and they are now casting for roles.   Executive producers David Garfinkle and Jay Renfoe couldn't be more excited as *Excused* distribution now has certainly put Renegade 83 Entertainment on the map.   This is the same production company that produced the reality show *Blind Date*.

Your reality business plan must also address is how you will seek distribution? Will you attend NAPTE or MIPCOM to get distributors or will you let the network seek foreign distributors. Some producers think it is best to self-distribute a reality show.   Frankly, in

MIPCOM 2010

my opinion it is best to leave the distribution aspect to companies that focus on distribution with you making the connections in the market.   That means, in your plan address that fact.

Also you must know that distributors will want to keep as much money as they can and pay out of pocket as little as they can. You must address in your plan that you will seek the best distribution deal for the most return on an investment.   This means you must find out all upfront costs to you in the deliverables expectations of a potential distributor.

Deliverables that a distributor may require a producer to provide a copy in high definition, stereo mix, dialog script (although a reality show is unscripted they may want it for closed captioning and English Subtitling); Music cue sheet; a copy of all actors contracts, advertising materials including all logos and graphics and production stills; a trailer; chain-of-title; errors and omission insurance and any behind the scenes footage.   Each distributor that I have worked with never requires the same thing. Be advised to get their requirements upfront and before you sign any deals. Don't let excitement of a possible distribution deal get in the way of logic and fact. Maintain your rights. The only way to do that is to know them. In this case, ignorance is not bliss.

After discovering this information you may not want to deal with that distribution company at all. You certainly have the option of self-distribution and going straight to DVD. When it comes to the end of the day, make sure before you sign anything your entertainment attorney has looked it over from every angle.

WRITING YOUR DISTRIBUTION STRATEGY

The heading Distribution Strategy is simple and forthcoming that maximizes the greatest return on an investment. The first statement you write is an opening statement just like the other subheadings that brings clarification to the reader. Suggested wording is:

> The Company will actively seek to negotiate with the following distribution companies known to distribute like genre programming the production and negotiate the best deal for the highest return on investments.

Once you have stated the above you are going to identify three to five distribution companies known to distribute the type of reality genre similar to yours. Suggested wording is:

> The following distribution companies are respected in this industry and have a reputation of getting results in a domestic market. These companies are: XXX, XXX, XXX, and XXX. Likewise, syndication will be sought. The

> Company will continue to seek other distribution companies in foreign markets which are eager for Western reality shows especially in the UK, Asia, and Indian markets. These companies include: XXX, XXX, and XXX.

Once domestic and foreign distribution companies have been identified the next portion of the section addresses how the producers will seek distribution by attending select conferences known for marketing. These include NATPE and MIPCOM. Suggested wording is:

> The producers of *XXX* reality show will actively seek distributors by attending and networking at NATPE, the national conference held each year in Las Vegas and MIPCOM. When appropriate, a completed show will also be taken to AFM to seek distribution.

The next section of your paragraph addresses the critical aspects distributors look for in a reality show project and how your show meets those areas. Suggested wording is:

> In acquiring a project, a distributor (studio or independent) looks for six basic elements within the show which includes: genre, the storyline, appeal of the cast members to the audience, success and experience of the production company, producer and director, cross-marketing platform with product placement and the amount of money, if any, that is attached to the show. *XXX* reality show addresses these six elements with a genre that continues to successful television programming, an appealing story with a charismatic cast, an experienced and successful production team and myriad opportunities for product-placement and cross-marketing.

Next address how you plan on capturing the distributors' attention. This is not the same thing as marketing. With marketing you are directing your attention toward a viewing audience. Capturing the attention of distributors are methods you use to bring your project to the forefront for distributors to buy. That is your goal.

These methods include the use of press releases, submitting your show to IMDB, and to trade magazines such as *Hollywood Reporter* and *Daily Variety* where distributors can find new shows. Suggested wording is:

> The Company will use publicity methods in an effort to gain the attention of distributors by releasing a Press Release four times: during pre-production, during production, during post-production and upon completion of project to trade industry magazines such as *Hollywood Reporter* and *Daily Variety* and through Internet Press Release sites such as PRWIRE.

> Also, The Company will submit production information to IMDB once production begins.

> There are several components in place that optimizes *XXX* reality show to get domestic and international distribution.

PUTTING THE DISTRIBUTION SECTION TOGETHER

You have the groundwork laid for a well put together distribution strategy that should meet the needs of network executives and production companies. Now make certain that it is in a format that investors and television executives are used to reviewing. When the business plan isn't in a recognizable format often intended readers won't read the document because they find it confusing. Don't put yourself in a category of losing funding opportunity with improper formatting.

To format the Distribution section follow these guidelines:

- Place graphic logo centered at the top of the page.

- Space down and flush right the heading Distribution Strategy. Use font size 14 and make it bold.
- Space down and flush left using font size 12 the opening statement.
- Complete body of section with either the suggested wording from above or one you created.

Refer to Diagram 12-1 as a visual example for formatting the Distribution Strategy section.

Diagram 12-1   Distribution Strategy from *Hoops: Life off the Court*

DISTRIBUTION STRATEGY

Hoops, LLC will actively seek to negotiate with the following distribution companies known to distribute like genre programming the production and negotiate the best deal for the highest return on investments.

The following distribution companies are respected in this industry and have a reputation of getting results in a domestic market. These companies are: Warner Brothers, CBS, Miramax, and CDT. Likewise, syndication will be sought. The Company will continue to seek other distribution companies in foreign markets which are eager for Western reality shows especially in the UK, Asia, and Indian markets. These companies include: Curb Entertainment, Fries Film Group and Show Case Entertainment.

The producers of *Hoops, Life off the Court* reality show will actively seek distributors by attending and networking at NATPE in November, the national conference held each year in Las Vegas in February and MIPCOM in October. When appropriate, a completed show will also be taken to AFM to seek distribution. This will ensure that exposure on both the international and domestic level occur.

In acquiring a project, a distributor (studio or independent) looks for six basic elements within the show which includes: genre, the storyline, appeal of the cast members to the audience, success and experience of the production company, producer and director, cross-marketing platform with product placement and the amount of money, if any, that is attached to the show. *Hoops, Life off the Court* reality show addresses these six elements with a genre that continues to successful television programming, an appealing story with a charismatic cast, an experienced and successful production team and myriad opportunities for product-placement and cross-marketing.

The Company will use publicity methods in an effort to gain the attention of distributors by releasing a Press Release four times: during pre-production, during production, during post-production and upon completion of project to trade industry magazines such as *The Hollywood Reporter* and *Daily Variety* and through Internet Press Release sites such as PRWIRE. Also, The Company will submit production information to IMDB once production begins. There are several components in place that optimizes *Hoops, Life off the Court* to increase the opportunity for domestic and international distribution.

I realize that the example above is very small and for the most part unreadable. I wanted you to see the style and format of a finished page. The following is an example of the contents of the Distribution Strategy from *Hoops: Life off the Court* for your review.

Example 1   Distribution Page Wording

Hoops, LLC will actively seek to negotiate with the following distribution companies known to distribute like genre programming the production and negotiate the best deal for the highest return on investments.

The following distribution companies are respected in this industry and have a reputation of getting results in a domestic market. These companies are: Warner Brothers, CBS, Miramax, and CDT. Likewise, syndication will be sought. The Company will continue to seek other distribution companies in foreign markets which are eager for Western reality shows especially in the UK, Asia, and Indian markets. These companies include: Curb Entertainment, Fries Film Group and Show Case Entertainment.

The producers of *Hoops, Life off the Court* reality show will actively seek distributors by attending and networking at NATPE in November and MIPCOM in October. When appropriate, a completed show will also be taken to AFM to seek distribution. This will ensure that exposure on both the international and domestic level occurs.

In acquiring a project, a distributor (studio or independent) looks for six basic elements within the show which includes: genre, the storyline, appeal of the cast members to the audience, success and experience of the production company, producer and director, cross-marketing platform with product placement and the amount of money, if any, that is attached to the show. *Hoops: Life off the Court* reality show addresses these six elements with a genre that continues to successful television programming, an appealing story with a charismatic cast, an experienced and successful production team and myriad opportunities for product-placement and cross-marketing.

The Company will use publicity methods in an effort to gain the attention of distributors by releasing a Press Release four times: during pre-production, during production, during post-production and upon completion of project to trade industry magazines such as *The Hollywood Reporter* and *Daily Variety* and through Internet Press Release sites such as PRWIRE. Also, The Company will submit production information to IMDB once production begins. There are several components in place that optimizes *Hoops: Life off the Court* to increase the opportunity for domestic and international distribution.

HOW TO WRITE A PRESS RELEASE

I am not afraid of the blank page when I sit down to write. From my books and articles to my screenplays words seem to come naturally to me. That is until I have to write a Press Release. Well, that was until a couple of years ago when I had the opportunity to be become a reporter with a newspaper after I had to evacuate my home after Hurricane Katrina. Then I realized that just about anybody could write them if they followed a format. So can you. The format for a well written Press Release is easy and I'll walk you through it. There are eight parts to a press release:

- Opening statement - declares the document is for immediate release or the date to be released.
- The Headline - always include the company name and the name of the reality show.
- Summary sentence - this sentence will appear below the headline usually in a smaller font but gives the reader a chance to know what the press release is about.
- Create a dateline - the first line of the body of your press release - that includes the city where the release

is generated and the date (New Orleans, LA. - January 16, 2011).

- The Press Release body - with the "5 Ws," who, what, when, where, and why.
- Call to action – what do you want people to do.
- Contact information – so people may contact you if they request interviews or need more Information.
- Last line - should always be three #; e.g., ###, to signal that this is the end of the press release.

Opening Statement

Anytime you write and submit a press release it will be looked at by news directors.   The first thing news desk editors look for are news stories that require their immediate attention. If you start your press release in a format in which news journalists are used to reading, you more than likely will not get noticed. I have included two examples. Both should always be written in a bold font and every letter all caps. You may choose to italicize the font if you which for impact. However, avoid making it any other of a color font than black. Suggested fonts are Times Roman, Courier, Calibri or Arial. Nothing fancy here.

Example 1

FOR IMMEDIATE RELEASE

Example 2

RELEASE MARCH 17, 2011

The Headline

The headline should be catchy and limited in the amount of words used if possible. The shorter the better and it does not have to be a complete sentence. When writing your headline think about getting across that the subject of the story does something exciting. Make the person want to read the story. In our case we want people to know what is going on with the reality show. Therefore, depending on the stage in development for my reality show dictates what I write for my headline. Remember, we already told our investors that we would issue a press release at four different times: pre-production, production, post-production, and upon completion of the project. These are the optimal time to issue press releases. The following four examples reflect the four different occasions for our press release headlines.

Example 1 – Pre-Production

> *The Baker Girls* get Green-Light from Oxygen Network

Example 2 - Production

> *The Baker Girls* Roll Cameras

Example 3 – Post-Production

> After 5 Months *Baker Girls* Turn off the Lights

Example 4 – Premier and Project Complete

> *The Baker Girls* Premiere Tonight

In the aforementioned headlines take note that they are all short and direct. It allows the reader to know what is going on without reading the rest of the article.

Summary Sentence

Immediately after the headline you will summarize the paragraph into one or two sentences. The reason is to make the reader familiar with the subject of the article before reading the entire press release. This provides for continuity and structure for a news director.

Look at the following examples.

Example 1 – Pre-Production

> After several months of negotiation On the Lot Productions, LLC has reached an agreement with Oxygen Network to co-produce a new reality series tentatively titled, *The Baker Girls: Sealed with a Kiss*.

Example 2- Production

> Cameras are rolling at the Esplanade Mall in New Orleans, Louisiana as production starts on a new reality show entitled *The Baker Girls: Sealed with a Kiss*. The show is a co-production between On the Lot Productions, LLC and Oxygen Network directed by New Orleans native local television and film producer Dr. Mel Caudle.

Example 3 – Post-Production

> Hollywood is packing up and heading back to Los Angeles as the reality series *The Baker Girls: Sealed with a Kiss* wraps up five months of production. Producer Dr. Mel Caudle says she hopes to see the show air this fall.

Example 4 – Completion and Premiere

> After one year of planning and filming the locally shot reality series *The Baker Girls: Sealed with a Kiss* premieres tonight on the Oxygen Channel. The cast of *The Baker Girls* glams it up for a private premier party at the Ritz Carlton.

With the four above examples you can get a complete understanding of what the four articles are without reading any of them. That is the advantage of the summary paragraph in a press release. Write them creatively to grab reader's attention.

Dateline

Once you have written your summary sentences place the dateline in the next section of the press release. The dateline is the first sentence you write that begins with the name of the city in which the incident takes place or has taken place followed by the date in which you submitted the Press Release. The dateline is at the left and is always followed by a dash. Suggested wording is:

Example 1

> New Orleans, LA. - January 16, 2011 -

Body of Press Release

The Body of the Press Release begins immediately after the dash of the dateline and follows what all good reporters would write – who, what, when, where and why.

I will provide the body of one article using the information for the pre-production stage. You are more than likely at this stage of development for your reality show. If you desire further information on development of press releases or additional examples of press releases for every stage of development purchase my book *A Producer's Press Kit: EPK Packaging (*ISBN-10: 1461049199) available from Amazon.com, CreateSpace eStore, www.onthelotpruductions.com, Barnes and Noble, CreateSpace Direct, and other retail outlets.

Example 1

> New Orleans, LA. - January 16, 2011 – On the Lot Productions, LLC has agreed to a deal with the Oxygen Network to produce a new reality show in New Orleans, LA. Tentatively the show will be called *The Baker Girls: Sealed with a Kiss* and stars five beautiful young women

between the ages of 18 to 30. The girls work together at a local mall shoe store.

The show follows these women as they juggle their daily home, social and work life. Having nothing in common, other than employment as sales clerks or managers at the store, these women find there's more to life and as friendships become real. When one girl gets pregnant they all come together to plan a wedding and a baby shower for the same day. Time is running out but will their friendship? "I love working with these girls," said Dr. Mel Caudle, producer and director. "I've never seen anything like it."

Caudle also states that she is excited to have the opportunity to bring the show to others through the deal she made with Oxygen Network. "The show was a prime example of woman's issues that the Oxygen Network likes to showcase." Cast members tend to agree and look forward to the next five months of filming. Monique XXX, the oldest cast member, said, "It's not at all what you might be expecting from a reality show. We don't eat bugs or have fist fights. We live our lives."

By reading the press release you can easily identify who, what, when, where, and why.

Call to Action

All well written press releases will have some sort of call to action. This means the producers, director or cast members want the readers to get involved with the show long before it airs. This statement encourages readers to participate in the social network sites created by cast and the website. Suggested wording is:

Example 1

> The producers and directors invite you to follow the girls on Twitter and Facebook. You can also catch bloopers and blunders posted by cast members from their cell phones from set. The Youtube Channel is called The Baker Girls Channel.

Contact Information

The last statement of your press release should include contact information for anyone that wants a full interview with cast or crew members. Suggested wording is:

> For more information contact Dr. Mel Caudle at XXX-XXX-XXXX or E-Mail her at drmelcaudle@google.com. Websites include: www.onthelotproductions.com and Thebakergirls.com

The End Signal

All news editors must know where to end of the article. You would think it would be obvious but it's not. Sometimes people submitting will add a note to the editor or a different contact phone number for day or night. Therefore, journalist standards call for the last line of the body of the press release to be indicated by typing in three ### centered directly below the last line of the body of the text. Sample is below:

###

PUT THE PRESS RELEASE ALL TOGETHER

Follow the above guidelines and put all of the pieces together on a single page.

- Logo is optional centered at the top of the page.
- Space down and center on page For Immediate Release.
- Space down and place the Headline in bold size 12 font.

- Space down and put the Opening Statement center on the first line in bold and size 14 to 16 fonts.
- Space down and put Summary sentence in font size.
- Space down and place dateline.
- Put a – and begin The Press Release Body.
- Space down and put the Call to Action paragraph.
- Space down and put Contact Information.
- Space down and type ### and center at the bottom of text.

The goal is to gain media attention in a variety of formats; e.g., written press as in newspapers, magazines and websites and in video media such as newscasts, blogs and podcasts. Send it out to as many media outlets as you can. Diagram 12-2 exemplifies a properly formatted press release targeted for all media.

Diagram 12-2   Press Release

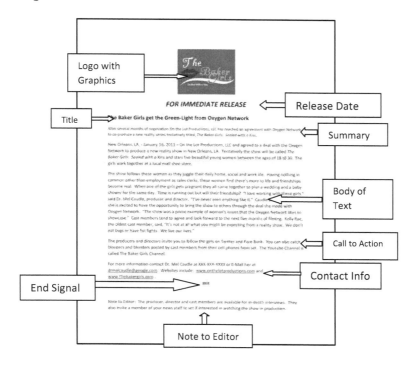

TIPS FOR EFFECTIVE PRESS RELEASES

- Write just the facts and don't exaggerate.
- Make sure that the press release if free of spelling and grammatical errors.
- Make certain that you provide the opportunity to meet with the cast and crew for additional interviews for feature length stories.
- Always follow-up on the press releases where you send them. You are more likely to get a feature story that way.
- Include a call for action of some sort. Ask them to visit the show's website, join in on blogging, follow stars on Twitter and Facebook or even call or start a writing campaign requesting the show with a particular network.
- All press releases are written in block style; therefore no indentions are needed.

FREE ON-LINE PRESS RELEASE SERVICES

The best supporter and promoter of your project is yourself. Never forget that. A sure-fire way to get free press is to author your own articles and press releases. Once you are proficient in writing press releases, it won't take any longer to start generating them and posting them for free on the internet.

It has been my experience that I gain the attention of distributors as well as other producers whenever I have taken this approach. It is also an easy way to include press releases into your reality show business documents. There are five main internet press release sites that I use:

1. Free Press Release Distribution Service - PR Log is easy, fast and free press release submission and distribution service located at www.prlog.org.

2. Daily News Online - Internet Marketing - Press release marketing service. Free to submit press news by county and by category located at www.free-press-release.com.

3. I-Newswire.com™ - The fastest and easiest press release distribution service and free press release submission online located at www.i-newswire.com

4. PRPRESS – A quick an easy way to get your press release out onto the web. Located at www.pr.com/pressreleases.

5. 1888 Press Release - This service provides free press releases to businesses and companies, including film production companies. Located at www.1888pressrelease.com.

Give all of the above companies a try and soon you will have an internet presence.

SELF DISTRIBUTION

It may come to a point where you will want to consider self-distribution. Why not? There are many advantages including maintaining the entire rights and profits. There are several services available such as CreateSpace from Amazon.com and Distribber.com from indiegogo. Netflix and HuluTV are also viable options. Submission guidelines are available on their websites. Netflix works fast. A friend of mine last year released a movie on Netflix and within one year made $1.6 million dollars. These options allow the owners of a reality show to offer their product to the public, both domestically and in foreign markets both in a print on demand (DVD) or immediate download. You don't have any upfront costs because they print on demand. You also don't have to worry about maintain inventory or mailing the products out either because they do so. You need only concentrate on marketing. There is a high demand for American made reality shows in the foreign market.

TIPS TO GET DISTRIBUTION

- Consider hiring a sales representative and a good entertainment attorney.
- Issue Press Releases.
- Call domestic and foreign distributors and ask to speak to a sales representative. Ask him or her as many questions that you can think of about your genre? Who's buying reality shows? What genre is selling best? What is the preferred format? What marketing tools should you start gathering? What is the average sale price of a reality show? Is it different for a seasoned producer?
- Attend as many of the six major markets for television which include: American Film Market held in Santa Monica, CA every November, Cannes Film Market held in Cannes France every May, MIFED Market held in Milan, Italy every October, MIPCOM held in October in Cannes France, European Film Market held every February in Berlin, Germany and FILMART held with the Hong Kong International Film and TV Market in March in Hong Kong.

CHAPTER SUMMARY

In this chapter distribution strategies were discussed. Also, suggested formatting and wording were included to provide the reader with enough information to begin formulating their distribution plan. Suggested tips were included on how to attract a distribution company toward your reality show product. The importance of Press Releases was discussed as well as a step-by-step guide on how to write press releases. A sample press release was provided.

PRACTICAL APPLICATION

1. Begin an internet search on reputable domestic and foreign distributors for reality shows.

2. Search the internet for sample press releases and become familiar with the formats.

3. Research the following Film Markets and locate the specifics on distribution companies.

- American Film Market held in Santa Monica, CA every November.
- Cannes Film Market held in Cannes France every May.
- MIFED Market held in Milan, Italy every October.
- MIPCOM held in October in Cannes France.
- European Film Market held every February in Berlin, Germany.
- FILMART held with the Hong Kong International Film and TV Market in March in Hong Kong.

4. Using the information in this chapter as a guide and write your Distribution Strategy into your reality show business document. Print a hardcopy and put into your binder.

5. Use Worksheet 29 to practice writing Press Releases.

6. Research and invest time in learning about self-distribution. Visit the following websites:

- Netflix
- HuluTV
- Createspace.com
- Outskirtspress.com
- Lulu.com
- Vimeo
- Youtube
- Distribber

PHOTOGRAPHY CREDIT FOR CHAPTER 12
Chapter 12 Photo taken by Renjith Krishnan
NATPE Floor Conference floor taken by Dr. Mel Caudle

WORKSHEET 29: PRESS RELEASES

Objective: To write effective Press Releases.

1. Using the 5 Ws of who, what, when, where and why, write and effective press release based off of the following information.

Who - Your Own Reality Show, LLC has joined with On the Lot Productions to produce your reality show.

What – The two companies will be producing the reality show, Making My Reality starring an up and coming first time creator and producer, which is you.

Where - You will be filming this show in your home town.

Why - You will be doing this show to enhance the careers of both production companies and show others the opportunity of creating shows.

When - Shooting is set to begin in three months.

Call to Action - You want people to come down and join the cast and be considered

2. Answer the following questions to generate your press release information.

1. Who is this press release about?

2. What is this press release about?

3. When will the event be happening?

4. Where will the event take place?

5. Why are you doing this?

3. Write your completed Press Release below.

CHAPTER 13

MARKETING STRATEGY

Mark Cuban, owner of the NBA team *Dallas Mavericks* and movie industry mogul with Magnolia Pictures, came up with an interesting question, "How can I market a film without spending $60 million?" Cuban was well aware of the fact that the more money he spent, the less money he earned. As a reality show producer and creator you must too ask the same type of question, "How can I market my reality show without spending money I haven't yet earned?" This area will be the key to your show's success or failure and could make the difference in whether or not your show attracts the attention needed for a network to decide to pick it up or for investors to fund. The more people that know about your show, the easier it will be to sell. That means you have to market your reality show without spending a lot money - a big task for producers but not impossible to accomplish with the right marketing tools and strategies in place. It's all about how creative you can be.

Believe it or not, your first marketing strategy is already in the works – your reality show business plan. You have been putting a great deal of effort formulating your plan, generating a logline and synopsis, getting a graphic logo in place as well as putting together you pitch package. You just may not be aware that you have been doing it. All of the work you are putting into your business plan will not go to waste. In fact, you will be relying on it to help market you reality show as well as tap into other creative and inexpensive ways. Future investors and television executives want to know what you have already done and plan on doing to market your show long before they decide to come on board. That is the purpose of the section Marketing Strategies in your business plan.

MARKETING IDEAS

There are many inexpensive ways to market your reality show. When the truth is known, your marketing strategy will be linked to your budget and how much money you can spend. But, with innovative approaches you can market your show with little out of pocket expense.

VIRAL MARKETING

Harvard Business School graduate, Tim Draper and faculty member Jeffrey Rayport successfully coined the term *Viral Marketing*. It sounds awful. Why would anyone deliberately want to give someone a virus? Well, that's not the intent. The intent is to generate a buzz through the internet and have it spread across platforms quickly multiplying each time mimicking the movement of a virus. Draper and Rayport completely understood how word of mouth techniques could successfully launch a new product. When applied to marketing your new reality show concept, often the least expensive method is word of mouth. The philosophy is that if I tell one person and they tell five, and that continues, then by the end of a day 625 people are going to know about the same thing. Multiply that by five and more than 3500 people know because you started with five. The only thing you did was to start the ignition and ripple effect.

E-Mail

One of the best viral marketing techniques was used by Hotmail when it first launched. Within a matter of 18 weeks from startup they had over 18 million subscribers without a "true" marketing campaign. How did they do it? They offered free E-mail to people on the internet. In exchange, on the bottom of every E-mail account, they had attached a statement that offered a free E-mail account to anybody. Word spread quickly and now I bet you know someone today that uses Hotmail as their choice of E-mail.

The same method can be applied to your reality show. Each time you E-mail somebody, put at the bottom of your E-mail a tagline announcing your new reality show. I use the following signature statement at the bottom of my E-mail signature:

Respectfully submitted,

Dr. Mel Caudle

Producer and Creator of *The Baker Girls: Sealed with a Kiss.*

"The Baker Girls: Sealed with a Kiss" currently in production. Visit www.onthelotproductions.com for more information.

Of course I save myself a great deal of time by having my signature set to automatically appear on all my E-mail correspondence. I often rotate different E-mail signatures to reflect a viral marketing strategy and to change things up. I have different shows always in production including films.

I also frequently send out an E-mail to everyone in my address book telling them of my new project and ask them to forward the information to five or more of their best friends. I point blank ask them to help me out. Of course I don't send this to people that are casual friends, but true friends. It is my friendship and business dealings that want to make people help me out. And they do.

What do they get in return? Entertainment. In trade, I provide a special link where they can view my sizzle reel for the new project or a mini-episode for free. Somehow, when people think they are in a special category they want to get involved. I guess the idea is that I thought of them enough to include them in my free give-away. In reality, I actually do. The end result is that I am generating a buzz and an audience for the show long before it airs.

I'm always surprised how many E-mails I get in return that are favorable and asking where they can watch more of the show. I use these to my utmost advantage and include these comments to help sell my reality show to the networks and potential investors in my business plan. I maintain copies and keep statistics on these E-mails. I also include a new section in my business plan with the subheading, "What Others Think of XXX" or I will include these statements in the section on target audience. I will place the quote along with the sex, race and age of the author. By doing so, I send a strong message as to who comprises the target audience for my show based on fact.

The Newsletter

Another freebie that I offer for my friends, family and newly acquired social network friends the opportunity to sign up for my free newsletter. Once a month I post a newsletter updating the status of my projects or new ones I'm creating. I also give tidbits on the status of reality shows in general. What my newsletter does is to keep my name in front of them as well as my shows. It also allows me to build my database for a potential audience for a show. Anytime one of the shows that I have worked on airs, I'll zap a note to my database members alerting them to the show. In essence, I'm advertising the show and increasing ratings at the same time. This is important to you because you will want people to keep informed of your progress. Then in your Marketing Strategy section you can identify how many people are on your database indicating you have a built in audience.

Social Networks

Social Networks are very popular these days so you may as well take full advantage of them. Don't limit yourself to just one but tap into all of them. Design a Facebook account for your show as well as a Myspace page. Also rely on a Twitter account. Have anybody and everybody you know sign up as friends or followers etc. I have to admit I personally don't like Twitter for my daily use. I don't really care to know when someone is eating or just got through watching a movie. But, Twitter is effective to get a following on your "Realebrities" and you should take advantage. Also, have your cast members sign up and follow anyone they can. You will attract others to your site that way. Then keep the pages active by providing updates. Also, encourage your cast and crew to start their own pages and direct their friends and followers to the reality show's page. It's a great viral marketing strategy that today's viewers utilize and word about your reality show will spread fast.

Youtube and Vimeo

In early 2006 three former PayPal employees revolutionized the way for filmmakers to broadcast their short films with the formation of Youtube.   Soon other channels like Vimeo surfaced and is a create resource for your reality show. The purpose is to build and generate interest as well as to build your viewer audience. You won't be posting your completed show, but you can post interviews with the creator, producer, and director and cast members to generate a buzz. Be careful not to post too much because you don't want the actual show up on the internet or even parts of it.

This marketing strategy provides you the ability to translate your channel subscriptions into real numbers for television executives and investors. If done correctly, your concept can go viral overnight and is a great marketing tool. The key is to keep the site active. One of my videos has over 1 million views. Of course I include this in my reality show business plan. What investor wouldn't know that something I produced has over a million views. That's a huge audience.

One goal is to try and have your reality show sizzle reel to become a viral sensation. Follow some simple techniques and start posting to generate an audience and buzz about your show. Here are some tips:

- Produce something that is short, under 2 minutes that is funny, and eye-catching.
- Make sure you push the boundaries, but not too far. Keep it PG rated. You don't want to run away potential audience.
- Make the video seem real, but not too real.

- Create a fake newscast of one of the cast members getting involved in something crazy. Use real actors as the newscasters.
- Be sure to include the name of the reality show and your graphic logo. Start getting your logo recognizable from the start.
- Include the message to sign up for more videos or your newsletter.
- Make sure you follow the simple rules of all productions by having a beginning, middle and end to the video.
- Make the video HD and of high quality. This will show off your work.

Blogging and Podcasts

Nielsen Company, the same company that provides the research data for television viewing, conducted a study that found that 23% of people between the ages of 18-24 follow blogs and podcasts. That means that approximately 1 out of 4 people in that age group tune in to read what someone has to say and then respond. Can you think of a better way to get an audience for your show than to find people that are interested in reality shows or a particular reality star?

Get creative and start a blog and initiate conversations on the topic of reality shows or narrow your focus to a particular genre of reality show. You must be willing to take the good with the bad. But what this does is allow you a forum to discuss your reality show and garner interest in it. It is also an excellent way to drive bloggers to your website. The  "Blogosphere" or the entire blog is often used by the media to gauge interest levels. Why not take advantage of this marketing viral strategy.

On the flipside of a blog cast is a podcast where instead of writing about a topic you create interest by talking about it and encourage others to comment back by posting their podcasts. It also is a great way to generate interest. There are many podcasts that you can respond back to if you choose. For instance, Podcast.com and Apple i-pod are two that offer free downloads of podcasts. The most popular podcast is *The American Life* with more than a half of million people downloading each episode. Use them to your advantage by responding and plug your reality show or have a cast member post their ideas. It's there for the using and it's a free marketing strategy. Soon you will have generated a built in audience without much effort and no cost to you but your time.

THE SIZZLE REEL

When presenting your reality show business plan you should also include a sizzle reel or teaser. A sizzle reel is a fantastic marketing strategy. Potential investors want to see and meet the people involved with the show. More than ever today's public is audio-visual. We've become accustomed to watching things and not reading them. That's why podcasts have increased in popularity not to account for Skype where you can see the other person you are having a conversation with. "It's all about relationships," according to reality show producer James Dubos. Dubos told me that he never gets involved with a reality show without having a relationship built with those involved. These relationships involve not only the cast but also the producer and director.

There are certain items that should be in a sizzle reel. Without exception start with the graphic logo and title of the reality show followed with about 30 seconds of quick clips of the stars in action put to music. Think of the opening of the 1970's sitcom *The Golden Girls*. This is a perfect opening style for a sizzle reel. Next include three clips from three different scenes. Try to make these no longer than one minute each. Once that is complete, introduce the main reality stars, again to music, but have them do something and superimpose their name. A good example of this is watch the 1970's opening credits for *Charlie's Angels.* In each case they show the three angels in at least five quick poses. Then end the sizzle reel with the production company's name and contact information.

For your sizzle reel you will not be telling a story or try to show the entire show. You want to tease the viewer into wanting to get to know the reality stars better and leave them wanting more.

Tips to Producing a Sizzle Reel for Next to Nothing

- Avoid having to pay for actors housing and travel by hiring locals.
- Avoid costs in wardrobe and makeup by having cast use their own clothing and supplies.
- The same thing applies to crew. Hire locals to avoid lodging and travel expenses.
- Go for either deferred payment or credit for both cast and crew.
- Find ways to cut down on your sizzle reel budget by limiting your location to outdoors during the day. That way lighting doesn't have to be an expense for the sizzle reel.
- Borrow or rent a HD camcorder such as the Cannon AX-H1 for the day.
- Borrow or rent sound equipment such as lapel microphones, shotgun microphones and audio mixer.
- Learn to do your own editing, graphics, and logos.
- Use non-union actors that need a reel. Instead of paying them, give them a copy of the sizzle reel to use as their actor's demo reel.

FOCUS GROUPS

To add to your marketing strategy don't overlook the impact a focus group can have on your show. Don't you want to know the strengths and weaknesses of your show before network executives and investors get a hold of them so you can make the necessary adjustments? I know I do.

To put together a focus group assemble a diverse group of people from a variety of ages, race and include both male and female.   Present your idea and concept as well as your breakdown of the episodes. If you have a sizzle reel show them. Listen to what they have to say and make the necessary adjustments. Include your results in your Marketing Strategy section of your business plan.

HOSTING SPECIAL EVENTS

A great way to generate a buzz is to hold a social event of some sort. If you advertise it, people will come. You don't have to spend any money either.   Put out a blast on all Twitter,

Facebook and Myspace accounts from all cast and crew that they will be meeting at a certain place and what time. Invite them to come out and meet the cast. Choose a public place like a local bar, bowling alley etc. and be sure to tell everybody that it is a cash bar.   As an incentive offer a free raffle for those in

Kelly and Jamie - *The Baker Girls: Sealed with a Kiss*

attendance for T-Shirts, or allow pictures to be taken with the cast. Be sure to invite the press. I once did this and over 600 people came. That's a lot of response for a word of mouth promotion. Be sure to keep cameras rolling for upload on the cast and reality show Youtube channel.

USING THE POWER OF THE PRESS

I often hear the saying, "There is no such thing as bad press." I tend to have to agree when it comes to generating interest in your reality show. Get all the press you can. This means creating and sending out press releases, getting interviewed by local radio and television stations, and having any newspaper coverage you can. Also, contact any television and film industry magazines to see if they would be willing to write an article on you and your show. If not, find a freelance writer to write an article and submit it for publication. Magazine editors are always looking for interesting material to publish. And, don't overlook online magazines either. The more the merrier. Don't limit yourself by having only the producer or director involved but also involve the entire cast. The goal is to keep the information flowing to the public.

Include all press releases and copies of articles published about your show, cast and production team in the Appendix of your reality show business plan.

FESTIVALS

With a feature film or documentary the producer will take the route of entering their work into film festivals. A reality show doesn't have this luxury. Or does it? If shot correctly and within a different structure you might. Why not consider making a behind the scenes documentary of your reality show and how you created it for entry into film festivals. You will generate interest in your show using this method. Be sure to have your One Pager with you just in case you find a potential investor. (More on the One Pager in Chapter 15).

CONTESTS

In today's television market there are many opportunities to enter your project concept into contests. There are contest specifically for pitching new television shows. Research them and enter as many as feasible. Just make certain that they are reputable. Anytime you win, make sure to include that information in your reality show business plan in your biography section.

TAPPING INTO UNIVERSITIES AND HIGH SCHOOL FILM CLUBS

More prevalent today is the fact that public schools, universities, and community centers offer classes in film and

television production. Use this to your advantage to start your grass root campaign and spread the word about your reality show project. The more people who know about your reality show the more interest that is generated. Volunteer to be a guest speaker. While there, take the opportunity to have the students sign up for your newsletter, blog, podcast and social networks. Remember, one person can add 625 people by the end of a day if word begins to spread.

NETWORKING THROUGH MEETUPS

Sometimes it's not what you know, it's who you know. The same holds true in the reality show production business. You can't go it alone. In fact, you need to be able to tap into a vast group of people to help you spread the word or to get your product produced. Network every opportunity you have and spread the word. Have professional business cards printed with the graphic logo of your show and don't hesitate to give them out. Don't print business cards yourself but use a company such as Vista Print that offers quality inexpensive business cards. If you meet someone of significance, send them an E-mail letting them know how much you enjoyed meeting them.

If they are a potential investor try sending a thank you letter with your logo stationary or a handwritten thank you card that has been printed with you logo. I have made my own thank you cards with my projects logo by using bright white card stock paper, folded in it half or half of a half, and printed my logo on it. This is a simple and inexpensive method to send a personal message. I have also had professional postcards printed fairly inexpensively from Vista Print with the logo of the show and sent them. This makes a great professional first impression.

CONFERENCES

Throughout the year there are several key conferences specifically designed for television programming. One of the biggest is the National Association of Producers and Television Executives (NAPTE). Two other yearly conferences are Mipcom TV Conference and The Future of Television. Speakers at these conferences have included some of the most powerful players in television including Leslie Moonves (Chairman, CBS), Mark Cuban (Chairman, HDNet /Owner, Dallas Mavericks), Jack Abernethy (CEO, Fox Television Stations), Bruce Rosenblum (President, Warner Bros. Television Group) and Tom Rogers (President and CEO, TiVo). The NAB Show in Las Vegas is attended by leading media, entertainment and communications

professionals who share a passion for delivering the next generation of audio, video, and filmed content across multiple platforms – from televisions, radios and computers to phones, the big screen and beyond. Don't miss the opportunity to be part of the exciting developments shaping the future of television! These conferences are a fantastic way to not only network but to also obtain distribution and hand deliver marketing tools. If you can afford to attend, I highly recommend it.

GIVE-A-WAYS

People love to get stuff free and there is no better way to generate interest in a reality show than to give something away. Items to can range from something as an inexpensive T-Shirt with the branded reality show logo to signed autograph pictures of the cast. You don't have to spend a lot of money, but hold a contest on your website by having people sign up for your newsletter for a chance to win a T-Shirt or a autographed picture of the entire cast. Make a small Youtube video announcing the contest and use press releases to announce it. You generate a buzz and a built in audience. Be creative with your give a ways. It could be a blind date with one of the cast members. I had a friend once auction a date with one of the cast members on E-bay. It generated a lot of buzz and made money. The money did go to a local charity but the press was unbelievable.

WEBSITE

One of the best marketing tools is the creation of your website for the show. Your website is a way to connect to the world and gain an intended audience. If at all possible make your website interactive where people can blog about your cast. If you can have it professionally created that's even better. You can run all of your contests, blogs and podcasts from the website and build in a visitor's page.

THE MARKETING STRATEGY OF YOUR BUSINESS PLAN

The past couple of pages presented 15 marketing strategy ideas. I'm positive that there are 100s more waiting to be used that I haven't thought of or tried. The more creative marketing strategies you generate the better results you will get. You will need to put these ideas in writing for inclusion into your reality show business plan in an individual section with the heading Marketing Strategy followed by a listing of the strategies you will be using to market your reality show.

The format follows the same style as the rest of the business plan:

- Place the graphic logo centered at the top of the page.
- Space down and flush to the right the heading Marketing Strategy.
- Space down and flush to the left the opening statement that introduces marketing strategy concept.
- Space down and put the subheadings for each marketing technique you will utilize followed by an explanation on how you plan on using the technique.

The following are examples of opening statements for the marketing strategy section.

Example 1: From the *Ace Mechanic*

Ace Mechanic, LLC will endeavor to use a variety of marketing strategies to promote the reality show *Ace Mechanic.*

Example 2: From *The Baker Girls: Sealed with a Kiss*

Tapping into a wide variety of proven marketing strategies, The Baker Girls, LLC, will generate interest and promote the reality show *The Baker Girls: Sealed with a Kiss*.

Example 3: from *Hoops: Life off the Court*

The key to a successful reality show is proportionately related to The Company's marketing campaign and strategy. Hoops, LLC will incorporate sound marketing strategies to promote the reality show *Hoops: Life off the Court.*

The above three examples are very simplistic in nature but all have several commonalities – the name of the production company, the name of the show and that a variety of marketing strategies will be used.

Let's look at one example broken down by the following sections:

1. The production company.

2. The multi-faceted strategies.

3. The name of the show.

(1) The key to a successful reality show is proportionately related to The Company's marketing campaign and strategy. (2) Hoops, LLC will incorporate sound marketing strategies to promote the reality show (3) *Hoops: Life off the Court.*

Although strategies will change you need not provide lengthy explanations for each strategy. Something succinct is far better. The idea is to get across to potential investors and television executives that marketing strategies are in place to build their confidence level. There is no standard wording. It is all about the marketing strategies and nothing else.

To format the Marketing Strategy page:

- Place logo graphic centered at the top.
- Space down and put heading in all caps font 14 bold.
- Put an opening statement about marketing strategies.
- Space down and begin listing marketing strategies with a brief explanation of each.

Now look Diagram 13-2 which is the Marketing Strategy page from *Hoops: Life off the Court*.

Diagram 13-2 Marketing Strategy

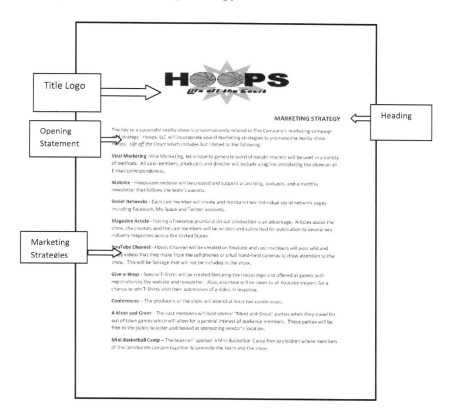

For your convenience I have listed below nine example market strategies from *Hoops: Life off the Court* that you can use as a guide when generating your Marketing Strategy section of your business plan.

Example 1

Viral Marketing - Viral Marketing, a technique to generate word of mouth interest will be used in a variety of methods. All cast members, producers and director will include a tagline introducing the show on all E-mail correspondences.

Example 2

Website - Hoops.com website will be created and support a cast blog, podcasts, and a monthly newsletter that follows the team's success. The domain site has already been obtained. The company is seeking a professional web designer company to design the website.

Example 3

Social Networks - Each cast member will create and maintain their individual social network pages including Facebook, Myspace and Twitter accounts.

Example 4

Magazine Article - Having a freelance journalist on our production team is an advantage. Articles about the show, the creators and the cast members will be written and submitted for publication to several key industry magazines across the United States.

Example 5

YouTube Channel - Hoops Channel will be created on Youtube and cast members will post wild and crazy videos that they make from the cell phones or small hand-held cameras to draw attention to the show. This will be footage that will not be included in the show.

Example 6

> **Give-a-Ways** - Special T-Shirts will be created featuring the Hoops logo and offered at games with registration to the website and newsletter. Also, a contest will be open to all Youtube viewers for a chance to win T-Shirts with their submission of a video in response.

Example 7

> **Conferences** – The producers of the show will attend at least two conferences to promote the reality series.

Example 8

> **A Meet and Greet** – The cast members will hold several "Meet and Greet" parties when they travel for out of town games which will allow for a general interest of audience members. These parties will be free to the public to enter and hosted at sponsoring vendor's location.

Example 9

> **Mini Basketball Camp** – The team will sponsor a Mini Basketball Camp free to children where members of the community can join together to promote the team and the show.

CHAPTER SUMMARY

In this chapter the section of your business plan Marketing Strategy was introduced. Fifteen marketing strategy ideas were presented as well as examples from the reality show business plan *Hoops: Life off the Court.*

PRACTICAL APPLICATION

1. Conduct an internet search on market strategies and generate a list of ideas that you find that you think would be beneficial to your show.

2. Research three different marketing strategies used by television companies to promote their shows.

3. Attend a social network meeting in your community and seek out ways producers have promoted their films and shows.

4. Research the following conferences and become familiar with what they have to offer.

- NATPE
- MIPCOM
- The Future of Television
- The NAB Show in Los Vegas

5. Research contests that accept television pilot episodes and consider submitting you logline and synopsis.

6. Using Worksheet 30, generate a list of marketing strategy ideas for your reality show.

7. Using Worksheet 31, write your Marketing Strategy Statement. Print a hardcopy and put in your binder.

8. If you come up with something unusually creative and want to share them with me send them to drmelcaudle@gmail.com. I would love to hear from you and read your ideas.

PHOTOGRAPHY CREDITS FOR CHAPTER 13
Chapter 13 photo taken by Renjith Krishnan
Email photo designed by JS Creations
Social Network photo designed by JS Creations
The Baker Girls photo taken by Erin Gamvrogianis
College Building photo taken by Dr. Mel Caudle
NAPTE Conference photo taken by Dr. Mel Caudle
Web photo taken by Salvatore Vuono
My Reality Logo photo designed and taken by Dr. Mel Caudle

WORKSHEET 30: MARKETING STRATEGIES

Objective: To identify marketing strategies that can be incorporated into your reality show business plan.

1. **Check the following market strategies that you could use in your reality business plan**.

☐ Viral Marketing   ☐ E-Mail Signature ☐ Website   ☐ Blog cast   ☐ Podcast   ☐ Newsletter

☐ Youtube   ☐ Vimeo   ☐ Contests   ☐ Give-a-ways ☐ Press Releases

2. **Generate 15 other marketing strategy ideas.**

1_____ 2. _____ 3. _____

4_____ 5. _____ 6. _____

1_____ 2. _____ 3. _____

7_____ 8. _____ 9. _____

10_____ 11. _____ 12. _____

13_____ 14. _____ 15. _____

3. **Ask at least 3 friends for their marketing strategy ideas. Include them in the space below if they are not already checked or listed above.**

4.   **Following the suggested format develop your opening statement for your Marketing Strategy section.**

WORKSHEET 31: MARKETING STATEMENT

Objective: To identify marketing strategies that can be incorporated into your reality show business plan.

1. Look up three reality shows and identify the marketing strategies.

Show 1 _____
Strategies:

Show 2 _____
Strategies:

Show 3 _____
Strategies:

Use the following format to create your Marketing Strategy Statement for your business plan.

1. Name of company

2. Varied marketing techniques

3. Name of show.

> (1) The key to a successful reality show is proportionately related to The Company's marketing campaign and strategy. (2) Hoops, LLC will incorporate sound marketing strategies to promote the reality show (3) *Hoops: Life off the Court.*

4. Print a hardcopy and put in your binder.

CHAPTER 14

INVESTMENT OPPORTUNITY

Money. Money. Money. I have yet to find a magical "Money Tree." I don't have a millionaire great-aunt or a rich husband. In fact, when I started into this business I didn't have any spare money at all. I did have ingenuity, creativity and a high definition camera at my disposal. I shot a couple of things and realized the potential of reality shows. In order to go bigger in my endeavors I had to have more money. I came up with over 200 ways to raise money and was able to produce more. Then I realized I really needed to find investors and the only way to find investors was to provide an investment opportunity in a business plan.

An investment opportunity is the chance to make an exceptional return on a financial investment usually in productions that are in the early stages development. The chance that an investor or network might have a significant return on the investment improves greatly with reality shows that have a dedicated production team, well thought out and comprehensive plans and various competitive advantages that include prior success. Basically, this type of production is a gem waiting to be found by networks and larger production companies. The problem for them in the past is to find the gem or diamond in the rough. A well thought out business plan which includes an opportunity for investment can make or break your deal. There are no big or Bonsai money trees out there, but there are investors if you know where to look.

WRITING THE INVESTMENT OPPORTUNITY SECTION

The Investment Opportunity section outlines the approximate amount of money you are seeking. It is straight forward and to the point. You are not offering securities, stocks or bonds. You

must make that clear. You are offering someone to put some money into a project if they choose to. The level of involvement will be up to them. You have to be honest and make no promises that they will get a return on their money. You must also be on target with the amount in which you are seeking. If you quote that you can produce an episode for $100,000 and you fall short, they investors will more than likely not give you more money. However, let's say you come in under budget, the next time you ask for money they will remember that.

You also must build confidence in you as a producer and your product to the investors. A reality show offer must be precise and with no promises or guarantee on the investor's return of the investment because you have no way of determining that factor. Unlike feature films where box office projections can be calculated, reality shows don't have that same opportunity. There are no box office tickets to be sold. The money comes from selling either a reality show idea or from selling the completed series. So don't back yourself into a corner. Rather, state the truth and that the success of the reality show depends on numerous factors such as audience appeal, marketing strategy and ratings.

Why would anyone invest in your project if you can't give them a projected amount for the return on their money? It will be because they have a gut feeling that the show will be a success or they believe in your abilities. Either way, it is your responsibility to make certain that anyone reading your reality show business plan is notified of the risk potential. The best way is to put it in writing is to begin the Investment Opportunity with a Risk Statement. The statement below is only intended for educational purposes. It cannot be construed as legal or tax advice since I am not an attorney or tax advisor.

Example 1: The Risk Statement

> Investing in any reality show is risky. This is a reality show business plan. It does **not imply** and **shall not be construed** as an offering of securities. Prospective investors are **not** to construe the contents of this document as investment, legal or tax advice from either the Company or the preparers of this document. *Any party considering a transaction with the Company agrees to look solely to its own due diligence. NOTHING IS GUARANTEED IN RETURN ON ANY INVESTMENT. AS WITH ANY INVESTMENT THERE ARE RISKS AND ACTUAL RETURNS, IF ANY, ARE UNPREDICTIBLE.* ALL prospective

investors ***should consult*** with professional investment advisors and a entertainment attorney to gain professional legal and tax advice. Each potential investor specifically understands and agrees that any estimates, projections, revenue models, forecasts or assumptions **are** by definition uncertain and thus possibly unreliable and therefore are not included. The return on any investment for a reality show depends on how much the network is willing to pay, audience appeal, advertising revenue and ratings.

Once you have clearly advised the reader that risk is involved then proceed to the amount you are seeking which should correlate directly with your estimated budget that you will create in chapter 16. For now you can assemble the template to use then plug in the numbers.

Example 2: The Investment Statement

(Name of Company) seeks $X to fund the reality show (Name of reality show). (Name of Company) desires to obtain all funding from private investors or from obtaining an additional production company to co-produce the show. Investing in any reality is risky and there is no guarantee that there will be a return on investment. **This is a reality show business pitch plan.** It does not imply and shall not be construed as an offering of securities. Prospective investors are not to construe the contents of this document as investment, legal or tax advice from either the Company or the preparers of this document. Any prospective investor should consult with professional investment advisors and gain professional legal and tax advice. Each potential investor specifically understands and agrees that any estimates, projections, revenue models, forecasts or assumptions are by definition uncertain and thus possibly unreliable. The amount of your investment return is open for negotiation. The

Company desires to pursue the best price for the reality show when negotiating the product for sale for distribution. Any party considering a transaction with the Company agrees to look solely to its own due diligence. It is impossible at this time to estimate a return amount of the investment. The return is highly correlated to how much the show sells for and if advertising revenue is generated.

Once you have clearly identified the risk and the amount you are seeking provide the contact information for the company representative that will be responsible for all negotiations. At the beginning, more than likely it will be your name and contact information.   Diagram 14-1 is from the reality show *Clean Sweep*. To format the Investment Opportunity Section use the following:

- Place title and logo graphic centered at the top page.
- Space down and flush right the heading INVESTMENT OPPORTUNITY in all caps. You can use a larger font if you desire.
- Space down and include the risk statement paragraph.
- Space down and include the amount you are seeking along with the statement that this is a reality show pitch business plan and not an offering of securities.
- Provide contact information.

Diagram 14-1 Investment Opportunity Page

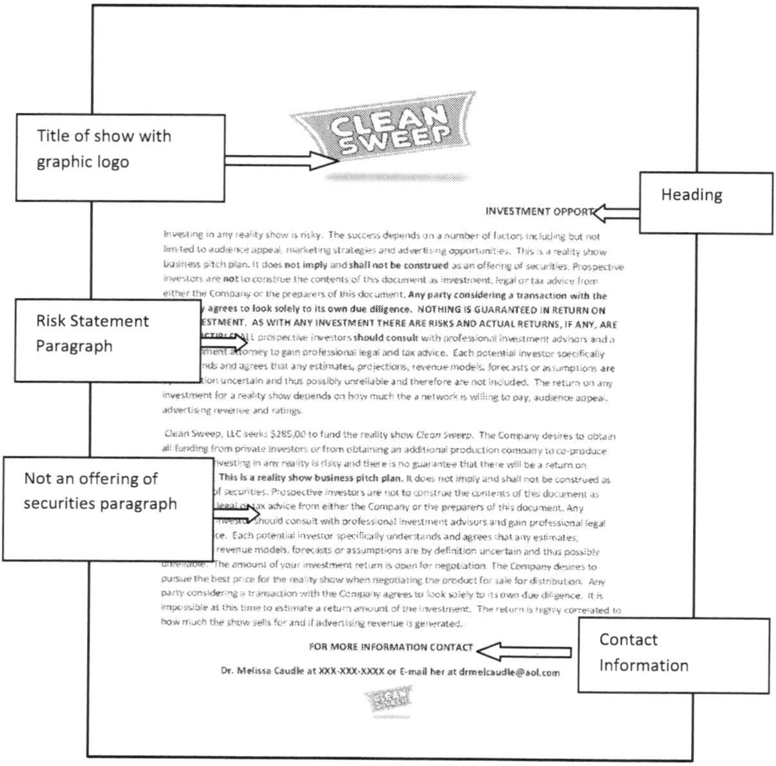
Title of show with graphic logo
CLEAN SWEEP
Heading
INVESTMENT OPPORT
Risk Statement Paragraph
Not an offering of securities paragraph
Contact Information
FOR MORE INFORMATION CONTACT
Dr. Melissa Caudle at XXX-XXX-XXXX or E-mail her at drmelcaudle@aol.com

WHERE TO FIND INVESTORS

More than anything a creator or producer wants to know is where they can find investors. I wish I had a magical answer for you but I don't. But what I do know the more relationships I form and the more products I put on the market the easier it becomes. It was finding that first investor that believed in me and trusted me that was the difficult part. I started out by working on reality shows as a crew member. I met a lot of producers and television executives that way. I also learned the ropes. I have yet to work on a show where I did not form a long-term relationship.

What if you don't have the opportunity to work on a reality show to form a relationship? You still can start forming relationships with a phone call to television executives and producers, by meeting them at national conferences such as NATPE and visiting Los Angeles and introducing yourself. I had a friend that attended the conference once and because she couldn't afford the conference ticket price she spent her entire time in the bathroom, in the lobby or at the venue bar. She met tons of people in the industry this way and made many connections.

It is my experience that A-list of Hollywood actors are not unreachable people. They breathe the same air we do. I have met and worked with a great number of famous individuals including the great actor James Woods.   Other actors include *Superman* claim to fame James Marsden and Kate Bosworth and *True Blood's* Alexander Skarsgard.   I have all of their private addresses and phone numbers.   I even text them. When working with them I have found out they are as normal as you and I.   Networking is the key and they often know someone else that can help me.

Alexander Skarsgard and Dr. Mel

I even met a famous producer chatting online and to this day we continue to chat. He was one of the first people I chatted with after Hurricane Katrina hit my city. The first person I spoke with was actor and comedian Brett Butler.   I was Brett's personal assistant on a film that was filming when we had to evacuate for Hurricane Katrina. It was days until our phone lines were established and she was the first call into my phone. She went as far as offering me and my family the use of her home until we got back on our feet.

Another source is your family and friends.   More than likely there is someone out there that knows somebody interested in getting into show business. You'd be surprised if you open up and tell people what you need and you are more likely to get it.

With all of this said, never submit a business plan or pitch an idea to a network executive or production company unsolicited. It's in bad taste and very unprofessional. The industry is a small one and they will remember you but in a bad way. Save the time, headache and money by only submitting to those who have agreed to review it. Remember, you don't want to kill your opportunity by presenting your idea in the wrong way or to too many people.

Quick Funding

There are two sites that offer a way for producers to raise funds for their projects. The first is indiegogo.com. The second is kickstart.com. Both sites allow you to set the amount of money you have as a target amount to raise. In return they get a small percentage. I prefer indiegogo.com because you get all of the  money even if you don't reach your target amount; whereas, kickstart.com does not give you the money pledged to you unless you reach your target. Both indiegogo.com and kickstart.com allows you post your project online free to receive funds. Indiegogo.com is a contribution site where you in return provide different levels of incentives for the amount contributed. Kickstart.com is a little different because people pledge a certain amount provided your target funding is achieved.

Listed below is an example of the level of participation I used on indiegogo.com for one of my projects. The advantage of a level of contribution is that it provides an opportunity for funding according to what a person can afford. That way everybody that is interested in your project can participate. You can devise your levels as you wish.

Level 1 – $10,000 and Above

- Receive Executive Producer credit in an opening single title card
- A dinner with the cast or producer and director
- A T-shirt
- Autographed picture of the cast
- A meet and greet with the cast
- Visit the set anytime during filming
- Attend Primer Night and After Party
- Autographed copy of DVD

Level 2 - Contribution of $ 5,000 - $9,999

- Receive Executive Producer credit in an opening double title card
- Dinner with Producer and Director
- A T-shirt
- Autographed copy of the cast
- A meet and greet with the cast
- Visit the set anytime during filming
- Attend Primer Night and After Party
- Autographed copy of DVD
-

Level 3 - Contribution of $1000

- Executive Producer's credit in a triple end title card
- A T-shirt
- An autographed copy of the cast
- A meet and greet with the cast
- One day to visit the set
- Attend Primer Night and After Party
- Your name in a raffle to have dinner with the Director and Producer

- Autographed copy of DVD

Level 4 - $500- $999

- Having a their name at the end credits as a thank you
- A T-shirt
- An autographed copy of the cast
- A meet and greet with the cast
- A day to visit the set
- Autographed copy of DVD
- Your name in a raffle to have dinner with the Director and Producer

Level 5 - $250- $499

- Having a their name at the end credits as a thank you
- A day to visit the set
- Attend Primer Night
- Attend Primer Night and After Party
- A T-shirt
- An autographed copy of the cast
- A meet and greet with the cast
- Your name in a raffle to have dinner with the Director and Producer, and an autographed copy of DVD

Level 6 - $100 - $249

- Having a their name at the end credits as a thank you
- Attend Primer Night and After Party
- A T-shirt
- An autographed copy of the cast
- A meet and greet with the cast
- Your name in a raffle to have dinner with the Director and Producer, and a Autographed copy of DVD

Level 7 - $50- $99

- A T-shirt
- An autographed copy of the cast
- Your name in a raffle for a chance to attend Premier Night and a meet and greet with the cast during a private party and an autographed copy of the DVD

Level 8 - $25 - $49

- An autographed copy of the cast
- Your name in a raffle for a chance to win a T-shirt, a chance to attend Premier Night and a meet and greet with the cast during a private party
- Your name in a raffle to have dinner with the Director and Producer and an autograph copy of the DVD

Level 9 - $15 - $24

- An autographed copy of the cast
- Your name in a raffle to have dinner with the Director and Producer
- Your name in a raffle for a chance to win an autograph copy of the cast, a T-shirt, a chance to attend Premier Night and a meet and greet with the cast during a private party and an autograph copy of the DVD

Level 10 - $1 - $14

- Your name in a raffle for a chance to win an autograph copy of the cast, a T-shirt, a chance to attend Premier Night and a meet and greet with the cast during a private party and an autographed copy of the DVD

150 WAYS TO FUND A REALITY SHOW

If you want to take a step in the right direction and start raising funds for your reality show I have written another book, *150 Ways to Fund a Reality Show* (ISBN: 146096715) available for purchase from Amazon.com, CreateSpace eStore, www.onthelotpruductions.com, Barnes and Noble, CreateSpace Direct, and other retail outlets. As the title suggests is a list of possible ways to raise money. I have also included a section in this book on additional marketing strategies.

CHAPTER SUMMARY

This chapter covered the topic of the Investment Opportunity of your reality show business plan. Examples and guided wording was provided; however, each producer or creator should contact their own entertainment attorney or CPA or legal and/or tax advice. The Investment Opportunity section is not an offering of securities, but rather placed to allow the readers to gain knowledge that there could be an investment opportunity if they so desire. Information on where to find investors was also included including to funding websites. A sample of level of participation was provided.

PRACTICAL APPLICATION

1. Use the information provided in this chapter to develop your Investment Opportunity section of your reality show business plan. Add it to your plan once complete.

2. Generate a list of possible investors for your reality show.

Note: There are no worksheets for Chapter 14.

PHOTOGRAPHY CREDITS FOR CHAPTER 14
Chapter 14 photo taken by Pixomar
Money photo taken by Salvatore Vuono

CHAPTER 15

THE ONE PAGER

A One Pager is also called a One Sheet. It really doesn't matter what you call it because both terms are used frequently. A One Pager is a single piece of paper that quickly lets anyone reading identify the name of the show, genre, logline, synopsis, number of episodes, the format filmed, target audience, creator and producer. It is an overall presentation of the show on one nice and neat page.

A One Pager is used as your calling card to the industry. You will need them to distribute at film festivals, NAPTE and to potential investors to generate interest. There are a variety of sizes of One Pagers including 6 X 9 inches, 5 X 7 inches and most frequently 8 X 10 inches. They are also usually printed on very nice paper. I personally use the glossy presentation paper. It makes for a nice first impression. Diagram 15-1 is an example of the One Pager I created for the fake reality show *The Man Behind #9*.

Diagram 15-1   Sample One Pager

Genre: Reality TV
Length: 22 Minutes
Episodes: 8
Format: 1020 HD

Logline

Drew Brees brings his leadership skills from the field to the city of New Orleans.

Synopsis

The Man Behind #9 is a celebrity style reality show with 8 episodes created by Dr. Melissa Caudle that follows Drew Brees, a Super Bowl Champion Quarterback, a father of two and a community advocate. Sport's Illustrated, " Man of the Year" has a direct way of getting things done on the field - with some of the best statics in the NFL. His sharpness and razor edge skill as a top quarterback translates to his off-the-field life in his community. He makes a difference to a city that was once devastated by Hurricane Katrina. For the past 6 years Drew Brees has brought hope to New Orleans, the city he now calls home. While off the field, Drew Brees raises awareness for the homeless, produces fund raising events for charities, brings laughter and joy to children stricken with terminal diseases, and more. On the Lot Productions, LLC, under the direction of Dr. Melissa Caudle presents a bold new reality series that steps into the life of a Super Bowl Champion Drew Brees. Throughout the 13 part series Drew Brees is joined by his closest friends in the NFL and community leaders. We got to know the man behind #9.

Target Audience Men and women of all ages.

I will go into detail later in this chapter on how to format and write it. I just wanted you to get a good conceptualization of what a One Pager looks like.

You already have generated the information for the One Pager section of your business plan if you have completed all of the practical application sections so far in this book. Since you already have the information stated elsewhere in your packet you may be asking "Why repeat it?" It goes back to an overall presentation of your reality show after having just presented some major budget and risky investment information. You want to re-direct your reader back to the excitement level of your reality show.

There is debate as to whether this page should be included immediately following the Investment Opportunity section or placed in the beginning of your business plan prior to or after the Executive Summary. I personally like it at the end because it serves as an overall reminder.

Diagram 15-3 is an example One Pager. The breakdown for the One Pager and format guidelines are below.

- Place centered on the first line your title graphics.
- Space down about half-way and flush right the words Genre, Length of Episodes, Number of Episodes and Format.
- Space down and flush left the sub-heading Logline followed by the logline on the next line.
- Space down and flush left the sub-heading Synopsis followed by the synopsis paragraph on the next line.
- Identify your target audience.
- Then at the bottom center, identify the creator, the name of your production company, and copyright statement.

Diagram 15-3 Sample One Pager

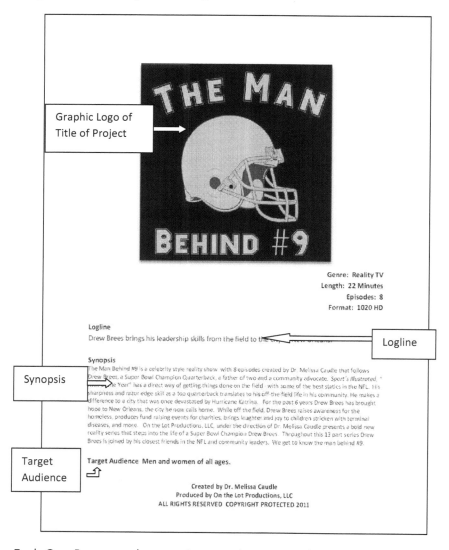

Each One Pager can be as unique as the creator desires and the information can be placed in various areas on the page. Diagram 15-4 is the example from the reality show I created called *Here Comes the Bride.*

Diagram 15-4 *Here Comes the Bride* **One Pager**

Notice that the format and graphics are different from the one I created for the fake reality show *The Man Behind #9*. All of the necessary components are included but it is in a different format that catches the reader's attention.

CHAPTER SUMMARY

In this chapter the One Pager heading of a reality show business plan was defined and how to generate one in a reality show business plan. The subheadings for the One Pager are: name of the show, genre, logline, synopsis, number of episodes, format, target audience, creator and producer. The purpose of the One Pager is to remind your investors in a succinct way your reality show concept.

PRACTICAL APPLICATION

1. Use Worksheet 32 to create the One Pager for your reality show and place it into your reality show business document. All information should already be generated if you have completed all Practical Applications in previous chapters.

2. Type the contents of your one pager into your reality show business plan according to the formatting instructions in this chapter.

- Title Graphics of your project that is centered.
- Space down about half-way and flush right the Genre, length of episode in minutes, number of episodes and format.
- Place your logline.
- Place your synopsis.
- Identify your target audience.
- Then at the bottom center, identify the creator and the name of your Production Company, and copyright statement.

3. Print a Hardcopy of your One Pager and put it in your binder.

PHOTOGRAPHY CREDITS FOR CHAPTER 15
Chapter 15 photo taken by Dr. Mel Caudle
Here Comes the Bride and The Man Behind #9 One Pagers were created and designed by Dr. Melissa Caudle. Photograph of the Bride also taken by Dr. Mel Caudle

WORKSHEET 32: THE ONE PAGER

Objective: To develop the One Pager for inclusion into your reality show business plan.

1. **Using the format below develop your One Pager.**

PLACE LOGO GRAPHICS
OF SHOW HERE

Genre: _____ Reality Show
Length: _____ Minutes
_____ Episodes
_____Format

LOGLINE:

SYNOPSIS:

TARGET AUDIENCE:

Name of Production Company
Contact Information

2. Formulate a different One Pager with a different font and use a jpeg image for your graphics along with the title of your show. Determine which one you like the best.

Place JPEG Image

TITLE OF YOUR REALITY SHOW HERE

Genre: _____ Reality Show

Length: _____ Minutes

_____ Episodes

_____Format

LOGLINE:

SYNOPSIS:

TARGET AUDIENCE:

Name of Production Company

Contact Information

CHAPTER 16

THE BUDGET

No one likes to do a budget much less follow one. But, a budget is a necessary evil in the reality show industry. You can't operate a business without one and a reality show LLC is a business. "Show me the money" is a common phrase for investors. The good news in your business plan you don't have to create the entire budget; that will be left up to a qualified line producer. The bad news, you will have to provide enough information in specific categories for investors to determine the feasibility of your show, the estimated cost to hire your cast, and the number of crew members along with the estimated cost to employ them from your area. Investors will ask:

- Where will my money be spent?
- Will the show be shot locally or will distance travel have to be budgeted for?
- How will housing be provided for cast and crew? Where will they live?

- How will the cast and crew get around?
- What equipment will be needed?
- How many cast members?
- How many crew members?
- Who will do the editing and log footage?
- What will be the above the line costs?
- What will be the below the line costs?
- What will be the deliverables?

There are a lot of questions you must consider when presenting your budget to potential investors. The more you can address the clearer it becomes for an investor. The first step is to calculate the number of days it will require you to shoot your

sizzle reel or pilot episode, how many cast, the number of crew, camera and lighting equipment, and general production costs. The calculation for the number of days for shooting was already completed in Chapter 9. Now you must consider the

reality of producing a reality show and calculate how many crew members it will take and what equipment you will need to make the show happen. Once you have a general idea, start making phone calls to potential cast, crew, locations and vendors to get a ball park figure of the cost involved in each aspect. This is the amount that you will present in a Summary Top Sheet. Keep in mind, the more you can get cast, crew, locations and equipment for free the better off you will be. Don't promise free if you can't deliver. In fact, the only time free should be considered is if you are producing a sizzle reel with the goal to get funding from a network or another larger production company.

So let's take a look at budget items. Budget items in any production are classified as above the line and below the line costs.

Above-the-line costs are costs that are attributed to writers, creators and rights, producers, directors, and actors; in essence, the creative people involved in making a reality. In a standard budget, the cost to hire these creative people are listed above items that involve equipment, expendables, fees, travel, wardrobe, hair and makeup and lodging which are placed after the above-the-line costs. Thus, the name derived below-the-line. Diagram 16-1 is the Production Top Sheet for the reality show *The Baker Girls.*

Diagram 16-1 Summary Top Sheet

PRODUCTION BUDGET

SUMMARY TOP SHEET

PROJECT:	The Baker Girls	BUDGET DATE:	1/22/2010
EXEC. PRODUCER:	TBD	VERSION:	1
PRODUCER:	Dr. Melissa Caudle	PROD. NO.:	OLTP 5
DIRECTOR:	Dr. Melissa Caudle	SCRIPT DATE:	Unscripted
PROD. COMPANY:	The Baker Girls, LLC	LOCATIONS:	5
ADDRESS:	XXX	START DATE:	12/5/2010
ADDRESS:	XXX	FINISH DATE:	6/22/2011
TELEPHONE:	XXX FAX: XXX	PREPARED BY:	Dr. Mel Caudle
E-MAIL:	XXX	PROD. MGR:	

ACCT	DESCRIPTION	GOTO ACCT	TOTAL ACCUM COST TO DATE	BUDGET	(OVER) or UNDER
	ABOVE THE LINE				
1100	STORY RIGHTS & CONTINUITY		12,000	0	(12,000)
1200	PRODUCERS UNIT		25,000	0	(25,000)
1300	DIRECTION		20,000	0	(20,000)
1400	CAST		15,000	0	(15,000)
1500	CAST - TRAVEL & LIVING		300	0	(300)
1900	CAST - FRINGES & TAXES		0	0	0
	TOTAL - ABOVE THE LINE		**72,300**	**0**	**(72,300)**
	BELOW THE LINE				
	PRODUCTION				
2000	PRODUCTION STAFF		1,000	0	(1,000)
2100	EXTRA TALENT & ATMOSPHERE		0	0	0
2200	ART DIRECTION		0	0	0
2300	SET CONSTRUCTION & STRIKE		0	0	0
2500	SET OPERATIONS		0	0	0
2600	SPECIAL EFFECTS		0	0	0
2700	SET DRESSING		0	0	0
2800	PROPERTY		0	0	0
2900	WARDROBE		0	0	0
3100	MAKE-UP & HAIRDRESSING		500	0	(500)
3200	LIGHTING		1,200	0	(1,200)
3300	CAMERA		35,000	0	(35,000)
3400	PRODUCTION SOUND		11,000	0	(11,000)
3500	TRANSPORTATION		2,000	0	(2,000)
3600	LOCATION		500	0	(500)
3700	PRODUCTION FILM & LAB		0	0	0
3800	PROCESS PHOTOGRAPHY		0	0	0
3900	TESTS		0	0	0
4000	SECOND UNIT		0	0	0
4200	FACILITY/PROD. EXPENSE		0	0	0
4300	PRODUCTION - FRINGES & TAXES		0	0	0
	TOTAL - PRODUCTION PERIOD		**51,200**	**0**	**(51,200)**
	POST PRODUCTION				
4500	EDITING		3,000	0	(3,000)
4600	MUSIC		1,500	0	(1,500)
4700	POST PRODUCTION SOUND		0	0	0
4800	POST PROD. FILM & LAB		0	0	0
4900	MAIN & END TITLES		1,000	0	(1,000)
5100	PROJECTION		0	0	0
5200	POST PROD. - FRINGES & TAXES		0	0	0
	TOTAL - POST PROD. PERIOD		**5,500**	**0**	**(5,500)**
	OTHER COSTS				
6500	PUBLICITY & PROMOTION		1,500	0	(1,500)
6600	LEGAL & ACCOUNTING		3,000	0	(3,000)
6700	INSURANCE		1,200	0	(1,200)
6800	OVERHEAD		1,500	0	(1,500)
6900	MISCELLANEOUS		750	0	(750)
	TOTAL - OTHER COSTS		**7,950**	**0**	**(7,950)**
	TOTAL ABOVE THE LINE		72,300	0	(72,300)
	TOTAL BELOW THE LINE		64,650	0	(64,650)
7000	FINANCE		0	0	0
7100	COMPLETION BOND		0	0	0
7200	CONTINGENCY		0	0	0
	GRAND TOTAL		**136,950**	**0**	**(136,950)**

Show Me the Money

When creating your reality show keep in mind the above and below the line costs. A solid formula to use to calculate each line item for your budget is:

> The number of days X cost per day of cast/crew/equipment = line item expense

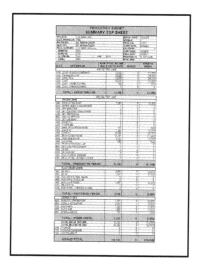

Once you have calculated each line item, add them together for the approximate budget of your reality show sizzle reel, pilot or all episodes. There are numerous budgeting software programs on the market that can create your budgets. You may also create your own budget template in Microsoft Excel. Production budgets rely on categories called line items and only the Top Sheet or Summary Sheet are submitted. The categories are usually identified by a number sequence beginning at 1100 and title of the area. Line items to you could possibly include in your reality show budget includes:

Above the Line Categories
1100 Story rights and Continuity
1200 Producer's Unit
1300 Director's Unit
1400 Cast
1500 Cast Travel and Lodging
1900 Cast Fringe Benefits and Taxes

Below the Line Categories for Production

2000 Production Staff
2100 Extra Talent and Atmosphere
2200 Art Direction
2300 Set Construction and Strike
2400 Set Operations
2500 Special Effects
2600 Set Dressing
2700 Property
2800 Wardrobe
2900 (Left Open)
3000 (Left Open)
3100 Lighting Equipment
3200 Camera Equipment
3300 Grip Gear
3400 Production Sound
3500 Transportation
3600 Location
3700 Production of Film & Lab
3800 Still Photography
3900 Test Shoots
4000 2nd Unit
4100 Production Office
4200 Production Office Supplies
4300 Production Fringe Benefits and Taxes
4400 (Left Open)

Below the Line Cost for Post Production

4500 Editing
4600 Music
4700 Post Production Sound
4800 Post Production Film & Lab
4900 Main & End Titles
5000 (Left Open)
5100 (Left Open)
5200 Post Production Fringe Benefits and Taxes

Other Below the Line Cost

6500   Publicity & Promotion

6600   Website and Graphics

6700   Insurance

6800   Overhead

6900   Miscellaneous

7000   Finance Fee

7100   Completion Bond

7200   Contingency

Anything that you can do to minimize cost is advised. The lower the production cost, the more return or prophet to the producers and investors. Cost consideration is a key factor for investors and networks when making the decision to produce a reality show. On average, one episode of a TV drama such as *Criminal Minds*, *CSI*, and *Dexter* cost in excess $1 million dollars. Shows with lots of special effects such as SyFy's show *V* can ultimately double or triple that figure. You can produce an entire pilot episode for a reality show for less than $5000. Also, you can produce a sizzle reel for less than $500 if you make the right connections.

Let's examine each area of a budget as it relates to a reality show production.

ABOVE THE LINE ITEMS

1100   Story rights and Continuity

Since there is no script, there is no cost for a writer or need for continuity. The only cost is to the creator of the show that is negotiable. On average, creators of a show get a one-time

payment per season between $15,000 and $35,000. If you had to follow union rules as it relates to WGA, you are looking at a minimum of $60,000 for story rights and more each time the script had to be revised. If you are the producer and the creator, you may never get money for your story rights. It all will depend on what you negotiate with a network.

1200 Producer's Unit

The salary for your producer's unit varies according to expertise and experience. These individuals can be negotiated with since they don't have to belong to The Producer's Guild of America. The most common pay for a reality show non-union producer and/or field producer ranges from $1,500 to $3,500 per episode. A more experienced producer can get up to $5,000 per episode. Of course as the popularity of the show increases so does your pay. Now the sad part – more than likely for your sizzle reel or pilot for your reality show you are the producer and won't get paid at all for your efforts. Consider it a work for hire and a way to get your foot into the door.

1300 Director's Unit

A reality show non-union director's salary is slightly less than that of a producer ranging from $1000 to $3000 per episode. Again, a more experienced director can demand more. And, you as creator of your sizzle reel will more than likely not get paid.

1400 Cast

The actor's fees on dramas shows are outrageous in comparison with "Realebrities." With the exception of the top ten reality star earnings, most are much more affordable. Eyeworks, a European production company, offered to pay OctoMom Nadya  Suleman and her 14 children $125,000 for 36 days of shooting their forthcoming reality show. The Osbournes reportedly paid each family member $5,000 per episode the first year. After the show became an overnight MTV sensation, each family member was paid $5 million per episode. Kristin Cavallari reportedly gets $63K per episode of *The Hills*. Meanwhile, Heidi Montag makes $100,000 per episode. *American Idol* judge Simon Cowell earned an estimated $36 million his last year on the show and turned down an offer of $80 million to continue.

Big Brother whose cast members make $750 a week, plus room and board for the duration of the show are offered a grand prize of $500,000 going to the winner, a second place winning of $50,000 and a $25,000 Viewer's Choice Award. *Dancing with the Stars* contestants earn a base salary of $125,000 and bonuses ranging from $10,000 to $50,000 according to the length of their stay. The *Real World* cast doesn't make much money at all but are provided free rent and the claim to their fifteen minutes of fame.

There is a lesson for you to learn. The less money you can pay a cast member the more profit potential. On average for a cast

member who is not known, is non-union and attached to the project can work for free or deferred payment hoping for stardom and their big chance. If payment is insisted upon, I wouldn't pay more than $100 a day as a contractual employee who is responsible for paying their own taxes and I would negotiate a deferred payment deal.

What if the cast member asks for part of the back end deal or part ownership? Don't agree and don't offer because the reality of reality shows there are truly no back end deals. Once your show is picked up by a network, they own it and it's not yours to give away in a back end deal.

Table 16-1   Table of Top Paid Reality Stars

TOP TEN PAID REALITY STARS IN 2011
1. **Kim Kardashian**: $6 million
2. **Lauren Conrad**: $5 million
3. **Bethenny Frankel**: $4 million
4. **Audrina Patridge**: $3.5 million
5. **Kate Gosselin**: $3.5 million
6. **Mike "The Situation" Sorrentino**: $3 million
7. **Khloe Kardashian**: $2.5 million
8. **Kourtney Kardashian**: $2.5 million
9. **DJ Pauly D**: $2 million
10. **Kendra Wilkinson**: $2 million

1500   Cast Travel and Lodging

If you plan your reality show with cost savings in mind, only hire local cast. If you do this, then there is no cost for cast travel and lodging. The cast member is responsible for reporting to set.

1900   Cast Fringe Benefits and Taxes

Reality show production companies don't have to hire union cast which is a major reduction in cost. No fringe benefits are

involved and they are responsible for their own taxes. In essence they are considered independent contractors or day players. Most cast members don't get paid anything at all for their appearance; instead the tradeoff is the possibility of fame and getting possible endorsements and speaking engagements. Matt Rolof from *Little People Big World* parlayed his appearance on the show with his family into a lucrative career. On average he gets up to $10,000 a speaking engagement. Sometimes, the incentive of being able to parlay is motivation enough for future cast members.

BELOW THE LINE PRODUCTION COST

2000 Production Staff
Your production staff is minimal for a reality show in comparison to a TV Drama, scripted comedy or feature film. It could take up to 30 people to run a production office for the aforementioned with a variety of crew including production manager, unit manager, first assistant director, and script supervisor. However, for a reality show typically there is not a home production office and it is done by the producer or field producer.   At most, the production company will hire a production coordinator and a couple production assistants. The average pay for a non-union production coordinator is $275 to $350 a day and production assistant $100 per day as an independent contractor.   On the reality show *The Girl's Next Door*, I was hired as the production coordinator for their New Orleans shoot during Mardi gras. As far as the production office went, I used a hotel room and hired three production assistants. To minimize cost, they hired local camera crews.   They did however, for consistency brought in the line-producer, field producer and production supervisor.   The crew for a reality show is nowhere near the size for films. The same held true for *The Little Couple*, there were only about nine of us, including the camera people that filmed the episode in New Orleans. The footage was then sent back to Houston for editing.

2100 Extra Talent and Atmosphere
It has been my experience that extras and atmosphere talent are not usually a part of a reality show. There are exceptions such as *The Colony* who hired extras to play the Marauders.

These extras got paid less than $100 daily. I know. Remember, I joined in on the fun on four different episodes.

As for *The Girls Next Door there* were plenty of extras and atmosphere. We were filming on Fat Tuesday where there was a million people walking and partying on the streets; however, none of them received any payment. Several production assistants were assigned to obtain signatures on personal release forms. The same held true for extras for *The Little Couple*. Again, plenty of extras and atmosphere people but none received payment of any kind.

2200 Art Direction
Depending on the genre of your reality show, you may or may not need an Art Department. Competition shows such as *American Idol* and *Dancing with the Stars* do because of the elaborate sets and artwork. Other shows such as a surveillance type that requires home living arrangements like *Big Brother*. Special care is taken to create the environment and living arrangements to meet the show's need. However, shows that feature celebrities, professionals and families filming takes place in their home or place of employment as in *The Osbournes*, *Keeping up with the Kardashians*, and *Miami Ink*. No special art direction needed. I followed suit in my reality show the *Ace Mechanic* where filming takes place in an automotive repair shop. Utilizing already established places for filming saves a great deal of money and no need for art direction.

2300 Set Construction and Strike
You won't need to include set construction or striking a set in your reality show budget unless you build a set specifically for your show. If you do you will need money to pay people to tear it down once and haul off the trash after filming is over.

My advice - film in locations already built to avoid this cost in your budget. Investors will be drawn to the fact and tell you that it is a fiscally sound decision on your part.

If you choose to go the other way and construct a set, plan on spending at minimum $100,000 to build and strike the set. Why would you want to spend this amount of money on a pilot or your sizzle reel?

2400 Set Operations
If you don't have a set you won't need Set Operations in your budget.

2500 Special Effects
Very few reality shows need special effects unless of course you create an experimental type reality show based on what it would be like to have to live on a colony on Mars. Then you might. I'd personally try to stay away from any extra costs involved in producing any reality show.

2600 Set Dressing
Set dressing line item is for decorations. If you build a set, you will need to dress it. You can't build a house and not furnish it. A more fiscal way is to find a location that is already functional then you won't need it in your budget.

2700 Property
Property are items that a production company purchases; e.g., computers, printers etc. Be very careful when you make these purchases or include them in your budget. Investors don't want to buy you a computer or printer. Only put items that are necessary and not considered for personal use.

2800 Wardrobe
Wardrobe is the clothing the cast wears. Most reality show actors provide their own uniforms and wardrobe. That is one

area that makes a person seem real. Again this saves tons of money in the budget.

3100 Lighting Equipment
Without proper lighting the quality of your project will be limited. There are plenty of ways to purchase inexpensive lighting without breaking the budget. Better yet, you might already have a lighting kit in your garage with work lights used on construction sites. An inexpensive place to purchase lighting kits is on EBay.

3200 Camera Equipment
Camera equipment line item is for all those things that can change the look of your results which includes tripods, dollies and jibs. Whenever possible try to avoid hand-held filming. Always use a tripod or "sticks" as they are called. Negotiate with your cameraman to include a camera package to avoid additional costs. Jibs are affordable on a day rental basis if you absolutely have to have one. You also can get really creative and use a wheelchair as a dolly for moving shots. I've done it.

3300 Camera
Cameramen make anywhere from $275 to $1200 a day as does an experienced Director of Photography. A feature film or drama TV crew can have up to 4 cameras, with 4 camera operators, 4 camera assistants and more. For your reality sizzle reel or pilot, usually a two camera shoot with 2 assistants can be used. During the production of *The Little Couple*, we had a nine member team to create one episode. This included camera, sound and lighting. The savings are enormous. As you can see, the production cost goes way down for non-union shows. It really depends on what you can do to negotiate an agreeable amount. At this price it should include the camera package. If not, then $150 to $275 for a day rate. A non-union camera assistant should make no more than $100.

3400   Production Sound
Quality sound to your final product is as important if not more important than lighting. Make sure you use a good microphone system to capture your sound. NEVER shoot anything without sound. I also advise going the cost of using an audio mixer. A non-union audio mixer with equipment can range from $200 to $450 a day. Audiences are forgiving when it comes to bad footage, but they are not as forgiving for bad sound.

3500   Transportation
In a reality show if you hire locals, transportation should not be an issue and can save you money.

3600   Location
A producer friend once told me that finding the right location for a shoot makes all the difference in the world. I would have to intend to agree with him. To reduce this line item in your budget, find locations that you don't have to construct and that you can use for free. By contacting your city or state film commission, they probably can provide you a suggested list of places to shoot for free.

3700   Production of Film & Lab
For a reality show you probably won't have to include production of film and lab line item. In essence, you will be delivering with your business plan a DVD for consideration. Then, once your show has been picked up by a network they become responsible for this expense. However, you will have to include numerous DVD for dailies and multiple hard drives to transfer you footage from if you are shooting digitally. It is my belief to always have at least two copies of the raw footage and never store them in the same location.

3800   Still Photography
Having still photos on your set is very important for marketing and distribution. I don't care if you have a friend that does it has a hobby or you contact a photography student at a local

college. Get photos and lots of them. Worst case scenario - have your production assistant take pictures. I actually was assigned this duty on the New Orleans shoot of *The Little Couple* for TLC.

4000   2nd Unit
The line item of 2nd Unit is when you need to do pick up shots or reshoots of something and you don't need the entire production crew. You probably won't need a second unit at this point for your sizzle reel or pilot. Therefore, you can probably eliminate this expense from your budget.

4100   Production Office
Unless a show has been picked up by a major network chances are you won't have an expense of a separate production office. That's reality. You will probably work from your home office to develop your project.   Therefore, at this junction you can probably eliminate this expense from your budget to present to your investors.

4200   Production Office Supplies
Production Office Supplies line item is a necessary evil. There are a lot of costs involved in preparing your reality show. You need paper, pens, highlighters, binders, dividers, a binding machine if you can afford one, ink cartridges, postage stamps and more. Whatever you think you need in this line item multiply it by 20. When I print five copies of my business plans in color and bind them. To print a copy in color is expensive and if you have them printed it could cost up to $1 dollar a page. Just think, if your business plan is 50 pages that is already $50 dollars for one reproduction. I probably spend easily on each packet. That's $50 dollars just to get a packet in somebody's hands.   It is cheaper for me to print them myself than have an office store or printing company print them. But, still the ink is still expensive and it really doesn't save me that much money. It's a good thing that you need to limit the number of people who receive your business plan. It gets pretty expensive. I try

to always include about $500 in my reality show budget just for office supplies and another $1000 for copies.

4300   Production Fringe Benefits and Taxes

Since the crew for your reality show should be hired as independent contractors responsible for their own taxes there is no need to add money to the Production Fringe Benefits and Taxes line item.

BELOW THE LINE COST FOR POST PRODUCTION

4500   Editing

For the purposes of your sizzle reel if you can edit it yourself, by all means do.   However, if you don't have the equipment, knowledge or skill then you will have to contract out this area which can be costly. A great editor is worth their weight in gold, but unfortunately your budget won't allow for this type of payment. I was lucky. I worked as the Program Director and Producer of Programming for a local television station for two years. Part of my job was to make sure our programs that we produced were of quality. Therefore, I would sit with our editor and watch him, make suggestions and before I knew it I understood the process. I eventually graduated to being able to edit. Not everybody has this luxury and will have to get their sizzle reel edited.   To cut post-production cost, consider contacting master level film students at your local university. Also try to find someone willing to edit your sizzle reel for credit. Last option is to pay out of pocket. Editors who charge by the hour are very expensive. I would try to negotiate by project instead.

4600 Music

For less than $100 you can buy a library of royalty free music to use in your sizzle reel. Once you have purchased a library you won't have to pay again to use the music as long as you list the company and give credit in the end title. The larger expense is when you want a song or jingle written especially for your show which could range in the thousands of dollars. I'd avoid original music at all cost and go for the royalty free music library. Once a network picks up your show, let them incur this expense. Your goal right now is to get a network to green-light your project and not to become a music label.

4700 Post-Production Sound
Your post-production of your sound for the purpose of your sizzle reel should be fairly easy to accomplish. Editing programs today have built in programs to enhance your sound. Be sure to talk with your editor about this area as well as your sound mixer. You probably won't incur a line item cost in this area for your sizzle reel and once your show is picked up by a network, the cost will be incurred by them.

4800 Post Production Film & Lab
You won't incur a significant cost at this time because you will be producing your sizzle reel onto a DVD and you can avoid the cost of having a print for theatrical distribution. Remember, a reality show goes to television and not theaters.

4900 Main & End Titles
Getting motion graphics for your main and end titles can be very expensive for a feature film ranging up to $5,000 for each. Lucky for you, this will not be necessary for your sizzle real. Most editing programs have built in title and end credit options and will become the editor's responsibility. Therefore, at this time it is not necessary to but this line item into your budget. Once your reality show is bought, they will incur this expense.

5200 Post Production Fringe Benefits and Taxes
Since your post production crew are non-union and hired as independent contractors and as day players they will be responsible for their own taxes.

6500 Publicity & Promotion

The Publicity and Promotion line item needs to be included in your budget. If you don't market your idea it may never get noticed. When determining your budget more than likely you will only have to come up with the costs to produce a three to four minute sizzle reel or teaser, the cost to replicate your reality show business plan and any marketing to seek distribution and a co-producer. When you are first starting out in this business it is very difficult to get anybody to notice you and your reality show that have completed episodes.

Networks prefer to buy the concept and rights and then come aboard as a co-producer or hire a production company with experience. With this in mind you could possibly shoot your sizzle reel for less than $1000.00. I can produce my own sizzle reels for no out of pocket expense because I own all of my own equipment, including HD camera, microphones, lighting gear, backdrops and editing suite. You may not have this luxury and will have to be creative and tap into a network of people in your area willing to do a sizzle reel on either a deferred payment or for credit. Try everything you can to get a sizzle reel to attach to your business plan.

6600 Website and Graphics

A website and graphics are two essential line items for your reality show and for your reality show business plan. One of the first steps I do is to purchase my reality shows domain name. I use GoDaddy.com and for less than $20 I can buy my domain. You need to plan on constructing a website for your reality show. To save money there are many "do it yourself" sites that include hosting for a year for less than $300. Also, consider purchasing a logo creator software program. There are several on the market for under $50. You can also contact a community college art department and see if the students would be interested in designing you a website, logo and graphics. If all else fails, be creative with the clip art program and fancy text fonts that comes with Microsoft Word.

My philosophy, if there is a will there is a way. The estimated cost for this line item would be no less than $350 and could go as high as you can afford to spend. Try not to spend a lot of money in this area because once the show is picked up, the network will take it over. Look at the bright side, if you get the exact domain name for your reality show and a network wants to buy it you could possibly recoup any expenditure to date as well as make money. I once was asked to sell my domain name for my company, On the Lot Productions at *www.onthelotproductions.com* for $25,000. I turned them down because I need it for my business. The moral of this story is to purchase any and all domain names that reflect your reality show.

6700 Insurance
Insurance is basically cheap for a reality show and in most cases you won't be able to rent equipment or obtain filming permits if you do not have it. I recently bought an insurance policy for $750 dollars to cover 10 days of shooting. If someone got hurt or I broke somebody's equipment, that insurance policy would have covered it. It makes me sleep better at night.

Do you need it for your sizzle reel? Probably not, but why take the chance. Investigate with local insurance companies. If you can't find one, ask your city or state film commission for a recommendation on companies to contact. The good thing is that once a network picks up your show, you will fall under their insurance umbrella at no cost to you.

6800 Overhead
You probably can avoid having to put this into your sizzle reel budget at this time. No production office and no production crew equates to no overhead.

6900 Miscellaneous
Just when you think you have everything covered you come up with an expense you didn't think about. Trust me it happens.

For example, parking, catering for lunches, bottled water, needing a gel, to buy batteries, a reflector and more. I always put in $500 for this area at a minimum and include 10% of the total budget for contingency.

7000 Finance Fee

A Finance Fee line item is more for feature films than reality shows. Hopefully with a little ingenuity, product-placement, and getting funding from a network you won't have to finance your project. As a general rule, avoid financing and using your own money. If all else fails try buying my *book 150 Ways to Finance a Reality Show* (ISBN 146096715) from Amazon.com, Create E Store, Barnes and Noble and other retail outlets for some easy and down to earth ideas to generate money.

7100 Completion Bond

Your investors may or may not require that you have a completion bond which serves as an insurance policy that if for some certain circumstances your show cannot be completed, the insurance completion bond pays back the investors. I have yet to see this included in any reality show budgets. This area is mostly used for feature films and is often difficult to obtain.

7200 Contingency

When developing your overall budget, add 10% to account for Murphy's Law.

TIPS FOR CREATING YOUR BUDGET

On the onset of your business plan your may not have to include a budget or Summary Top Sheet. When pitching your reality show, networks will be more interested in your concept, story development details, cast and your production team. However, to demonstrate the cost effectiveness of your reality show you may want to include the Summary Top Sheet. There are several budgeting software programs available on the market to create a budget for you. However, I recommend using an experience reality show line producer.

To minimize cost utilize the following cost saving tips:

- Use non-union and first time actors and have them work for free in exchange for a shot at stardom.
- Seek recent college graduates or aspiring filmmakers in your city who would be willing to work for the experience and an opportunity to add to their production resume.
- Contact a local film rental firm or production company and see if they would be willing to donate their equipment.
- Use actor's homes, places of business, and public areas in your community for locations.
- Look around your own home for resources for lighting equipment. You just might find something useful.
- Restrict the number of shooting days. The less days to shoot, the less it will cost to produce.
- Shoot during the day and not at night to avoid significant lighting costs.

DO I HAVE TO INCLUDE A BUDGET IN MY PLAN?

There are two rules of thought about whether or not someone should include the budget in your business plan. The first thought is that a creator of a reality show seeking a television network to pick up their show would not need to submit a budget. Why? Because if a network green-lights the project, they will set the budget, bring in their team and you will become a part of that. In essence, you submitted a reality pitch packet. The only difference between a reality pitch packet and a reality show business plan is the inclusion of the budget. The second rule of thought is how can you ask an investor to invest if you don't know the amount you need? I lean toward the second rule of thinking. I am experienced at production and I'm also used to creating budgets for films and reality shows. So, I feel very comfortable in preparing a budget.   However, for someone that doesn't have experience it might be best to leave that up to the professional line producers and not include the budget or any wording to the effect that you are seeking investors, rather make it a true pitch packet dealing with the concept of the show.

CHAPTER SUMMARY

This chapter covered a reality show budget and presented a listing of line items that are included in above the line and below the line expenditures. Each line item was discussed and where applicable approximations for cost were included. The recommendation was made to only include a budget if a network or potential investor wants to see one in your business plan. If they ask you to remove all budget items, then you have a reality show pitch packet and you should name your document accordingly. One way is not better than the other. It is a matter of what the production company or network wants to see.

PRACTICAL APPLICATION

1. Research budgeting software programs for the feasibility of purchasing one.

2. Using Worksheet 33, begin to isolate the line items that best could be associated with your reality show.

3. Using Worksheet 34, generate a list of people you know with production equipment for a crew list.

4. Using Worksheet 35 assemble a potential vendor list.

5. Consider placing an ad on Craig's list and begin gathering resumes of potential crew members. Investigate how much

they charge and if they have their own equipment. This is a sure fire way to know what your area crew are charging for their services. Be sure to ask for resumes for all the following departments:

- Director of Photography
- Cameraman
- Camera Assistant
- Production Assistant
- Editor
- Sound Mixer
- Craft Services
- Catering
- Location Manager
- Production Coordinator

6. Using Worksheet 36 generate a location list. Print a hardcopy and place in your binder.

7. Using Worksheet 37 generate your Budget Summary Top Sheet for your reality show business plan document. Print a hardcopy and place in your binder.

PHOTOGRAPHY CREDITS FOR CHAPTER 16
Chapter 16 photo taken by Pixomar
Money photo taken by Salvatore Vuono
Calculator and Money photo taken by Pixomar
Copyright Symbol created by JS Creations
Taxes photo taken by Arvind Balarman

WORKSHEET 33: LINE ITEMS

Objective: Identify Line items as it relates to your project.

1. Using the following line items circle the ones that you will need to include for your production of your sizzle reel and/or pilot reality show.

Above the Line Categories

1100 Story rights and Continuity
1200 Producer's Unit
1300 Director's Unit
1400 Cast
1500 Cast Travel and Lodging
1900 Cast Fringe Benefits and Taxes

3900 Test Shoots
4000 2nd Unit
4100 Production Office
4200 Production Office Supplies
4300 Production Fringe Benefits and Taxes
4400 (Left Open)

Below the Line Categories for Production

2000 Production Staff
2100 Extra Talent and Atmosphere
2200 Art Direction
2300 Set Construction and Strike
2400 Set Operations
2500 Special Effects
2600 Set Dressing
2700 Property
2800 Wardrobe
2900 (Left Open)
3000 (Left Open)
3100 Lighting Equipment
3200 Camera Equipment
3300 Grip Gear
3400 Production Sound
3500 Transportation
3600 Location
3700 Production of Film & Lab
3800 Still Photography

Below the Line Cost for Post Production

4500 Editing
4600 Music
4700 Post Production Sound
4800 Post Production Film & Lab
4900 Main & End Titles
5000 (Left Open)
5100 (Left Open)
5200 Post Production Fringe Benefits and Taxes

Other Below the Line Cost

6500 Publicity & Promotion
6600 Website and Graphics
6700 Insurance
6800 Overhead
6900 Miscellaneous
7000 Finance Fee
7100 Completion Bond
7200 Contingency

2. How many days of production are you planning?

3. How many locations will you need and what are the cost per day for their usage?

4. What equipment do you currently have on hand that you would not need to purchase or rent?

5. Using the formula below calculate your approximate cost for each line item.

Line Item is:

Number of days X number of cast/crew/equipment = Line item Cost

WORKSHEET 34: POTENTIAL CREW

Objective: To identify potential crew and vendors for the production of your reality show sizzle reel and/or pilot episode.

Answer the following questions.

1. Make a list of people you know that own film equipment.

Name: _____

Equipment: _____

Name: _____

Equipment: _____

Name: _____

Equipment: _____

Name: _____

Equipment: _____

Name: _____

Equipment: _____

Name: _____

Equipment: _____

Name: _____

Equipment: _____

WORKSHEET 35: POTENTIAL VENDORS

1. Identify vendors in your computer that rent production equipment.

Name: _____

Equipment: _____

Name: _____

Equipment: _____

Name: _____

Name: _____

Equipment: _____

Name: _____

Equipment: _____

Name: _____

Equipment: _____

Name: _____

Equipment: _____

Name: _____

Equipment: _____

WORKSHEET 36: LOCATIONS

1. Make a list of business owners you know that may allow you to use their places as locations.

Name: _____

Location: _____

Name: _____

Location: _____

Name: _____

Name: _____

Location: _____

Name: _____

Location: _____

Name: _____

Name: _____

Location: _____

Name: _____

3. Contact everybody on your list above and see if they are interested in participating in your reality show.

WORKSHEET 37: BUDGET PROJECTION

1. Use the following table to generate your Summary Top Sheet. Use the circled line items categories circled from Worksheet 32 to generate your line items needed for your production. You will need to make enough copies in accordance with the number of line items as well as for above-the-line and below the line costs.

Example:

Line Item No	Description	Cost	X	Number of Days	=	Total of Line Item
1200	Producer	1000	X	4 Days	=	1000
3200	Camera Equipment	375	X	2 Days	=	750

List the Line Items that you need for your production.

Line Item No	Description	Cost	X	Number of Days	=	Total Amount of Line Item
			X		=	
			X		=	
			X		=	
			X		=	
			X		=	
			X		=	
			X		=	
			X		=	
			X		=	
			X		=	
			X		=	
			X		=	
			X		=	
			X		=	
			X		=	
			X		=	
			X		=	
			X		=	
			X		=	
			X		=	

TOTAL
OF LINE ITEMS:

_____

2. Formulate your Budget Top Sheet using the information above.

CHAPTER 17

PUTTING IT ALL TOGETHER

You now have come close to the end of this book and with that you should be close to finishing up your reality show business plan. CONGRATULATIONS! It is a huge undertaking and you should be very proud. You are hopefully proud enough to want to get it into people's hands so that you can make your reality show. Not so fast. Just take time to take a deep breath and gather your thoughts. You don't want to present something that isn't ready. You have a couple of more steps to undertake which includes: re-visiting your Executive Summary, proof reading your document, gathering your items for your Appendix section, placing individual production team members complete resumes into the document , and formatting your Table of Contents. These steps should not be excluded and YOU need do these tasks in the order. Otherwise you will be wasting valuable time and effort. You will be taken through these steps throughout this chapter and then when you get to the practical application section you will follow through to completion of your reality show business plan. The order of the next tasks I recommend is:

1. Re-visit your Executive Summary.

2. Proof read your document for spelling and grammar.

3. Add any pictures are graphics to the document that would enhance the overall presentation.

4. Establish Appendix.

5. Double check for consistent formatting.

6. Formulate Table of Contents.

7. Print a Hard Copy.

8. Save several copies of business plan on numerous jump drives.

9. E-Mail a copy to yourself. Save it.

10. Register Document with WGA.

STEP 1: RE-VISIT THE EXECUTIVE SUMMARY

You have spent days, maybe weeks or months writing your reality show business plan. You diligently finished all of the practical application sections and wrote your plan as you went through the book. That's fantastic. Now step back and look at your document as a whole document and not individual pieces. Does it flow? Do you have all of the parts completed in the plan? Is it put together with consistent formatting? All of these questions need to be addressed, especially to determine whether or not you have all the necessary parts to your reality show business plan.

The first place to start is to re-visit your Executive Summary section. Remember when I first brought up the idea I suggested that the Executive Summary section should be completed last, but you could design the template upfront? So now go back, re-read and drop in the real figures to replace the XXs or blank information. Abstract it from the sections that you developed as a result of going through the step-by-step approach in the previous chapters. Make certain all information is complete in your Executive Summary. For example, the following is the product-placement statement that you had previously typed in from during the practical application section for the Executive Summary.

> Many opportunities for segment/demo-specific are available for (Name of reality show.) They include but are not limited to: XXXXXX, XXXXX, XXXXX and blank. (Name of Company) will actively seek product endorsements to increase market appeal and advertising revenue sources.

Now that you have completed the entire product-placement section in your business plan re-visit the Executive Summary section of your reality show business plan and remove the Xs that represented a potential company and replace with the ones you now have identified. The new statement in your Executive Summary becomes:

> Many opportunities for segment/demo-specific are available for *The Baker Girls: Sealed with a Kiss.* They include but are not limited to: T-Mobile, Goody Hair Products, Maxfactor, and Baker Shoes. Baker Girls, LLC will actively seek additional product endorsements to increase market appeal and advertising revenue sources.

Go through your entire Executive Summary section of your reality show pitch packet and/or business plan and make all modifications in every area.

STEP 2: PROOF READ DOCUMENT

What good is it to have a GR8T docament if it had speling and gramma mestakes? See what I mean? It really distracts from the final presentation doesn't it? The people reading your pitch packet and/or business plan will notice all spelling and grammatical mistakes. It will be distracting and will also put you in the ranks of an amateur if you present a document full of errors. You know what type of document is the hardest to proof read? The document that you write is without a shadow of a doubt the hardest one to edit. I know this first-hand. I can look at a document written by other people and find all of the typographical and grammatical mistakes. But when it comes to mine, I hardly ever catch them. That is why I get two to three trusted and reliable friends and intelligent family members to read all of my books and articles prior to going to publication. They always find something I missed or spell check didn't find.

Although it is a good idea to run the spell check and grammar check program that comes with your writing software, it too is not 100% accurate. You can have a word such as "there" and "their" and both be spelled correctly, but which one you really are supposed to use can only be determined by the content. A spell check will not identify this for you because both words were spelt correctly. There are plenty of keywords that are commonly misspelled. Appendix A in this book contains a list of the most frequently misspelled words in the English language. Get to know them and how to spell each correctly. It will save you a future headache.

You should also allow your document to sit for three or more days without you having looked at it prior to proof reading. Why? You can get a better feel for the flow as well as catch more errors that way. I do practice what I preach. It took me longer to proof this book than it did to write it. First, after I wrote this book, I let it sit. In fact, I filmed my movie *DARK BLUE* that I am co-producing with New Guy Films. That's how important proof-reading is for a writer. I also always proofread my documents several times prior to making the first printed copy. Once printed, I edit onto the hardcopy and transfer the corrections. Once I make the necessary corrections I'm back to square one and have to proof edit again. That is another reason I like to have two or three people at my disposal to assist me in editing.

I have had on occasions had complete strangers edit my book. Especially if they are interested in learning about the topic in which I chose to write. I did that for this book. I had plenty of takers who wanted to learn how to write a business plan for a reality show. I also received feedback on areas they wanted me to further develop or information they wanted to know and didn't get. It is a great way in getting your feedback on your plan long before any investors reads it.

You can also use a professional editing service if you can't find a qualified individual or two to edit for you. However, this can get rather expensive and I don't recommend it this option.

STEP 3: ADD PICTURES AND GRAPHICS

If a picture is worth a thousand words then why not use them to your advantage? I do. I always add as many pictures of the people involved in the project from production team members to cast into my business plans. I also add graphics. Since your reality show business plan is not going to be published like a book you need not worry about copyright and trademark issues. You can use as much clip art as you want. You don't want to overdo this, but you do want to provide a nice break from text and jazz things up a bit. I try to have at least one image on every page if it is appropriate.

STEP 4: APPENIX PREPARATION

Oh happy days are here. You have every piece of the puzzle together. Do You? Not exactly because you must now concentrate on your Appendix for your reality show business plan. This is where you are going to place any supporting documents to help pitch your idea. Items to include but not limited for inclusion are:

- Letters of Intent from crew and cast.
- List of locations that you have secured.
- Resumes of key team production members.
- Any news clippings or magazine articles.
- Production Tax Incentives

It is my belief that anything that you put into your Appendix should be of high quality. Don't continually make copies to attach. Instead, have all documents such as articles and newspaper clippings put in a PDF file and placed in the document itself. Type all resumes using the same format. Make them professional and not something that you cut and paste from IMDB.

STEP 5: DOUBLE CHECK FORMATTING ISSUES

Now that you have edited your document, inserted graphics and images and added the documents for the Appendix, recheck your formatting. Look for the following common formatting issues:

- Make sure graphic logos are centered at the top of each section heading. The size of the logos can be different.
- Make certain that all Headings are either flushed to the right or to the left and a larger font than the subheadings. I recommend font size 14 for headings and font size 12 for all subheadings.
- Make sure all headings and subheadings are in a bold font to make them stand out.
- Make sure that you have consistently used the same formatting for paragraph separations. Some people prefer indenting five spaces for each paragraph whereas I prefer all paragraphs to remain flush left with two spaces separating each

paragraph. It is a matter of preference not a hard set rule. Just make sure your document is formatted the same way throughout.

- Make sure you keep the same font size and font type throughout the document. This is especially important if you have cut and pasted something from another document that was written in a different font. I like to use Calibri, Arial and Georgia as my preferred fonts. I think they are easier on the eye for readers. This book is written in Calibri.

STEP 6: FORMULATE TABLE OF CONTENTS

You will need to formulate a Table of Contents once you have everything in place. Some word processing programs such as Microsoft Word and Corel Word Perfect have the software already included to accomplish this task. When you present your pitch packet or business plan it makes it very easy for the reader to find different components by referring to the Table of Contents. Once you have succeeded in formulating the Table of Contents, be sure to proofread it as well making sure there are no errors. It is also important that the page numbers do correspond with the correct section of your plan. I have on several occasions used Skype to pitch a project and the person on the other end of the conversation kept referring to my sections by the page numbers. He wanted to make certain we were literally on the same page.

STEP 7: PRINT A COPY OF YOUR BUSINESS PLAN

By the time you are to this point in your preparation of your plan you should be able to print a master copy for safekeeping. I always file one in a filing cabinet and put another into a fire and water proof box. I learned the hard way after Hurricane Katrina when I lost a lot of documents and files. Now I probably go overboard to protect them and make sure I have a copy at my disposal.

STEP 8: SAVE MULTIPLE COPIES

After Hurricane Katrina took everything from me, I had no copies anywhere of anything. My computer was wiped out and all my files were soggy to say the least. That is when I started making backup copies of everything and stored in multiple places. I always put my plans on three different jump drives (even as I write them), and now I have a company that I pay that backs up and stores all of my documents offsite. That way, if my computer crashes, I still have my documents. I like the security of knowing that a small jump drive is in my safety deposit box with key business plans, books, articles and screenplays that I have written.

STEP 9 – E-MAIL A COPY TO YOUR-SELF

I always E-mail a copy of my business plan to myself and save it in my file cabinet online. Sometimes you don't have your jump drive with you or a copy and you run across somebody that wants to see it.   You can always access your E-mail from anyone's computer and provide them with a copy. Remember to get them to sign the Confidentiality Agreement which you should also email to yourself just in case you need it.

STEP 10: REGISTER WITH WGA

To safe guard yourself, always register your document with the WGA.   It is well worth the $20. Remember that this number also goes on the cover page of your business plan.

You can go one step further and register your business plan with the US Copyright service section of the US Library of Congress for $35 dollars. It is always to your advantage to document that you are the owner and creator of your document.

By the way, don't rely on the poor man's method of copyrighting a document by thinking you can mail a copy to your-self and be done with it. It really isn't advisable and investors and television executives won't accept this method.

In the long run, it will only cause you heartaches and trouble when it comes to distribution. So copyright your reality show and business plan the correct way through the U.S. Library of Congress.   You can even process your information online through their website.

CHAPTER SUMMARY

In this chapter the final preparations to your reality show business plan was discussed. These included:

- Re-visit your Executive Summary.
- Proof read your document for spelling and grammar.
- Add any pictures are graphics to the document that would enhance the overall presentation.
- Establish Appendix.
- Double check for consistent formatting.
- Formulate Table of Contents.
- Print a Hard Copy.
- Save several copies of business plan on numerous jump drives.
- E-Mail a copy to yourself. Save it.
- Register Document with WGA.
- Copyright your document through the U.S. Library of Congress.

PRACTICAL APPLICATION

1. Re-visit your Executive Summary section and replace any missing data in the appropriate spaces. Print the final version and add to your binder.

2. Use Worksheet 38 to identify any missing sections of your reality show business plan. Complete any section of your reality show business plan prior to advancing to the next one.

3. Look at the formatting of your business plan. Make any adjustments to your document needed to create visually appealing flow to your document.

4. Gather all resumes of key production team members.

5. Gather all letters of intent from those that are attached.

6. Gather all news clippings and articles from magazines. Make a PDF file of each for inclusion into your document Appendix.

7. Proof read your document and make sure it is free of errors.

8. Add page numbers to your document.

9. Give you document to a couple of trusted friends that can also proof read your document for errors. And don't forget to have them sign the Confidentiality Agreement.

10. Formulate a Table of Contents using the correct headings and place the appropriate page numbers in your document.

11. Using Worksheet 39 double check your document and make sure all of the necessary parts to the plan have been included. If not, go back and fix the gap.

12. Print a copy of your document to file in your records.

13. Register Document with the WGA

14. Register Document with the Library of Congress.

PHOTOGRAPHY CREDITS FOR CHAPTER 17
Chapter 17 photo taken by Simon Howden and graphic design by Dr. Mel Caudle

WORKSHEET 38: EDITING AND FORMATTING

Objective: To review your reality show business plan to make certain that all criteria have been adhered to.

Review your business plan document adhering to the following benchmarks. Check off completed tasks.

☐ I have re-visited my Executive Summary section and replaced on XXXs with appropriate data.

☐ I have proof read my plan for spelling and grammar errors.

☐ I have added pictures and graphics to the document that enhances the overall presentation.

☐ I have established the Appendix section.

☐ All headings and subheadings are consistent in format.

☐ My Table of Contents has been created and page numbers reflected.

☐ Several people have proof read my business plan.

☐ I have printed and filed away a hard copy of my final plan.

☐ I have saved several copies of my business plan on numerous jump drives and stored safely in different locations.

☐ I have E-Mailed a copy to my own E-Mail address.

☐ I have registered my business plan Document with WGA.

☐ I have put my WGA number on the cover sheet of my business plan.

WORKSHEET 39: PARTS OF THE BUSINESS PLAN

Objective: To identify and complete all parts of a reality show business plan.

Check all parts that have been completed in your reality show business plan.

- ☐ The Cover
- ☐ The Confidentiality Agreement
- ☐ Table of Contents
- ☐ The Executive Summary
- ☐ The Logline and Synopsis
- ☐ The Structure of the Show
- ☐ The Cast Members
- ☐ The Production Team
- ☐ Production and Production Schedule
- ☐ The Market
- ☐ Product Placement
- ☐ Distribution
- ☐ Marketing Strategy
- ☐ Investment Opportunity
- ☐ The One-Pager
- ☐ The Budget
- ☐ The Appendix Cover Sheet
- ☐ Resumes
- ☐ Letters of intent for:
- ☐ Producer ☐ Production Company ☐ Director ☐ Cast
- ☐ News clippings

CHAPTER 18

FIRST CONTACT

The most frequent question I get from creators of reality shows is, "How do I find television executives and investors to green-light my reality show?" There are several paths that you can take besides winning the lottery or waiting on a rich relative to die and leave you money. There is no real tried and true method and I won't profess that I have all the answers. I don't. What I can offer is the path that I find most effective. I go directly to one of two sources.

TELEVISION NETWORKS

The first source is to make contact with a television network program development department with a phone call. I pitch my show in one minute and ask if I can forward to them my reality show business plan. Networks do not accept pitch packets or business plans that are unsolicited. Once you have received the go ahead from a network executive your plan is not longer consider unsolicited. They usually provide you with a private E-mail address. That's when I follow-up and ask them to sign the Confidentiality Agreement. By doing so, they know immediately that I am a professional.

Sometimes, a network executive likes my idea, but instead of giving me permission to send my business plan they ask that I have either my agent or entertainment attorney forward the copy. I completely understand where they are coming from. It provides protection to both parties involved. First, they are protecting themselves. Believe me when I tell you that there are several other people with similar reality show concepts just like yours. In fact, at the time you place your call, there could be one just like yours in the developmental stage at the network. The networks don't want to get into a legal battle with you by you claiming they stole your idea. When an attorney or agent submits your idea to them there is a Confidentiality Statement from them that informs you that it is your understanding that similar programs could already be in development. Likewise, when an agent or attorney forwards your business plan to a network executive, it protects you as well. You have a formal chain of distribution that you can maintain.

Prior to making the initial phone call I have done extensive research on these networks and the people that run them. I

don't waste my time pitching a reality show idea that a network wouldn't already have an interest in that type of genre. A good example is my show *The Baker Girls: Sealed with a Kiss*. I'm not going to waste my time and submit it to HGTV or to The Discovery Channel. Why? These two networks do not typically air programs about five twenty-something beautiful girls. However, Bravo, VH1 and

MTV all do. How do I know this? I know because I have done my research. I have made it a point to visit each network's website, and make a list of current reality show programs. I then go to several resources; e.g., Internet Movie Data Base Pro (IMDBPRO) and to the National Cable and Television Association (NCTA) to identify the producers, directors and the name of production companies for each show. I did not include a list of the executives for each network because by the time I publish this book, the list will be outdated. It seems that television executives jobs are very fluid in nature so don't get sucked up into buying a list. The only source book I would ever recommend is *The Hollywood Creative Directory* which is updated a couple times a year. Even with this, names change so always make a phone call and inquire the name of the current executive in charge of reality show program development.

I also make it a point to watch reality TV shows by networks. I call it my "Reality Show Viewathon." I can't wait for a rainy day or a day where I have all to myself and can watch one channel's reality shows. I do so in an active manner with my pen and paper in hand to acquire all the notes I need. By doing so, I get a sense of the programming styles of each network. I have been able to ascertain that some networks like the cast members to have the equivalent to a confession testimony booth where they can spill the beans on other cast members while other networks just like a single cast member to provide a testimonial of what they felt at a certain point. This is key information in designing your show with a particular network in mind. If you provide a certain familiarity in the format of your show it sublimely provides a comfort zone. When you couple a comfort zone with a new and fresh take, it is easier to for television executives and investors to digest and comprehend.

Reflect back to the information I provided in Chapter 6 on the format of a reality television show. The only way to obtain this knowledge is by watching the program yourself. I hope you discovered patterns in each show by networks. If not, re-visit a couple of reality shows with formatting similarities between them.

First you need to be able to identify the television stations that air reality television programs and find out their submission rules and guidelines. Almost without an exception, networks do not accept unsolicited material. I have provided a list of the stations and a partial list of the reality shows they air. Use this information wisely to begin your research and to help you identify what type of reality genre each network is known to include in their line-up. That is the intent of this section.

ABC - (www.abc.com) – ABC has always provided a myriad of programs that meet the supply and demand of its audience. This includes popular reality shows such as: *Extreme Makeover*, *Dance War*, *The Bachelor*, *The Bachelorette* and more. They are introducing the new reality show *True Beauty* in 2011. They will not accept unsolicited concepts, business plans or treatments. You must go through an agent. (Main Phone: 818-560-1000)

- *All American Girl - ABC*
- *American Inventor - ABC*
- *American Supergirl - ABC*
- *Are You Hot? - ABC*
- *The Bachelor*
- *The Bachelorette - ABC*
- *The Benefactor - ABC*
- *Boss Swap - ABC*
- *Boston 24/7 - ABC*
- *Brat Camp - ABC*
- *The Chair - ABC*
- *Dance War - ABC*
- *Dancing With the Stars - ABC*
- *Dating Experiment - ABC*
- *Dating in the Dark - ABC*
- *Dot Comedy - ABC*
- *Duel - ABC*

- *Extreme Makeover - ABC*
- *Extreme Makeover: Home Edition - ABC*
- *Extreme Makeover: How'd They Do That - ABC*
- *Extreme Makeover: Wedding Edition - ABC*
- *EX Wives Club - ABC*
- *The Family - ABC*
- *Fast Cars and Superstars - ABC*
- *Fat March - ABC*
- *The Hamptons - ABC*
- *Here Come the Newlyweds - ABC*
- *Hooking Up - ABC*
- *Hopkins 24/7-ABC*
- *Houston Medical - ABC*
- *i-Caught - ABC*
- *Houston Medical - ABC*
- *I Survived a Japanese Game Show - ABC*
- *Just for Laughs - ABC*
- *Master of Champions - ABC*
- *Miracle Workers - ABC*
- *The Mole - ABC*
- *My Kind of Town - ABC*
- *National Bingo Night - ABC*
- *The Next Best Thing - ABC*
- *The One: Making a Music Star - ABC*
- *One Ocean View - ABC*
- *Oprah's Big Give - ABC*
- *The People Versus - ABC*
- *Pepsi Play for a Billion - ABC*
- *Public Property - ABC*
- *Set for Life - ABC*
- *The Next Best Thing - ABC*
- *This is Your Life - ABC*
- *The Runner-ABC*
- *The Scholar - ABC*
- *Set for Life - ABC*

- *Shaq's Big Challenge - ABC*
- *Show Me the Money - ABC*
- *True Beauty*
- *You Don't Know Jack - ABC*

A & E - (www.aetv.com) A & E is a powerhouse for reality television with shows like *Hoarders, Dog the Bounty Hunter, Gene Simmons Family Jewels*, and *Flip This House*. A & E does not accept any unsolicited reality show ideas. You must submit through an agent or entertainment attorney. (Main phone: 212-210-1400)

- *Caesars 24/7 - A&E*
- *Dog the Bounty Hunter - A&E*
- *Dream Chasers - A&E*
- *Family Plots - A&E*
- *Flip This House – A & E*
- *Gene Simmons Family Jewels - A&E*
- *Growing Up Gotti - A&E*
- *Hoarders – A & E*
- *House of Dreams - A&E*
- *Inked - A&E*
- *Knievel's Wild Ride - A&E*
- *Parking Wars - A&E*
- *Rollergirls - A&E*
- *Sons of Hollywood - A&E*
- *The Two Coreys - A&E*
- *Outback House - A&E*
- *Random 1 - A&E*

BET – (www.bet.com) BET is a subsidiary of Viacom, Inc. and is one of the leading networks to broadcast reality shows that feature African Americans such as *The Monique Show* and *Tiny and Toya*. In 2011 they are introducing four new reality shows: *DMX: Soul of Man, Lil Kim: Countdown to Lockdown, Next Level: Vince Young and Committed* and *The Christies*. I am also currently trying to get my reality show *Darren: Sharper than*

Ever on this network.   BET does not accept unsolicited reality show ideas and to submit you must submit through an agent. If you choose to send a show idea to BET they acknowledge that you forfeit your right and claim to the show. (Main phone: 202-608-2000)

- *The Monique Show – BET*
- *Tiny and Toya – BET*
- *Keisha Cole: The way it is – BET*
- *College Hill – BET*
- *DMX: Soul of Man*
- *Lil Kim: Countdown to Lockdown*
- *Next Level: Vince Young*
- *Committed: The Christies*

BRAVO – (www.bravotv.com) Bravo is a cable network with a wide-range of programming including reality shows such as *Project Runway, Basketball Wives, Tabatha's Salon Takeover, Real Housewives of Orange County, Top Chef* and *Real Housewives of New Jersey*. New shows for 2011 include *Monica Still Standing* and *Harlem Heights*.   No unsolicited reality show projects will be accepted.   You must be represented by an agent. (Main Phone: 212-664-4444)

- *Basketball Wives - Bravo*
- *Battle of the Network Reality Stars - Bravo*
- *Being Bobby Brown - Bravo*
- *Better Half - Bravo*
- *Blow Out - Bravo*
- *Boy Meets Boy - Bravo*
- *Celebrity Poker - Bravo*
- *Flipping Out - Bravo*
- *Hey Paula - Bravo*
- *Hidden Howie - Bravo*
- *Kell on Earth - Bravo*
- *Long Way Round - Bravo*
- *Make Me a Supermodel - Bravo*

- *Manhunt - Bravo*
- *Million Dollar Listing - Bravo*
- *The Millionaire Matchmaker - Bravo*
- *Situation: Comedy - Bravo*
- *NYC Prep - Bravo*
- *Shear Genius - Bravo*
- *Tabloid Wars - Bravo*
- *Tim Gunn's Guide to Style - Bravo*
- *Top Chef - Bravo*
- *Top Design - Bravo*
- *Project Greenlight - Bravo*
- *Project Runway*
- *Queer Eye for the Straight Girl - Bravo*
- *Queer Eye for the Straight Guy - Bravo*
- *The Real Housewives of New York City - Bravo*
- *The Real Housewives of Orange County - Bravo*
- *Sports Kids Moms & Dads - Bravo*
- *Step It Up and Dance - Bravo*
- *Tabloid Wars - Bravo*
- *Welcome to the Parker - Bravo*

CBS – (www.cbs.com) CBS has always brought great drama and comedy programming and with the *Amazing Race* soaring in ratings, they continue to find new reality shows to bring to the public. They have also had hits in the genre of game shows. No unsolicited reality show projects will be accepted. You must be represented by an agent. (Main Phone: 323-575-2747)

- *Amazing Race - CBS*
- *American Fighter Pilots - CBS*
- *Armed and Famous - CBS*
- *Big Brother Seasons 1-12 - CBS*
- *Cupid - CBS*
- *The Cut - CBS*
- *Cupid - CBS*
- *The Cut - CBS*

- *Do You Trust Me? - CBS*
- *Fire Me Please - CBS*
- *Kid Nation - CBS*
- *Gameshow Marathon - CBS*
- *Million Dollar Password - CBS*
- *Pirate Master - CBS*
- *Power of 10 - CBS*
- *Real Beverly Hillbillies - CBS*
- *Rock Star: INXS - CBS*
- *Rock Star: Supernova - CBS*
- *Star Search - CBS*
- *Survivor-CBS*
- *Wickedly Perfect - CBS*
- *The Will - CBS*

The CW – (www.cw.com) CW is mostly known for programming with more of a country theme until they became a big hit in the reality world genre. With the banner show, *America's Next Top Model*, they are ready to find more hits. They are hoping their new 2011 reality show *Shedding for the Wedding* will do just that. It's just a matter of time. No unsolicited reality show projects will be accepted. You must be represented by an agent. (Main Phone: No phone listed: Contact through website)

- *America's Next Top Model - The CW*
- *Beauty and the Geek - The CW*
- *Blonde Charity Mafia - The CW*
- *Crowned - The CW*
- *Farmer Wants A Wife - The CW*
- *Fly Girls - The CW*
- *High Society - The CW*
- *Hitched or Ditched - The CW*
- *Online Nation - The CW*
- *Pussycat Dolls Present: Girlicious - CW*
- *Pussycat Dolls: The Search for the Next Doll - CW*
- *Shedding for the Wedding - CW*

Discovery Channel – (www.discovery.com) Discovery Channel Network is a very strong network that owns and operates numerous other channels including TLC. They concentrate on real-life programming and scientific discovery. Their standard is high and they require all pitch packets meet certain criteria. Reality shows include: *American Chopper, Gold Rush, Dirtiest Jobs, Deadliest Catch, Storm Chasers, Swamp Loggers, Flying Wild in Alaska, Fishing Kings* and more. No unsolicited business plans or pitches of any nature. They will only take calls from an agent and entertainment attorney. (Main Phone: 240-662-2000)

- *Kevin & Drew Unleashed - Discovery*
- *Man vs. Wild - Discovery*
- *American Chopper - Discovery*
- *Gold Rush- Discovery*
- *Dirtiest Jobs- Discovery*
- *Deadliest Catch- Discovery*
- *Storm Chasers- Discovery*
- *Swamp Loggers- Discovery*
- *Flying Wild in Alaska- Discovery*
- *Fishing Kings- Discovery*

E! – (www.eonline.com) E! specializes in bringing viewers what they call high impact entertainment shows. That is, shows that have a high following with popular people such as *Keeping up with the Kardashians*. No unsolicited reality show projects will be accepted. You must be represented by an agent. (Main Phone: 323-954-2400)

- *Anna Nicole Smith Show - E!*
- *The Entertainer - E!*
- *The Girls Next Door - E!*
- *Kill Reality - E!*
- *House of Carters - E!*
- *Katie and Peter - E!*

- *Keeping Up With the Kardashians - E!*
- *Kendra - E!*
- *Paradise City - E!*
- *Simple Life - E!*
- *Snoop Dogg's Father Hood - E!*
- *Star Dates - E!*

ESPN – (www.espn.com) ESPN is known for its sports broadcasting. However, they have moved to providing several reality shows such as *Dream Job, The Contender, NBA Live: Bring it Home, Varsity Inc, The American Gladiators*, and *Battle of the Gridiron Stars*. No unsolicited pitches or treatments. You must go through an agent. (Main Phone: 860-766-2000)

- *The Contender - ESPN*
- *NBA Live: Bring it Home – ESPN*
- *Varsity Inc. – ESPN*
- *The American Gladiators – ESPN*
- *Battle of the Gridiron Stars - ESPN*

Fox Reality – (www.foxreality.com) Fox Reality is probably the most dedicated network that thrives on reality television. They are always looking for new and exciting programs submitted by an agent or entertainment attorney. Shows include: *Gimme my Reality Show, House Husbands of Hollywood, My Bare Lady, Smile: You're Under Arrest, The Academy, The Next Elvira, and Paradise Hotel*. No unsolicited treatments, pitches or business plans. Must go through an agent not an entertainment attorney. (Main Phone: 310-689-1500)

- *All You Need is Love - FOX*
- *American Idol Seasons 1-11 - FOX*
- *American Juniors - FOX*
- *Anchorwoman - FOX*
- *Anything for Love - FOX*
- *Are You Smarter Than a Fifth Grader? - FOX*

- *Bachelorettes in Alaska - FOX*
- *Banzai - FOX*
- *Boot Camp - FOX*
- *The Casino - FOX*
- *Celebrity Boxing - FOX*
- *Celebrity Duets - FOX*
- *The Chamber - FOX*
- *The Complex - FOX*
- *Don't Forget the Lyrics - FOX*
- *Exhausted - FOX*
- *Forever Eden - FOX*
- *Hell's Kitchen - FOX*
- *Ivana Young Man - FOX*
- *I Want a Divorce-FOX*
- *Invasion of Hidden Cameras - FOX*
- *Joe Millionaire - FOX*
- *Kitchen Nightmares - FOX*
- *Krypton Factor - FOX*
- *The Littlest Groom - FOX*
- *Married by America - FOX*
- *Meet the Marks - FOX*
- *Miss Dog Beauty Pageant - FOX*
- *The Moment of Truth - FOX*
- *Mr. Personality - FOX*
- *Murder in Small Town X - FOX*
- *My Big Fat Obnoxious Boss - FOX*
- *My Big Fat Obnoxious Fiancé - FOX*
- *Nanny 911 - FOX*
- *Nashville - FOX*
- *The Next Great American Band - FOX*
- *Next Great Champ - FOX*
- *On the Lot - FOX*
- *Outback Jack - FOX*
- *Paradise Hotel - FOX*
- *Performing As - FOX*
- *Playing it Straight - FOX*

- *The Princes of Malibu - FOX*
- *The Rebel Billionaire - FOX*
- *Renovate My Family - FOX*
- *The Rich List - FOX*
- *Search for a Playboy Centerfold - FOX*
- *Second Chance Idol - FOX*
- *Sexiest Bachelor Contest- FOX*
- *Skating With Celebrities - FOX*
- *So You Think You Can Dance - FOX*
- *Star Chamber - FOX*
- *The Swan - FOX*
- *Temptation Island - FOX*
- *Thirty Seconds to Fame - FOX*
- *Todd TV - FX*
- *Trading Spouses - FOX*
- *Trailer Fabulous - FOX*
- *Trading Spouses - FOX*
- *Trailer Fabulous - FOX*
- *Unan1mous - FOX*
- *Wanted- FOX*
- *The X Factor - FOX*
- *Wanted- FOX*
- *Who Wants to Marry a Multi-Millionaire-FOX*
- *Who's Your Daddy - FOX*
- *World Idol - FOX*

FX – (www.fxnetworks.com) FX has typically been associated with high powered action. When they began to tap into the reality show production they tried to stay true to their calling with shows such as Justified coming out 2011. No unsolicited reality show projects will be accepted. You must be represented by an agent. (Main Phone: 310-369-1000)

- *30 Days - FX*
- *Todd TV - FX*
- *Justified - FX*

GSN – (www.gsn.com) GSN is known for competitive game shows and tournaments. Shows include *The Newlywed Game, High Stakes Poker, Catch 21, Game Show* Liars and more. No unsolicited material of any kind. They are also reluctant to accept anything even from an agent. (Main Phone: 310-255-6800)

- *High Stakes Poker - GSN*
- *The Newlywed Game - GSN*
- *Catch 21 - GSN*
- *Game Show Liars - GSN*
- *Who Wants to be a Millionaire - GSN*
- *$20,000 Pyramid - GSN*

HBO – (www.hbo.com) HBO isn't often associated with reality television programming but they should not be overlooked. They have aired numerous reality shows including: *Cat House: Back in the Saddle, 24/7, Hard Knocks, Taxi Cab Confessions, Real Life with Bill Maher, G-String Divas, Reverb, Lucky* and more. No unsolicited treatments, pitches or business plans. (Main Phone: 212-512-1000)

- *Cathouse - HBO*
- *Hard Knocks - HBO*
- *House Arrest - HBO*
- *Cat House- HBO*
- *Back in the Saddle- HBO*
- *24/7- HBO*
- *Hard Knocks- HBO*
- *Taxi Cab Confessions- HBO*
- *Real Life with Bill Maher- HBO*
- *G-String Divas- HBO*
- *Reverb- HBO*
- *Lucky- HBO*

HGTV – (www.hgtv.com) HGTV specialty genre of reality show programming is renovation and makeover shows such as *Design Star, Tough as Nails, Cash & Cari, Color Splash, House Hunters, Marriage Under Construction* and more. No unsolicited pitches or treatments. You must go through an agent. (Main Phone: 865-694-2700)

- *Design Star - HGTV*
- *Tough as Nails- HGTV*
- *Cash & Cari- HGTV*
- *Color Splash- HGTV*
- *House Hunters- HGTV*
- *House Hunters International- HGTV*

THE HISTORY CHANNEL – *(www.history.com)* The History Channel mostly focuses on documentary and educational programming; that is until recently when they jumped onto the bandwagon of reality TV with programs like *Ice Road Truckers*. No unsolicited reality show projects will be accepted. You must be represented by an agent. (Main Phone: 212-210-1400)

- *Expedition Africa - History* Channel
- *Ice Road Truckers - History Channel*

LIFETIME- *(www.lifetimetv.com)* Lifetime is known best for producing movies made for television that chronicles real lives and issues. When they jumped onto the bandwagon they moved slowly and still are with only a couple of reality shows to their line-up. No unsolicited reality show projects will be accepted. You must be represented by an agent. (Main Phone: 212-424-7000)

- *Cheerleader Nation - Lifetime*
- *Final Justice - Lifetime*

TLC – (www.tlc.com) - TLC probably has more reality shows on their network than any other including Fox Reality. The have made it a point to follow unusual people with unusual lifestyles. Some of their programming includes: *19 Kids and Counting, Kate Plus 8, Sarah Palin's Alaska, Mom Ink, Eat, Drink and Be Married, The Little Couple, Wedded to Perfection, Wild Weddings, Freakin Fabulous with Clinton Kelly, Making Over America with Trinny & Susannah, The General, Restorer Guy, Stager Invasion, Cake Boss, Ultimate Cake-Off* and *The Police Women Project.* No unsolicited pitches or treatments. You must go through an agent or entertainment attorney. (Main Phone: 240-662-2000)

- *19 Kids and Counting - TLC*
- *Kate Plus 8 - TLC*
- *Sarah Palin's Alaska - TLC*
- *Mom Ink - TLC*
- *Eat, Drink and be Married - TLC*
- *The Little Couple - TLC*
- *Wedded to Perfection - TLC*
- *Wild Weddings - TLC*
- *Freakin Fabulous with Clinton Kelly - TLC*
- *Making Over America with Trinny & Susannah - TLC*
- *The General - TLC*
- *Restorer Guy - TLC*
- *Stager Invasion - TLC*
- *Cake Boss - TLC*
- *Ultimate Cake-Off - TLC*
- *The Police Women Project - TLC*

MTV – (www.mtv.com) MTV having started with the focus on music quickly came to the conclusion that they wouldn't be able to sustain the revenue needed and moved into reality television programming. Some of their programs include: *Silent Library, Teen Cribs, America's Best Dance Crew, 16 and Pregnant, A Double Shot at Love, MTV Cribs, Celebrity Rap Superstar* and more. On February 4, 2011 MTV took a stand and cancelled Lauren Conrad's reality show stating that audience viewers didn't appreciate it and it was too raunchy. They didn't put all their eggs in one basket. Also new to MTV's lineup for 2011 include *Bromance, Janet Jackson, and a Double Shot at Love*. No unsolicited pitches or treatments. You must go through an agent. (Main Phone: 212-258-8000)

- *The 70's House - MTV*
- *8th and Ocean - MTV*
- *Adventures in HollyHood - MTV*
- *America's Best Dance Crew - MTV*
- *The Andy Milonakis Show - MTV*
- *artistLaunch - MTV*
- *The Ashlee Simpson Show - MTV*
- *The Assistant - MTV*
- *Bam's Unholy Union - MTV*
- *Battle for Ozzfest - MTV*
- *Battle of the Sexes - MTV*
- *Bromance - MTV*
- *Celebrity Rap Superstar -MTV*
- *Cheyenne - MTV*
- *Crashing With - MTV*
- *DanceLife - MTV*
- *The Duel - MTV*
- *Engaged and Underage - MTV*
- *FM Nation - MTV*
- *Fraternity Life - MTV*
- *Fresh Meat - MTV*
- *The Gauntlet - MTV*
- *The Hills - MTV*
- *I'm From Rolling Stone - MTV*
- *The Inferno - MTV*
- *I Want a Famous Face - MTV*
- *Jamie Kennedy's Blowin Up - MTV*
- *Juvies - MTV*
- *Laguna Beach - MTV*
- *Life of Ryan - MTV*
- *Made - MTV*

- *Newlyweds - MTV*
- *Score - MTV*
- *The Shop - MTV*
- *Road Rules 1-14 - MTV*
- *The Osbournes - MTV*
- *Rich Girls - MTV*
- *Sorority Life - MTV*
- *A Shot at Love With Tila Tequila - MTV*
- *Surf Girls - MTV*
- *Suspect: True Crime Stories - MTV*
- *Til Death Us Do Part: Carmen & Dave - MTV*
- *Who's Got Game? - MTV*
- *Wild n Out - MTV*
- *Wrestling Society X - MTV*
- *WWF Tough Enough - MTV*
- *Yo Momma - MTV*
- *You've Got a Friend - MTV*
- *Making Menudo - MTV*
- *Making the Band - MTV*
- *My Super Sweet 16 - MTV*
- *Newlyweds - MTV*
- *Newport Harbor - MTV*
- *Pageant Place - MTV*
- *Pimp My Ride - MTV*
- *PoweR Girls - MTV*
- *Punk'd - MTV*
- *The Real World - MTV*
- *Rob & Big - MTV*
- *Twentyfourseven - MTV*
- *Two a Days - MTV*
- *Road Rules 1-14 - MTV*
- *Run's House - MTV*
- *Score - MTV*
- *The Shop - MTV*

NBC – (www.nbc.com) NBC offers the public a variety of programming from talk shows to dramas. They too have followed suit by producing reality shows that have become fan favorites such as The *Apprentice* and the summer hit *America's Got Talent*.   No unsolicited reality show projects will be accepted. You must be represented by an agent. (Main Phone: 201-583-5000)

- *Adrenaline X - NBC*
- *Age of Love - NBC*
- *American Gladiators - NBC*
- *America's Got Talent - NBC*
- *Amnesia - NBC*
- *The Apprentice & Celebrity Apprentice - NBC*
- *The Apprentice Martha Stewart - NBC*
- *Average Joe - NBC*
- *Baby Borrowers - NBC*
- *The Biggest Loser - NBC*
- *Celebrity Cooking Showdown - NBC*
- *Clash of the Choirs - NBC*
- *Crime & Punishment - NBC*
- *Deal or No Deal - NBC*
- *Destination Space - NBC*
- *Dog Eat Dog - NBC*
- *Fame - NBC*
- *Fantasy Island - NBC*
- *Fear Factor - NBC*
- *For Love or Money - NBC*
- *Grease: You're The One That I Want - NBC*
- *Great American Road Trip - NBC*
- *Hit Me Baby One More Time - NBC*
- *Identity - NBC*
- *I'm a Celebrity But I Want to Be a Popstar - NBC*
- *I'm a Celebrity, Get Me Out of Here - NBC*
- *I Want to Be a Hilton - NBC*
- *Grease: You're The One That I Want - NBC*

- *Great American Road Trip - NBC*
- *Hit Me Baby One More Time - NBC*
- *Identity - NBC*
- *I'm a Celebrity But I Want to Be a Popstar - NBC*
- *I'm a Celebrity, Get Me Out of Here - NBC*
- *I Want to Be a Hilton - NBC*
- *Last Comic Standing - NBC*
- *Last Comic Standing - NBC*
- *Meet Mr. Mom - NBC*
- *Meet My Folks - NBC*
- *My Dad is Better Than Your Dad - NBC*
- *Spy TV - NBC*
- *Next Action Star - NBC*
- *The Law Firm - NBC*
- *Let's Make a Deal - NBC*
- *The Law Firm - NBC*
- *Let's Make a Deal - NBC*
- *Lost - NBC*
- *Tommy Lee Goes to College - NBC*
- *Treasure Hunters - NBC*
- *Weakest Link-NBC*
- *Who Do You Think You Are? NBC*
- *Who Wants to Marry My Dad - NBC*
- *World Moves - NBC*

SyFy – (www.scifi.com) SyFy is best known for their science fiction shoes such as Stargate, and Star Trek. They have had two unsuccessful attempts at reality show programming. But I think if the right one came along they would be open. I met with the president of SyFy and he was optimistic about the future of them finding the perfect SyFy reality show. It looks like they may have. In 2011 they started *Face Off*. No unsolicited reality show projects will be accepted. You must be represented by an agent. (Main Phone: 212-664-4444)

- *Who Wants to be a Superhero? - SyFy*

- *Mad Mad House* - SyFy
- *Face Off – SyFy*
- Marcel's Quantum Kitchen - SyFy

THE SCIENCE CHANNEL – *(*www.science.discovery.com) The Science Channel can boast on excellence in programming when it comes to shows relating to science. However, they are having some difficulty in finding the reality show niche. The only successful attempt has been Survivorman. I can't be certain if they will continue in the reality show genre programming in the future. I wouldn't let that stop you if you have the one pitch that would be a great match. No unsolicited reality show projects will be accepted. You must be represented by an agent. (Main Phone: 240-662-2000)

- *Survivorman - The Science Channel*

SPIKE – (www.spiketv.com) Spike is known to attract mostly male audiences and just recently made the move to try and gain female viewers. One way to increase viewership was to add reality television programs such as *Joe Schmo, Scrapers, Coal, 4ᵗʰ and Long, The Ultimate* Fighter and more hoping to increase the women's audience members. However, most of the programming is still geared toward men and woman are slowly taking notice. Hopefully this will be the home to my reality show the *Ace Mechanic*. No unsolicited pitches or treatments. You must go through an agent. (Main Phone: 212-767-8705)

- *The Club - Spike TV*
- *I Hate My Job - Spike TV*
- *Invasion Iowa - Spike TV*
- *Joe Schmo - Spike TV*
- *Murder - Spike TV*
- *Super Agent - Spike TV*
- *Pros vs. Joes - Spike TV*
- *Ultimate Fighter - Spike TV*

SHOWTIME – (www.showtime.com) Showtime has a huge following for their drama programs and movies. However, they have been slow to attract a reality show crowd. This seems to be changing with their connection to Netflix and HuluTVPLUS. I predict more reality shows for them in the future, but nothing for 2011. So if you have that one show, I'd try to get it into their hands because there shouldn't be that much competition that you would face with FOX, NBC and MTV. No unsolicited reality show projects will be accepted. You must be represented by an agent. (Main Phone: 212-708-3200)

- *American Candidate - Showtime*
- *Fat Actress - Showtime*
- *Freshman Diaries - Showtime*

TBS – (www.tbs.com) TBS has a wide range of programming available. Reality shows include: *The Real Gilligan's Island, He's a Lady, Undercover Karaoke with Jewel, House Rules, The Mansion* and more. TBS hasn't been as successful in airing hit reality shows although they are most certainly looking for a breakthrough hit. No unsolicited pitches or treatments. You must go through an agent. (Main Phone: 404-827-1700)

- *Daisy Does America - TBS*
- *He's a Lady - TBS*
- *House Rules - TBS*
- *The Real Gilligan's Island - TBS*
- *He's a Lady - TBS*
- *Undercover Karaoke with Jewel - TBS*
- *House Rules - TBS*
- *The Mansion - TBS*
- *Worst Case Scenario - TBS*

TLC – (www.tlc.com) TLC has made rather a name for itself for what I call unique programming in reality shows. They appear to have captured the market on the unusual for cast members.

With shows like *The Little Couple* I'm certain they will continue to find more reality show programming. While I was working on the show *The Little Couple* I had the chance to talk with Bill about how his show came to be. It was a matter of making contact. No unsolicited reality show projects will be accepted. You must be represented by an agent. (Main Phone:240-662-2000)

- *Faking It - TLC*
- *What Not to Wear - TLC*
- *Trading Spaces - TLC*
- *LA Ink - TLC*
- *A Model Life - TLC*
- *The Monastery - TLC*
- *Miami Ink   - TLC*
- *Miss America - Reality Check - TLC*
- *Outback Jack - TLC*
- *The Real Gilligan's Island - TLC*
- *Small People, Big World - TLC*

OXYGEN – (www.oxygen.com) Oxygen network is for woman as Spike TV is for men. Oxygen has tapped into the woman audience and continues to move forward at a rapid pace keeping up with popular television shows and turning them into reality. Shows like *The Glee Reality Show, All About Aubrey* and more are making their mark on reality TV. No unsolicited pitches or treatments. You must go through an agent. (Main Phone: 212-651-2070)

- *The Glee Reality Show - Oxygen*
- *All About Aubrey - Oxygen*

OWN – www.own.com) OWN is the newest network to pop up with Oprah Winfrey at the helm. Reality shows include: *Your Own Show, Deliver Me, Christine Ferrare's Big Bowl of Love, Kidnapped by the Kids* and more to come. This network also has Your Own Channel, where viewers can submit their own videos and obtain a following. Yes Unsolicited. You can film something and possibly get it on her website immediately and who knows if it becomes popular might get picked up. No unsolicited written pitches or treatments are accepted. You must go through an agent. However, there are numerous contests for opportunities as she develops this channel. This is probably your best bet in getting you show on air if it meets with Oprah's approval. However, read the rules and guidelines. If you submit to her show, she is in no obligation to pay you and the idea becomes property of Harpo Productions. However, it could be your foot in the door. Contact your entertainment attorney for advice. (Main Phone: 312-591-9222)

- *Your Own Show - OWN*
- *Deliver Me - OWN*
- *Christine Ferrare's Big Bowl of Love - OWN*
- *Kidnapped by the Kids - OWN*

UPN – (www.cw.com) UPN has now merged with The CW. But during their prime they did produce several reality shows. If you have a reality show similar to the ones listed below, consider taking your project to The CW network.

- *Amish in the City - UPN*
- *Britney and Kevin: Chaotic - UPN*
- *Chains of Love - UPN*
- *Challenge America – UPN*
- *Get This Party Started - UPN*
- *The Missy Elliot Project - UPN*
- *R U the Girl With T-Boz and Chilli - UPN*
- *Under One Roof - UPN*
- *I Dare You – UPN*
- *I'm Still Alive – UPN*
- *Manhunt – UPN*
- *The 5th Wheel – UPN*
- *The Player – UPN*
- *The Paranormal Borderline – UPN*
- *Crossing over with John Edwards – UPN*

USA – (www.usanetwork.com) USA is most known for other types of programming such as drama; however, they just recently have begun to join the bandwagon of reality TV with shows such as *Made in America*. No unsolicited pitches or treatments. You must go through an agent. (Main Phone: 212-664-4444)

- *Cannonball Run - USA*
- *Combat Missions - USA*
- *Break In - USA*
- *Eco-Challenge - USA*
- *Nashville Star - USA*
- *Made in the USA - USA*

VH1 – (www.vh1.com) VH1 started big in bringing audiences the number one rated videos on the market. It was in direct competition with MTV. When MTV started airing reality shows, VH1 was far behind. It became an economical decision. The most popular reality show is *Celebrity Fit Club* and *Celebrity Rehab* with Dr. Drew. Their latest show starting in 2011 is *You're Cut Off.* No unsolicited pitches or treatments. You must go through an agent. (Main Phone: 212-846-6000)

- *The Agency - VH1*
- *America's Most Smartest Model - VH1*
- *Bands on the Run - VH1*
- *Breaking Bonaduce - VH1*
- *BSTV - VH1*
- *But Can They Sing - VH1*
- *Celebrity Fit Club - VH1*
- *Celebrity Rehab With Dr. Drew - VH1*
- *Dice Undisputed - VH1*
- *Flavor of Love - VH1*
- *Gene Simmons Rock School - VH1*
- *Hogan Knows Best VH1*

- *I Love New York - VH1*
- *In Search of the Partridge Family - VH1*
- *Jessica Simpson's The Price of Beauty - VH1*
- *Kept - VH1*
- *Liza and David - VH1*
- *Strange Love - VH1*
- *Strip Search - VH1*
- *The Salt N Pepa Show - VH1*
- *Scott Baio is 45 and Single - VH1*
- *Scott Baio is 46 and Pregnant - VH1*
- *Mission Man Band - VH1*
- *My Fair Brady - VH1*
- *Rock of Love - VH1*
- *The Springer Hustle - VH1*
- *Shooting Sizemore - VH1*
- *You're Cut Off – VH1*
- *The White Rapper Show - VH1*

WB *(www.wb.com)* WB had a variety of programming. When they moved into the reality show genre some of their shows was met with hostility by woman. In 2006 WB merged with CW. So if you have a reality show similar to the ones listed below consider taking your pitch to CW. You will have to submit and make contact through their website.

- *Big Man on Campus - WB*
- *Boarding House: North Shore - WB*
- *Celebrity Look Alike Dating - WB*
- *Elimidate Deluxe - WB*
- *High School Reunion - WB*
- *The Starlet - WB*
- *Lost in the USA - WB*
- *Surreal Life - WB*
- *Survival of the Richest - WB*
- *Superstar USA - WB*
- *No Boundaries- WB*

- *Pepsi Smash - WB*
- *Popstars - WB*
- *Studio 7 - WB*

WE – (www.we.tv) – WE is similar in design to Oxygen in that it targets their programming toward women. New reality shows for 2011 include *Braxton Family Values* and *Staten Island Cakes*. No unsolicited pitches or treatments. You must go through an agent. (Main Phone: 516-803-3000)

- *Amazing Wedding Cakes - WE*
- *Platinum Weddings - WE*
- *My Fair Wedding with David Tutera - WE*
- *Bridezillas - WE*
- *The Cupcake Girls - WE*
- *The Locator - WE*
- *Downsized - WE*
- *Alien Abduction-True Confessions - WE*

NETWORK AFFILIATE CONTACT INFORMATION

I have provided a list of the network affiliates contact information in Table 17-1. They are as up to date as possible at the time of this printing. It is your responsibility to re-verify the names of the presidents of the company because they could possibly change. Remember that the positions are very fluid and change rapidly. Also, don't send unsolicited scripts to executives.

Also as a reminder, never send anyone an unsolicited reality show concept or business plan, always make a PDF version, and always have it registered with the WGA and U.S. Library of Congress.

Table 17-1 TELEVISION NETWORK CONTACT INFORMATION

Mr. Jeff Zucker, President **NBC Entertainment** 30 Rockefeller Plaza New York, NY 10112 818-840-4444	Ms. Nina Tassler President, CBS Entertainment **CBS Entertainment** 7800 Beverly Blvd Los Angeles, CA 90039-2112 (323) 575-2747	Anne Sweeney, President **ABC Entertainment** 500 S. Buena Vista St Burbank, CA 91521-4551 818-560-1000
Ms Gail Berman, President **Fox Broadcasting Co.** P.O. Box 900 Beverly Hills, CA 90213 (310) 369-1000	Mr. Dean Goodman, President ***Paxson* Communications Corp (*i*)** 601 Clearwater Park Road West Palm Beach, FL 33401 (561) 659-4122	Dawn Ostroff, President **CW Network** 11800 Wilshire Blvd. Los Angeles, CA 90025 (310) 575-7000 (818) 977-5000
Joh F. Swope, President **Public Broadcasting Service** 1320 Braddock Pl. Alexandria, VA 22314 709-739-5000	**ABC Family Channel** Paul Lee, President 3800 West Alameda Ave. Burbank, CA 91505 Phone: 818-560-1000	**A&E Television Networks** 235 East 45th Street New York, NY 10017 (212) 210-1340
AMC 200 Jericho Quadrangle Jericho, NY 11753 (516) 803-4360	**A&E Television Networks** 235 E. 45th St.New York, NY 10017 (212) 210-1400	**BET** 1900 W. Street, NE Washington, DC 20018 (202) 608-4BET
Bravo c/o NBC Entertainment 3000 W. Alameda Avenue Burbank, CA 90036	**Cartoon Network** 1050 Techwood Drive Atlanta, GA 30318 404.885.2263	**Court TV** Viewer Comments 600 Third Avenue New York, NY 10016 (800) COURT-56
Discovery Communications, LLC John S. Hendricks 1 Discovery Place Silver Spring, MD 20910 Phone: 240-662-2000 Fax: 240-662-1868	**The Disney Channel** 3800 W. Alameda Ave. Burbank, CA 91505 (818) 569-7500	**E! Entertainment TV** 5750 Wilshire Boulevard Los Angeles, CA 90036 (323) 954-2400
ESPN / ESPN2 ESPN Plaza 935 Middle Street Bristol, CT 06010 (860) 585-2236	**Fuse** 11 Penn Plaza, 15th Floor New York, NY 10001 (212) 324-3460	**FX** P.O. BOX 900 BEVERLY HILLS, CA 90213

Game Show Network, LLC	Home Box Office (HBO)	Lifetime Television
Jen Minezaki Director of Public Relations 2150 Colorado Ave. Ste. 100 Santa Monica, CA 90404 Phone: 310-255-6933 Fax: 310-255-6810	1100 Avenue of the Americas New York, NY 10036-6737 (212) 512-1000	309 W. 49th Street New York, NY 10019 (212) 424-7293
MTV Networks c/o MTV Studios 1515 Broadway New York, New York 10036	**Nickelodeon** Viewer Services 1633 Broadway New York, NY 10019 (212) 258-7579	**Oxygen** 75 Ninth Avenue New York, NY 10011
SyFy Channel 8800 W. Sunset Blvd, 4th Fl. West Hollywood, CA 90069 310-360-2300	**Showtime Network** 1633 Broadway New York, NY 10019 212-708-1600	**Spike TV** 1633 Broadway New York, NY 10019 (212) 846-2566
TBS 1 CNN Center PO BOX 105366 Atlanta, GA 30348-5366 404-827-1700	**Telemundo Cable** 10360 USA Today Way Miramar, FL 33025 (305) 889-7143	**TLC** - Owned by Discovery Communications, LLC John S. Hendricks Chairman 1 Discovery Place Silver Spring, MD 20910 Phone: 240-662-2000 Fax: 240-662-1868
TNT 1010 Techwood Drive Atlanta, GA 30318 Phone: 404-885-4538	**USA Network** 1230 Avenue of the Americas New York, NY 10020	**VH1** 1515 Broadway New York, NY 10036 212-258-6000

PRODUCTION COMPANIES IN THE GROVE

Just when you think you get a break and you talked with a network executive that sits in the ivory tower of "Green-light" the door slams shut. They say "No" and your hopes and dream seem to flutter in the wind. Not so fast. You still have another option – go directly to a larger production company that already has a connection with a television network and is established in producing reality shows. Pitch your show to them. This is often the quickest route to take and the most lucrative. It does take a little homework in finding these production companies, but they do exist. And, for the most part they are looking for projects. If you bring them a fantastic concept and fully developed show, it saves them time and money. Having worked in the reality show aspect business of production, I have established many relationships that I can count on. You too will have to begin. Start by doing some research of the newest reality shows and pay attention to the credits. Writing down the names of the companies is a great way to start to develop your contact list.

For your convenience I have listed several top production companies that I know who produce reality shows. There are about a dozen more larger production companies that are involved with producing reality television shows but very difficult to contact. These companies have made a name for themselves. The list continues to grow as does the popularity of reality TV.

To keep up to date on the ever growing list, subscribe to IMDBPRO and start a research campaign to identify the hottest reality shows and the production companies associated with them. Try contacting the company first to see if they would be interested in your idea. Always register your idea with WGA and/or copyright it with the United States Library of Congress. It protects everybody. If this doesn't work, then you will have to acquire the services of an agent to have them submit for you. The following production companies have made a name for themselves in reality show program production:

- Bunim-Murray Productions
- GRB Entertainment
- James Dubois
- Jag Productions, Inc
- LMNO
- Mark Burnett Productions

- Mindless Entertainment
- On the Lot Productions, LLC
- Peter Rosen Productions, Inc
- Pie Town Productions
- Screaming Flea Productions
- On the Lot Productions, LLC

NEW TO REALITY PRODUCTION BUT WORTHY

The newest production company is G3 Productions with Kelsey Grammer. Remember him from the sitcoms *Cheers* and *Frasier?* He has joined his efforts with reality TV veteran Stella Bulochnikov-Stolper to develop reality series concepts and formats. G3 Productions projects will be pushed to be sold and distributed around the world through Zodiac USA's extensive international infrastructure.

People magazine has reported early in 2011 Spencer Pratt, from the reality show *The Hills,* has started Pratt Productions and first up on the list for production *is* a reality dating show for Snooki's ex-boyfriend, Emilio Masella after he was dumped tentatively titled, *Fist Pumping for Love.* This production company may well be worth contacting since he has the reality show bug and the financing to go with it.

American Artist, which was coproduced by actress Sarah Jessica Parker in 2008, shows a progression of celebrities getting into the reality show production arena. Even Drew Barrymore has gotten into the act with her production of *Tough Love.* Lisa Kudrow followed suit with her show currently sponsored by Ancestry.com - *Who Do You Think You Are*? This show is increasing in popularity and I have created a spin-off called *Does A Name Make a Difference.*

The aforementioned examples gives an indication that if you have a really good idea about a show that fits in with a celebrity that has a production company, you might want to pitch them your reality show idea and see what develops. Other celebrities with production companies that are rumored to be entering the reality show production side of things include:

- Tim Allen's Boxing Cat Productions
- Tom Arnold's Clean Break Productions
- Alec Baldwin's El Dorado Pictures
- Sandra Bullock's Fortis Films
- Penny Marshall's Parkway Productions
- Henry Winkler
- Drew Barrymore

However, like the networks these production companies do not accept unsolicited material. Therefore it is imperative that you obtain an agent to submit your ideas or call and speak with individuals.

I would be remiss if I didn't include my own production company, On the Lot Productions, LLC located in New Orleans, LA. To see if I'd be interested in producing your show, first send me an E-mail with your One-Pager to drmelcaudle@gmail.com. Then, if I like your concept I'll respond and ask for the entire packet and sign a Confidentiality Agreement. That way it won't be unsolicited. I WILL NOT ACCEPT ONE PAGERS OR BUSINESS PLANS THAT ARE NOT REGISTERED WITH THE WGA.

GETTING AN AGENT

Just like actors, producers, writers and directors have agents. I do. In fact I have two agents. One agent handles my literary work such as my reality shows, books and screenplays and the other agent for my acting career. I am a SAG actor. Funny I'd say that. I have never really been in my reality shows although I make cameos. But I have had a couple speaking roles in films. Most notably, I deliver Leonie in the film *Leonie*. In the scene I am with Emily Mortimer who is giving birth and I'm the Maternity Ward Physician.

It wasn't easy getting either agent. In fact, it was harder to get a literary agent that it was for me to become a SAG actor with an agent. But that shouldn't stop you because if you are serious about this business you are going to have to find one and a good one. The answer is always no until you ask.

The first place to start is if you already are an actor and have an agent, ask your agent for a referral. Also ask to find out if they serve as a literary agent. Often, an agent may not, but another agent in the same company does. Next, ask anybody and everybody you know if they know or have a literary agent. If so, ask them for a recommendation. You can also go to WGA and search for a list of agencies.

Once you have established a list of potential agents you are going to start making contact with them. Call and see who is accepting clients and ask if you can send a query letter along with your One Pager.

A query serves as your introduction to an agent and explains in very few words your credentials followed by asking them to become your agent. Remember the One Pager I had you write. Attach it to the query letter and send them out. DO NOT E-MAIL OR FAX A POTENTIAL AGENT unless they ask you too. Be respectful.

THE QUERY LETTER

There are three things that must be included in your query letter: the hook, the synopsis and your short and very brief bio. By the time you have written your business plan you have already developed the information that goes into a query letter. The only thing you will need to do is shorten everything. Let's look at constructing a query letter.

The Hook

The first part of the query letter is the hook. You grab their attention. Does this sound familiar? It should because you already developed your hook with your logline. So let's stick with the logline for our make belief reality show *The Man Behind #9*.

> Logline:

> Drew Brees brings his leadership skills from the field to the city of New Orleans.

This sentence now is your hook and the beginning of your query letter.

The Synopsis

The next part of your query letter is the synopsis and a quick introduction to the show. Look at the synopsis below from make belief reality show *The Man Behind #9*.

> Synopsis:

> The Man Behind #9 is a celebrity style reality show with eight episodes created by Dr. Melissa Caudle that follows Drew Brees, a Super Bowl Champion Quarterback, a father of two and a community advocate. *Sports Illustrated,* "Man of the Year" has a direct way of getting things done on the field - with some of the best statics in the NFL. His sharpness and razor edge skill as a top quarterback translates to his off-the-field life in his community. He makes a difference to a city once devastated by Hurricane Katrina. For the past six years Drew Brees has brought hope to New Orleans, the city he now calls home. While off the field, Drew Brees raises awareness for the homeless, produces fund raising events for charities, brings laughter and joy to children stricken with terminal diseases, and more. On the Lot Productions, LLC, under the direction of Dr. Melissa Caudle presents

a bold new reality series which steps into the life of a Super Bowl Champion Drew Brees. Throughout this eight part series Drew Brees is joined by his closest friends in the NFL and community leaders. We get to know the man behind #9.

I can either choose to use the entire synopsis are make it shorter. I don't want my query letter to be more than a page. In this case, less is better than more. Try to extract key elements that explain the show and the contents without going into dialogue and episode arcs and conflicts. This isn't the time. You goal is to sell yourself, not the project so you can obtain a literary agent.

YOUR BIOGRAPHY

Now that you have the first two parts of the query letter, you now have the third by extracting a couple of things from your biography that you had to include in the section of your plan for the management team. Here is my short bio from one of my plans.

Short Biography

On the Lot Productions, LLC, under the direction of Dr. Melissa Caudle presents *The Man Behind #9*, a bold new reality series which steps into the life of a Super Bowl Champion Drew Brees. Dr. Mel has built a solid reputation as a reality show creator having started as a production coordinator in New Orleans, La on the reality show, *The Girls Next Door* featuring the three Playmates and Hugh Hefner. Dr. Mel is also a film producer. Her three films include *Dark Blue*, *Varla Jean and The Mushroomheads* and *Girls Gone Gangsta*. Her book, *The Reality of Reality TV* is on sale now.

THE QUERY LETTER ASSEMBLED

For your review I have included a sample query letter that extracts the information from my reality show business plan.

Sample 1 – Query Letter Put together from Business Plan

Dear Agent:

Drew Brees brings his leadership skills from the field to the city of New Orleans. *The Man Behind #9* is a celebrity style reality show with 8 episodes created by Dr. Melissa Caudle that follows Drew Brees, a Super Bowl Champion Quarterback, a father of two and a community advocate. For the past 6 years Drew Brees has brought hope to New Orleans, the city he now calls home. While off the field, Drew Brees raises awareness for the homeless, produces fund raising events for charities, brings laughter and joy to children stricken with terminal diseases, and more.

Dr. Melissa Caudle presents a bold new reality series which steps into the life of a Super Bowl Champion Drew Brees. Dr. Mel has built a solid reputation as a reality show creator having started as a production coordinator in New Orleans, La on the reality show, *The Girls Next Door* featuring the three Playmates and Hugh Hefner. Dr. Mel is also a film producer. Her book, *The Reality of Reality TV* is on sale now.

Dr. Mel is seeking a literary agent to present the entire show's concept to the television executives at ESPN and The Learning Channel. Both networks have already expressed interest in the show but require that the structure, format and episode breakdown be presented through my agent. I can be reached at XXX-XXX-XXXX between the hours of 9:00AM and 6:00PM. For your convenience I have included the One Pager for the reality show. I look forward to hearing from you soon.

Sincerely,

Dr. Mel Caudle

Notice how the information was extracted from the One Pager and from the biography information. Also, notice that it will fit on a single sheet of letterhead paper.

As with all formal letters, use your letterhead, address the letter to the recipient, correct date, the greetings, body of letter, and the salutation. You want to present yourself professionally.

Use the following format:

- Letterhead on top line.
- Space down and place recipients name and address.
- Date.
- Reason for letter.
- Greeting.
- Body of letter.
- Salutatory signature.

Diagram 18-1 Sample Query Letter

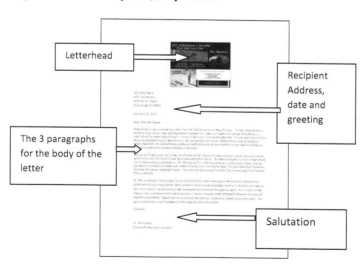

Let's say that you want to seek an agent but you don't have any of the information written succinctly in a business plan. Now what? You can still write a query letter using the same format of hook them in, tell them about the project and tell them a little bit about yourself.

Sample 2: Query Letter Seeking an Agent

Dear Ms. Literary Agent:

I am Dr. Mel Caudle and I am writing to direct your attention to a new reality show that I created called, *The Baker Girls: Sealed with a Kiss*. This show follows the careers and lives of five beautiful young women from 18 to 30 as they form friendships. The girls help each other by providing advice and emotional support to one another.

I am an established reality show producer having created 4 other shows including *The Ace Mechanic, Clean Sweep, Hoops: Life off the Court,* and *Post Season.* I have also worked on several other reality shows including *The Girls Next Door* on E! network and *The Little Couple on TLC.*   Prior to reality show programming, I wrote seven screenplays, several books and dozens of articles. My new book, *The Reality of Reality TV* is now available on Amazon.com.

I have several networks interested in reviewing my concept development plan for *The Baker Girls: Sealed with a Kiss*, but will not do so without it first going through an agent. Therefore, I am submitting to you the One Pager for the show which describes the format of the show and the synopsis and I would like for you to represent me as my agent. I can be reached at XXX-XXX-XXXX between the hours of 9:00AM and 6:00PM. Please feel free to contact me with any concerns or questions you may have.

Sincerely,

Dr. Mel Caudle, Producer and Writer

The above sample tells just enough about the show and the creator without going into great detail. That is the purpose of the query letter. You want to be able to grab the agent's attention quickly.

The next example is for a query letter that is a little more informal because you were recommended by someone that had an agent and you have talked with the agent. Prior to sending this letter you should always talk with the recipient first. Never say you know somebody that you don't. Name dropping isn't the answer and in fact could harm you. What happens if they have had a bad dealing with the person you are name dropping? Do you really want to be associated with them at this point?

Sample 3: Query Letter with a Referral

> Dear Tom:
>
> My colleague and your client, Dr. Mel Caudle, spoke with you recently about my first reality show creation. I submitted it to a production company who says they are interested in working together, so I am seeking representation.
>
> Thank you for agreeing to look at my Proposal for possible consideration for representation. I look forward to speaking with you soon. If you have any questions, please feel free to call me at your convenience at XXX-XXX-XXXX.
> Sincerely,
>
> XXX
> Producer and Reality Show Creator

Once you send the query letter and One Pager wait two to three weeks and then follow up with another phone call. Persistence will be the key. As with the controlled copies and maintaining documentation, always keep track of the literary agents you have contacted using the Telephone Log presented earlier in this book.

OTHER USE OF YOUR QUERY LETTER

Query letters aren't just for getting a literary agent but can also be used when contacting networks and production companies. The basic structure remains the same. What changes is that instead of asking for literary representation, you are asking if you can submit your business plan or pitch packet. Often, if you send a query letter first, you will get an E-mail or phone call asking for your plan to be submitted. This is exactly what you want. Below is the same query letter we just formulated to seek a literary agent. However, the third paragraph is replaced by the following one which is directed toward seeking a production company rather than an agent.

> I am Dr. Mel Caudle and I am writing to direct your attention to a new reality show that I created called, *The Baker Girls: Sealed with a Kiss*. This show follows the careers and lives of five beautiful young women from 18 to 30 as they form friendships. The girls help each other by providing advice and emotional support to one another.

> I am an established reality show producer having created 4 other shows including *The Ace Mechanic, Clean Sweep, Hoops: Life off the Court,* and *Post Season.* I have also worked on several other reality shows including *The Girls Next Door* on E! Network and *The Little Couple on TLC.* Prior to reality show programming, I wrote seven screenplays, several books and dozens of articles. My new book, *The Reality of Reality TV* is now available on Amazon.com.

I am seeking a television network and/or production company, to green-light *The Baker Girls: Sealed with a Kiss*. I feel Oxygen is the best match for this reality show because the show's audience is mostly woman. I would welcome the opportunity to send you the show's business plan that outlines the production team, cast members, format of the show and the episode breakdowns. Also, this show is perfect for product-placement opportunities. I can be reached at XXX-XXX-XXXX between the hours of 9:00AM and 6:00PM. Please feel free to contact me with any concerns or questions you may have. For your convenience I have included the One Pager for the reality show.

Sincerely,

Dr. Mel Caudle
Producer/Creator

CHAPTER SUMMARY

This chapter was all about making contact with the right people and production companies that can bring life to your reality show. A list of networks was provided that also included some of the reality shows on those networks. Information was presented on how to seek out networks and production companies and how to obtain an agent if you can't break through on your one. Instructions were provided on how to construct a query letter to obtain a literary agent and how to make changes to query letter to attract attention from a network or larger production company. Sample wording was provided as well as examples.

PRACTICAL APPLICATION

1. Re-read the information about each network and the types of shows they have on their schedule. Use Worksheet 39 to

make a list of the networks that your television show would be fit in on the line-up.

2.   Using Worksheet 40 Construct a Query Letter to send to obtain a literary agent.

3.   Using Worksheet 41 Construct a Query Letter to send to a television network.

4.   Using Worksheet 42 Construct a Query Letter to send to television production companies.

5.   Start making contact with literary agents. Don't stop until you are signed on by one.

6. Send out Query Letters.

PHOTOGRAPHY CREDIT FOR CHAPTER 18
Chapter 18 photo by Simon Howden
Here Comes the Bride One Pager

A One Pager used to attract Network Executives at NATPE

WORKSHEET 40: NETWORK CONTACTS

Objective: Make contact with television networks.

1. Mark the Television Network that your show would best fit into their existing line-up. Check all that apply.

☐ ABC ☐ NBC ☐ A & E ☐ CBS ☐ FOX ☐ FX ☐ PBS ☐ CW
☐ BET ☐ BRAVO

☐ MTV ☐ DISCOVERY ☐ ESPN ☐ OXYGEN ☐ TLC ☐ USA

☐ VH1 ☐ OTHER: _____

2. Indentify production companies that would most likely be interested in your type of reality show.

Name of Company	Contact Information	Shows They Produced

3. Identify 10 Literary Agents.

NAME OF AGENT OR AGENCY	CONTACT INFORMATION

4.   Begin contacting all television networks, production companies and agents listed above. Be sure to maintain a contact log so you can follow up.

WORKSHEET 41: THE AGENT QUERY LETTER

Objective: To construct a query letter for literary agent acquisition.

Query letters have three parts: hook, synopsis, bio information and end with your request.

1. **Complete the following to write your query letter to obtain an agent.**

THE HOOK: (Write logline in the space below)

THE SYNOPSIS: (Write the shortened version of the logline here)

BIO: (Write a smaller version of your bio here)

REQUEST: (Write your statement that you are seeking a literary agent)

2. **Using word processing software format your query letter and have it ready to go.**

WORKSHEET 42: NETWORK QUERY LETTER

Objective: To construct a query letter to send to a television network.

Query letters have three parts: hook, synopsis, bio information and end with your request.

1. Complete the following to write your query letter to a television network.

THE HOOK: (Write logline in the space below)

HOW YOUR SHOW FITS WITH THE NETWORK

THE SYNOPSIS: (Write the shortened version of the logline here)

BIO: (Write a smaller version of your bio here)

REQUEST: (Write your statement that you are seeking to green-light your project from a production company)

2. Using word processing software format your television query letter and have it ready to go.

WORKSHEET 43: PRODUCTION QUERY LETTER

Objective: To construct a query letter to send to a production company.

Query letters have three parts: hook, synopsis, bio information and end with your request.

1. Complete the following to write your query letter to a production company.

THE HOOK: (Write logline in the space below)

THE SYNOPSIS: (Write the shortened version of the logline here)

BIO: (Write a smaller version of your bio here)

REQUEST: (Write your statement that you are seeking to green-light your project from a production company)

2. Using word processing software format your production query letter and have it ready to go.

CHAPTER 19

SAMPLE REALITY SHOW BUSINESS PLAN

You have consistently been dedicated to reading this book and applying yourself during the practical applications. Congratulations. It has been an amazing journey for you. I hope you have taken away new knowledge and a skill that you can use again in the near future and be successful. Don't stop at creating just one reality show but create as many as you can. One of them is bound to land on the desk of a Hollywood Insider. Good luck with your journey and I look forward to seeing what you have created.

The remainder of this chapter is devoted to the presentation of an example of a reality show business plan for *Hoops: Life off the Court*. When you have completed your plan send me a query letter to **drmelcaudle@gmail.com** . Be sure to put in the subject line "Query as a result of your book" and the WGA registration number. I will not open any plan that isn't WGA registered for both of our protection.

SAMPLE REALITY SHOW BUSINESS PLAN

A Reality Show Business Proposal

Prepared by: Dr. Melissa Caudle

For

Hoops, LLC

CREATED BY DR. MELISSA CAUDLE 2010
ALL RIGHTS RESEVERD © 2010   REGISTERED WITH THE WGA: #54298571847

Table of Contents

CONFIDENTIALITY AGREEMENT

This document and the information contained herein are provided solely for the purpose of acquainting the reader with My Reality Show, LLC which is a Limited Liability Company. This reality business plan does not constitute an offer to sell nor is it a solicitation of an offer to purchase securities. It has been submitted on a confidential basis solely for the benefit of selected, highly qualified investors and is not for use by any other persons.   By accepting delivery of this business plan, the recipient acknowledges and agrees that: (i) in the event the recipient does not wish to pursue this matter, the recipient will return this copy to My Reality Show, LLC as soon as practical; (ii) the recipient will not copy, fax, reproduce, or distribute this confidential business plan, in whole or in part, without permission; and (iii) all of the information contained herein will be treated as confidential material. It is hereby acknowledged by the undersigned that the information to be furnished in this business plan is in all respects confidential in nature (other than such information which is already in the public domain through other means) and that any disclosure or use of same by the undersigned may cause serious harm or damage to My Reality Show, LLC.

_____

Signature of Recipient   Date

CONTROLLED COPY

Issued to: _____

Issue Date: _____

Copy No: _____

RETURN IMMEDIATELY UPON REQUEST BY PRODUCER TO:
NAME
STREET ADDRESS
CITY, STATE   ZIP CODE

1

The Executive Summary

Hoops LLC, hereafter called "The Company," is a Louisiana Limited Liability Company seeking $475,000 for the production of *Hoops: Life off the Court* a 13 episode reality show. Each episode consists of 22 minutes of programming and product placement endorsements allowing for 8 minutes for advertisement placement. *Hoops: Life of the Court* will be filmed in Louisville, Kentucky, the home of some of the most revered basketball fans and audience team members. *Hoops: Life off the Court* six college basketball players coming together with the common goal of helping their team go to the Final Four. The Company has attached Lebron XXX to our project as the host with the intention to bring NBA fans to cross-over into the reality show market (Letter of Intent attached). It is our hold open auditions to secure cast members appropriate for our project that have the necessary basketball skills and personality to enhance audience appeal and commercial value.

The market for reality shows grossed $25.9 dollars in 2010 in the U.S. and $18.3 billion worldwide respectively. The success of reality shows similar to *Hoops: Life off the Court* is evident as shows like UPN's *The Player* and *Challenge America* and Showtime's *Freshman Diaries* continue to air. Audience market appeal for reality and sports theme programming continues as networks strive to fulfill the demand. *Hoops: Life off the Court* offers an opportunity to tap into this market and offers the dimension for high returns with low production cost.

Hoops, LLC in association with On the Lot Productions, LLC will be producing *Hoops: Life off the Court*. This is the fourth OTLP production has reality show including *The Baker Girls: Sealed With a Kiss, Post Season,* and *The Ace Mechanic.*

Dr. Mel Caudle is the producer for the show. Melissa Caudle, Ph.D., is the author of several books including the books *The Reality of Reality TV and Writing Reality Show Query Pitches.* She also pens screenplays and is the creator of more than five reality shows. Having gotten her start in reality show world on the shows *The Girls Next Door* and *The Little Couple* she went on to create and develop five other reality shows. She is currently developing a TV Pilot series titled *"Does a Name Make a Difference?"* She also is a producer of the feature film *Dark Blue* and the associate producer of *Varla Jean and the Mushroomheads.* Her documentary films include *Dolphins of Terry Cove, Living out Death Row* and *A Heart for Mexico Missions.*

Many opportunities for segment/demo-specific product-placement are available for *Hoops: Life off the Court.* They include but are not limited to: Nike, Gatorade, Ray-ban sunglasses and Burger King. Hoops, LLC will actively seek product endorsements to increase market appeal and advertising revenue sources.

The success of reality shows is directly related to the distribution and marketing strategy. Hoops, LLC will not sit idle and intends to pitch *Hoops: Life off the Court* to the National Association of Television Producers and Executives annual conference in 2011 as well as appropriate festivals. Likewise Hoops, LLC will actively seek to negotiate with appropriate distribution companies known to distribute like genre programming the production. All best efforts to market *Hoops: Life off the Court* will begin during production that includes: establishing a website, Twitter and Facebook accounts for said reality show and cast members, create an EPK package, and seek publicity in magazines and newspapers for the show and cast members. The distribution and marketing strategies are likely to maximize Hoops, LLC's position for future acquisition by networks and distributors as well as increase future profit that *Hoops: Life off the Court* may earn.

Hoops, LLC seeks $475.000 to fund the reality show *Hoops: Life off the Court.* Hoops, LLC desires to obtain all funding from private investors. Investing in any reality is risky and there is no guarantee that there will be a return on investment. **This is a reality show business plan.** It does not imply and shall not be construed as an offering of securities. Prospective investors are not to

3

construe any content of this document as investment, legal or tax advice from either the Company or the preparers of this document. Any prospective investor should consult with professional investment advisors and gain professional legal and tax advice.   Each potential investor specifically understands and agrees that any estimates, projections, revenue models, forecasts or assumptions are by definition uncertain and impossible to obtain from reality show programming. Any party considering a transaction with the Company agrees to look solely to its own due diligence.

An original reality show concept created by Dr. Melissa Caudle

4

The Logline and Synopsis

Logline:

A group of college basketball players engage in life of the court as they develop team dynamics.

Synopsis:

Hoops: Life off the Court, a 13 docudrama reality show, created by Dr. Mel Caudle follows six college basketball players from diverse multi-ethnic economic backgrounds as they come together with the goal of getting to the Final Four. Lebron XXX brings his NBA skills to the platform as he becomes a mentor to the basketball players. On board is their Coach who not only demands perfection but also cohesive team spirit. Throughout each episode, Lebron and their Coach bring challenges for the group hoping that each challenge will help each player become a more confident and professional player. Stakes are heightened when the group realizes they have nothing in common and they don't like each other which is a challenge for their Coach. He is determined differences will not stand in the way of a Final Four Championship.

5

Format and Show Breakdown

FORMAT

Hoops: Life off the Court **is a 13 Episode reality show that follows six college basketball players off the court as they balance studying, practice, friendships and girlfriends. Each episode is 22 minutes.**

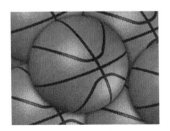

Each show begins by introducing six college basketball players showcasing their individual strengths on the court. They are true athletes in every sense. A challenge is presented by the Coach who makes each player think about what they are doing with the sole purpose of developing team group dynamics and teamwork. He is determined that differences of players will not stand in the way of a Final Four Championship. The Coach offers advice and solutions to help each succeed in their effort and to become a cohesive team. That is the only way that they will become champions. As the players go about their lives trying to incorporate the challenges, they face obstacles of peer pressure, lack of time, physical endurance, and having to maintain a high grade point average for their scholarships. There are surprises and pitfalls along the way they must endure before getting to March Madness and the Final Four in New Orleans, LA. However, each player somehow manages to overcome each obstacle and as a result becomes a better person. The ultimate goal is for the team to get into the Final Four and win a championship. Will they triumph?

Blueprint Structure of Hoops: Life off the Court

4 MINUTES: Opening and introduction of cast.
2 MINUTES: Challenge presentation.
8 MINUTES: Working on the challenge.
5 MINUTES: Obstacle to challenge.
2 MINUTES: Reconciliation.
1 MINUTE: Closure with an outcome to the challenge.

Episode 1 - *Anyone up for a Team?*

Team basketball tryouts for a college championship team occur as the six college basketball players are chosen for the reality show. The six team members are given the challenge to get to know each other off the court. Problems surface when the group discovers they have nothing in common but basketball. They all came from different backgrounds and egos get in the way of true team spirit. Coach intervenes by taking the team on a bowling trip where they discover they have more in common than originally thought. They bring their new friendship to the court during practice and demonstrate their different lifestyles, backgrounds and skills.

Episode 2 - *Walk in my Shoes*

After realizing the team is not coming together on the court, Coach challenges the players to "walk in a different persons shoes" for a weekend. Each player trades places at their day jobs, their home and even swap girlfriends so they can get to know the other. When one of the team members steps out of line with another's girlfriend, the team must find a way to overcome the tension and animosity during an all important basketball game. Coach will except nothing but the best performance and won't allow the conflict to stand in the way of victory. After the game, the team discuss what they learned by walking in another players shoes.

Episode 3 - *Winning isn't Everything*

The team loses an all important game in overtime and feels defeated. Coach steps in to teach the six basketball players the concept - winning isn't everything, but it is the character of the team that counts. He challenges each to whether or not they gave their best performance or did something else stand in the way. Coach sends the team to volunteer for one day at a children's hospital where one player discovers the meaning of giving to others. The team comes together on the court and when one player is injured the game is on the line. The team applies what they learned from one of the children at the hospital.

Episode 4 - *Frat Party*

Overcoming defeat is the most important element to the team. After winning a tough game the team decides to attend a frat party given by the team captain. The all-nighter proves to be more than the team can handle as they have a little too much to drink in violation of the team's unspoken "Code of Conduct." At practice, Coach pushes them to their limit as hangovers interfere. As punishment, Coach brings in a group leader from a local AA meeting. A shocking twist occurs as one of the boy's breakdown and confesses that his father is an alcoholic and suggests he may be as well. The team come together to bring comfort and support and now put the "Code of Conduct" in writing. Coach takes the opportunity to teach the boys that obstacles in life can be overturned with the help of good friends and that a setback is nothing more than a setup for a comeback.

Episode 5 - *Too Little Too Late*

The boys are excited as they win another game. However, after seeing their opponents new uniforms the team decides they want new ones as well. They confront Coach only to be told there isn't any money in the budget for uniforms but if they raise the money themselves they could purchase the uniforms. The team gets together and brainstorm ways to raise money. They decide on putting a "Kissing Booth" on campus and have the team members take turns. One team member contracts Mono from the experience and may have to quit the team while another has a fight with his girlfriend because he participated. Coach comes in and tells the boys their "Kissing Booth" didn't raise enough money for new uniforms and they put another plan into action.

Episode 6 - *Exams*

End of the semester exams adds pressure to an already stressed out team. Coach tries to teach the team time management but it backfires as the team members protests that there simply isn't enough time in the day for the amount of practice Coach wants them to put in. Coach threatens to quit. The team members get into a state of panic as a big game approaches without a coach. The team captain calls a meeting and they decide to apologize to the coach. Will he or won't he come back. Coach puts the team to a test.

Episode 7 – *What Happened to The Scout?*

The team's new uniforms have been delayed. The team learns that a NBA scout will be attending tonight's game. Nerves overwhelm the team and Coach tries to calm the young team down to no avail. One team member, who is still weak from Mono, is told he might not get to play. He gets hysterical because this maybe his only chance to prove he is NBA quality to a scout since this is his senior year. The team awaits the doctor's final recommendation which was bad news for the senior team member. At the start of the game, there is no sign of the professional scout nor the new uniforms. Later the team hears devastating news that the scout was involved in a head-on collision and is in the intensive care unit. The news motivates the team to victory as they dedicate the game to Mother's Against Drunken Drivers (MADD).

Episode 8 – *Things go Bump in the Night*

One of the team members come up missing at practice. When Coach investigates, the team member in question is nowhere to be found. After 24 hours and the player is still missing Coach notifies campus security who in turn notifies the police because they suspect foul play. A city-wide search ensues and the police have identified a person in a hospital who matches the missing team member's description. Coach and team players head to the hospital, but the nursing staff won't let them see the unidentified person because they are not next of kin. They patiently await the arrival of the missing team member's parents hoping for answers. While waiting, the missing team member walks out into the waiting room. He confesses to the team that he is diabetic and that he had kept it a secret and that last night he had an insulin reaction and took off for the hospital to receive help. The team has to play that night's game without him and lose.

Episode 9 – *Secret Santa is for Girls not Boys*

In an effort to build team spirit and bring the boys closer together Coach decides that the basketball team will play "Secret Santa." The team is shaken by the news and don't want to participate in the stupid game, "It's for girls, not boys," the team captain proclaims. However, Coach is adamant about the game and issues an ultimatum – either you participate or you sit the next game out. The team members give in. When one player chooses Coach as his

"Secret Santa" he struggles with what gift he should purchase. He seeks assistance from his other team members. At the party gifts are exchanged and one gift holds a special memory to a teammate that was in foster care.

Episode 10 – *Final Four*

The word is out that the SEC is about to announce the team that goes into the Final Four. The new uniforms arrive as they struggle to find out if they will be included. Being in the Final Four is the biggest question on the minds of the team players and Coach. Coach prepares them for the possibility that the team might not advance and as a result challenges the team to focus on positive outcomes. The countdown begins as anticipation builds. One player breaks up with his girlfriend who thinks he is spending too much time with the team. An ultimatum is given, but will it be accepted.

Episode 11 – *Travel in the Future*

The team learns that they have been selected to go to New Orleans, LA to play in the Final Four Tournament during March Madness. They make their plans and travel by bus. One team member over sleeps and misses the bus. He has to find another way to either catch up with the bus or get to New Orleans by different means and on time in order to play. The team arrives in New Orleans to a party like atmosphere. A dose of reality is given when Coach reminds them of the "Code of Conduct."

Episode 12 – *Bourbon Street Blues*

After a couple of days of travel the team settles into their hotel in New Orleans for participation in March Madness and the Final Four. They take it upon themselves to find out the nightlife of Bourbon Street which defies the "Code of Conduct." One team member spouts off that "At least he didn't break the pre-marital sex scandal of BYU" which infuriates Coach. When Coach finds out that the team went to Bourbon Street he threatens to pull the team from the Final Four tournament hosted by Tulane University. There is a possibility that they came all the way for nothing. The team plays their first opponent and advances.

Episode 13 – *We are the Champions or Not*

The day has arrived for the team to play the final game. Coach brings in Lebron X for a pep talk with the boys. Another surprise for the team as they learn that NBA scouts will also be present. This makes the team nervous as they recall that the first agent had been in a severe car wreck and was injured. They now think they may have a jinx on them and since they are in New Orleans they decide to find a Voodoo Priest to get rid of the jinx. Coach sets out to get the team heads back into the game and not to rely on myth or voodoo but on their skills that they have worked hard on all year. The team arrives to the practice gym and watches the warm-ups of the other teams which intimidate them. They now feel less than secure of their preparation for the Final Four March Madness and question each other. Coach can't believe his ears and for the first time comes down hard on the guys for their lack of confidence and low self-esteem. A special appearance by the NBA scout that was injured in a head-on collision speaks to the team just before they take center court. He delivers a powerful motivational speech which the team takes to heart. Does his speech work? Does the team win the Final Four?

11

Cast Members

The cast for *Hoops: Life off the Court* is a group of talented college-age basketball players from diverse backgrounds.

"Lil Jumper"   "Ice"   "Hooper"   "JC"   "T-Man"   "Bones"

"Lil Jumper" - Jeremy L. XXX, known as "Lil Jumper," is the team captain and there is nothing little about him. Measuring a 6' 11", Jeremy is the tallest of the team members. He is studying to be an attorney and thinks his size will be an asset in the courtroom. He was an All-Star high school basketball player and dreams of moving on to the NBA upon graduation. His enjoys playing video games and listening to rap music during his spare time. He most admires Michael Jordon and what he has done for the game of basketball. He is attached to this project.

"Ice" – Malcolm C. XXX, known as "Ice", has a reputation of being the coldest member of the team and anti-social. "I've never felt that I fit in anywhere unless I was on a basketball court," Malcolm says. He learned to play basketball in the Eastside of New York on the streets and brings that mentality to the court. He considers himself a lady magnet. He is studying to be a technical engineer and one day wants to work for NASA. He most admires Vince Carter and one day wants to play with him on the same team. He is attached to this project.

"Hooper" - Michael XXX, known as "Hooper" won a Hoops contest at the early age of 12. It was then that he got his nickname. His love for basketball came early since his dad has played for the NBA. "Basketball is in my blood," Michael said. "It would be even if my dad didn't play the sport." He is studying geology and one day wants to go on an expedition to Antarctica. He most admires Larry Byrd and likes to think of himself in following in his shoes. He is attached to this project.

"JC" - James XXX, is known as "JC," comes from a small rural community in Mississippi to the big city. He got his nickname because he was named after his father and wanted to be different. "Basketball is my life." JC says. "Every year since I can remember my aunt would give me something to do with basketball. It kinda of stuck. And look at me now." JC is studying business and hopes to one day own his own flight school. He entertains his friends at frat parties by juggling and performing magic tricks. A skill he learned from his granddad. He admires Kobe Bryant the most. He is attached to this project.

"T-Man"- Sam J. XXX, known as T-Man started playing basketball during night tournaments in his hometown of Chicago. "If it weren't for night basketball sponsored by our city I probably would have wound up in jail," Terry says. He got the name T-Man because at the gym people would laugh at him when he stretched out his arms. They were so long that his body made the shape of a "T." Sam is studying architectural design. He most admires Charles Barkley and would like to think they have humor in common. He is attached to this project.

"Bones" - Tso T., known as "Bones" comes from Japan where he is somewhat considered unusual. "I'm taller than most Japanese men," he says. "I knew I'd be tall when I was in the fifth grade. I was at least a foot taller than my classmates." His elementary school classmates gave Tso his nickname because he was so tall and boney. Tso came to America as a foreign exchange student and didn't start playing basketball until his first year in college when Coach saw him walking the campus and recruited him. Tso is studying mathematics, physics and forensics and wants to work as a member of a crime scene unit someday. He admires Yao Ming the most because he says he can identify with him on a cultural basis. He is attached to this project.

"Coach" - Coach Andy XXX is known for recruiting the best college basketball players. Having had his team in the Final Four seven times, Coach knows what it takes to make a winning team. He expects high performance at all times from his team. "You don't get winners unless you expect them to win," Coach says. "I'm looked at as being a hard nose tough guy, but this is no sissy game." Coach has been at the University for 17 years and just recently turned down an assistant coaching job with the Dallas Mavericks. He is attached to this project.

14

The Production Team

Hoops: Life off the Court, LLC is a limited liability corporation that is comprised of professional reality show producers and team members.

The Executive Producer

James XXX is the Executive Producer for *Hoops: Life off the Court*. He brings extensive experience to the production having produced five feature films, two documentaries and two reality shows. He also has directed the feature film *Private Life*.

The Producer/Director

Melissa Caudle, Ph.D., is the author of several books including *The Reality of Reality TV*. Dr. Mel also writes screenplays and is the creator of more than five reality shows such as *The Baker Girls: Sealed with a Kiss*, *Ace Mechanic* and *Post Season*. Having gotten her start in reality show world on the shows *The Girls Next Door* and *The Little Couple* she went on to create and develop five other reality shows. She is currently developing a TV Pilot series titled *"Does a Name Make a Difference?"* She also is a producer of the feature film *Dark Blue* and the associate producer of *Varla Jean and the Mushroomheads*. Her documentary films include *Dolphins of Terry Cove*, *Living out Death Row* and *A Heart for Mexico Missions*.

The Director of Photography

Whitmore XXX is the Director of Photography. His creative talent has been used on a variety of reality shows including *Survivor* and *Celebrity Apprentice*.

Production and Production Schedule

There are three stages to producing a reality show: pre-production, production and post-production. During the pre-production stage all decisions regarding the production itself will be identified, cast members will be secured, crew will be attached, all locations for shooting will be identified, vendors will be identified with appropriate contracts and product placement will be considered. Pre-production will take 6 weeks.

Once pre-production is completed, Hoops, LLC will move into the production phase or principal photography for *Hoops: Life off the Court*. During this time 13 episodes will be filmed. One episode will be filmed each week until the story is completely developed. Principal photography will last 13 weeks.

The Company upon completion of principal photography will immediately transition into post-production. All titling, music and sound will be inserted as well as clearly defined episodes that meet the story development arc. While in post-production, The Company will seek a distributor for the project. Post-production will last 12 weeks.

Production Timeline of Production

Preproduction	6 Weeks
Production	13 Weeks
Post Production	12 Weeks

The Market and Reality Show Trend

THE MARKET

Hoops: Life off the Court offers the viewing audience pure entertainment which is in line with other shows currently on the market that include *The American Challenge, College Life* and *The Player*. Although there are similarities between these shows, *Hoops: Life off the Court* is different in the following ways. *First, Life off the Court* offers a combination of a surveillance type of reality show combines with the competitive sport of basketball. This show also provides tips and coping skills for youth. Audience members that comprise a multi-age-range as well as both male and females will be interested in *Hoops: Life off the Court* because of the social dynamics combined with sports. The *Frat Boy's* reality show is most like *Hoops: Life off the Court*.

THE TREND

According to News Corporation an increase of $121 million in its 2010 fiscal year's second quarter has been reported. Much of that revenue comes from successful reality television programs such as *American Idol*. Top executives at Fox Broadcasting Company are elated too also report that second quarter contributions increased more than 50% from the same period last year. This growth reflects stronger advertising market, particularly to reality shows.

Other networks including but not limited to CBS, NBC, TLC, Fox and BET also have reported in 2010 increased advertising revenue that is coupled with

17

Reality shows market trends. They attributed the results to increased advertising revenue by the National Football League and interest of the American public to watch sports. Other networks such as A&E, TLC, The Discovery Channel, and BET also report an increase in fiscal year 2010 in relationship to advertising dollars when it comes to reality shows.

According to *Forbes* Magazine, the trend of increased spending in advertising began about 6 years ago and continues to spiral upward as the popularity of reality television remains in high demand throughout 2011. Nielsen Company found that the reality television industry continues to gain in popularity with more than 70% of viewers in 2010 say that they watch reality television programming. According to the *Daily Variety* and *the Hollywood Reporter more* than 122 new reality show programs are slated to be produced in 2011, an increase each year since 2006. A recent 2009 study by Nielsen Company ratings reported that when age is a factor, people 18 and younger report that 3 out 4 individuals prefer reality television programming; an industry that is worth an estimated 2.1 billion dollars in the United States as reported by *Advertising Ad Magazine*.

18

Product-Placement

Increasing revenue for advertisers should always be a goal for a reality show and *Hoops: Life off the Court* is perfect for product-placement. Throughout the show, each cast member uses a variety of sporting equipment and clothing. What better way to highlight *Nike* shoes are *Varsity Basketballs* than by naturally using it and having Lil Jumper or Hooper comment on why they insists on wearing *Nike* shoes or *Columbia Sports Wear* off the court. Also, what better way than for cast members to speak of the quality of cell phone service of Verizon and Dell laptops a perfect studying tool. This isn't a throw it your face advertisement but rather a natural progression of how and why Nike shoes and Columbia Sports Wear is the preferred choice. *Hoops: Life off the Court* holds unlimited potential for product placement to increase advertising revenue. Listed below are several companies and their products that would be a perfect match for *Hoops: Life off the Court*.

Listed below are potential companies for product-placement consideration:

Columbia Sports Wear	IBM
Nike	Wilson
Reebok	Spalding
Gatorade	McDavid Hex Pads
Aquafina Water	Attack Jump Ropes
Varsity Sports Wear	Bioflex
Dell	Northface

Distribution

Hoops, LLC will actively seek to negotiate with the following distribution companies known to distribute like genre programming the production and negotiate the best deal for the highest return on investments.

The following distribution companies are respected in this industry and have a reputation of getting results in a domestic market. These companies are: DCT, AXA Distributors, Roxie Releasing Inc., and Seventh Art Releasing, Inc. Likewise, syndication will be sought. The Company will continue to seek other distribution companies in foreign markets which are eager for Western reality shows especially in the UK, Asia, and Indian markets. These companies include: Shadow Distribution, Canadian Warehouse Inc., Variance House, and Northrop Media.

The producers of *Hoops: Life off the Court* reality show will actively seek distributors by attending and networking at NATPE, the national conference held each year in Las Vegas and MIPCOM. When appropriate, a completed show will also be taken to AFM to seek distribution in the television division.

In acquiring a project, a distributor (studio or independent) looks for six basic elements within the show which includes: genre, the storyline, appeal of the cast members to the audience, success and experience of the production company, producer and director, cross-marketing platform with product placement and the amount of money, if any, that is attached to the show.

20

Hoops: Life off the Court reality show addresses these six elements with a genre that continues to successful television programming, an appealing story with a charismatic cast, an experienced and successful production team and myriad opportunities for product-placement and cross-marketing.

Hoops, LLC will use publicity methods in an effort to gain the attention of distributors by releasing a Press Release four times: during pre-production, during production, during post-production and upon completion of project to trade industry magazines such as The *Hollywood Reporter* and *Daily Variety* and through Internet Press Release sites such as PRWIRE.

Also, *Hoops: Life off the Court* will submit production information to IMDB once production begins.

There are several components in place that optimizes *Hoops: Life off the Court* to get domestic and international distribution.

21

Marketing Strategy

The Producers of Hoops: Life off the Court has in place a variety of marketing strategies to not only to gain the attention of viewers but to also attract distribution. The key to a successful reality show is proportionately related to The Company's marketing campaign and strategy. Hoops, LLC will incorporate sound marketing strategies to promote the reality show *Hoops: Life off the Court* which includes but not limited to the following:

Viral Marketing - Viral Marketing, technique to generate word of mouth interest will be used in a variety of methods. All cast members, producers and director will include a tagline introducing the show on all E-mail correspondences.

Website - Hoops.com website will be created and support a cast blog, podcasts, and a monthly newsletter that follows the team's success. The domain site has already been obtained. The company is seeking a professional web designer company to design the website.

Social Networks - Each cast member will create and maintain their individual social network pages including Facebook, Myspace and Twitter accounts.

Magazine Article - Having a freelance journalist on our production is an advantage. Articles about the show, the creators and the cast members will be written and submitted for publication to several key industry magazines across the United States.

YouTube Channel - Hoops Channel will be created on Youtube and cast members will post wild and crazy videos that they make from the cell phones and small hand-held cameras to draw attention to the show. This will be footage that will not be included in the show.

Conferences – The producers of the show will attend at least two of the major marketing conferences in an attempt to obtain distribution.

A Meet and Greet – The cast members will hold several "Meet and Greet" parties when they travel for out of town games which will allow for a general interest of audience members. These parties will be free to the public to enter and hosted at sponsoring vendor's location.

Mini Basketball Camp – The team will sponsor a Mini Basketball Camp free to children where members of the community can join together to promote the team and the show.

Give-a-Ways - Special T-Shirts will be created featuring the Hoops logo and offered at games with registration to the website and newsletter. Also, a Contest will be open to all Youtube viewers for a chance to win T-Shirts with their submission of a video in response.

23

Investment Opportunity

Investing in any reality show is risky. This is a reality show business plan. It does **not imply** and **shall not be construed** as an offering of securities. Prospective investors are **not** to construe the contents of this document as investment, legal or tax advice from either the Company or the preparers of this document. *Any party considering a transaction with the Company agrees to look solely to its own due diligence. NOTHING IS GUARANTEED IN RETURN ON ANY INVESTMENT. AS WITH ANY INVESTMENT THERE ARE RISKS AND ACTUAL RETURNS, IF ANY, ARE UNPREDICTIBLE.* ALL prospective investors **should consult** with professional investment advisors and an entertainment attorney to gain professional legal and tax advice. Each potential investor specifically understands and agrees that any estimates, projections, revenue models, forecasts or assumptions **are** by definition uncertain and thus possibly unreliable and therefore are not included. The return on any investment for a reality show depends on how much the network is willing to pay, audience appeal, advertising revenue and ratings.

Hoops, LLC seeks $475,000 to fund the reality show *Hoops: Life off the Court*. Hoops, LLC desires to obtain all funding from private investors or from obtaining an additional production company to co-produce the show. Investing in any reality is risky and there is no guarantee that there will be a return on investment. **This is a reality show business pitch plan.** It does not imply and shall not be construed as an offering of securities. Prospective investors are not to construe the contents of this document as investment, legal or tax advice from either the Company or the preparers of this document. Any prospective investor should consult with a professional

Investment advisor and gain professional legal and tax advice. Each potential investor specifically understands and agrees that any estimates, projections, revenue models, forecasts or assumptions are by definition uncertain and thus possibly unreliable.   The amount of your investment return is open for negotiation. The Company desires to pursue the best price for the reality show when negotiating the product for sale for distribution. Any party considering a transaction with the Company agrees to look solely to its own due diligence. It is impossible at this time to estimate a return amount of the investment. The return is highly correlated to how much the show sells for and if advertising revenue is generated.

FOR ADDITIONAL INFORMATION CONTACT:

Dr. Mel Caudle
XXX Street
New Orleans, LA 70012
E-mail: drmelcaudle@gmail.com

25

The One-Pager

Genre: Reality Show
Length: 22 Minutes
Episodes: 13
Format: HD 1020

LOGLINE: A group of college basketball players engage in life off the court as they develop team dynamics.

SYNOPSIS: A 13 episode docudrama that follows six college basketball players from diverse multi-ethnic backgrounds as they strive to go to the Final Four. In each episode the players are met with a challenge from their Coach. Lebron X brings his wisdom and expertise as host.

TARGET AUDIENCE: Male/Female - All age ranges

XXX-555-1345
Producer/Director: Dr. Mel Caudle

26

The Budget

PRODUCTION BUDGET					
SUMMARY TOP SHEET					

PROJECT:	Hoops, Life off the Court			BUDGET DATE:	9/5/2010
EXEC. PRODUCER:	James XXX			VERSION:	1
PRODUCER:	Dr. Mel Caudle			PROD. NO.:	sit752
DIRECTOR:	Dr. Mel Caudle			SCRIPT DATE:	Unscripted
PROD. COMPANY:	Hoops, LLC			LOCATIONS:	0
ADDRESS:	XXX			START DATE:	1/5/2010
ADDRESS:	XXX			FINISH DATE:	5/12/2011
TELEPHONE:	XXX	FAX:	0	PREPARED BY:	Mel Caudle
E-MAIL:	XXX			PROD. MGR:	Monique XX

ACCT	DESCRIPTION	GO TO ACCT	TOTAL ACCUM COST TO DATE	BUDGET	(OVER) or UNDER
	ABOVE THE LINE				
1100	STORY RIGHTS & CONTINUITY		0	0	35,000
1200	PRODUCER'S UNIT		0	0	100,000
1300	DIRECTION		0	0	50,000
1400	CAST		0	0	30,000
1500	CAST - TRAVEL & LIVING		0	0	40,000
1900	CAST - FRINGES & TAXES		0	0	1,200
	TOTAL - ABOVE THE LINE		**0**	**0**	**256,200**
	BELOW THE LINE				
	PRODUCTION				
2000	PRODUCTION STAFF		0	0	35,000
2100	EXTRA TALENT & ATMOSPHERE		0	0	0
2200	ART DIRECTION		0	0	0
2300	SET CONSTRUCTION & STRIKE		0	0	0
2500	SET OPERATIONS		0	0	0
2600	SPECIAL EFFECTS		0	0	0
2700	SET DRESSING		0	0	0
2800	PROPERTY		0	0	10,000
2900	WARDROBE		0	0	0
3100	MAKE-UP & HAIRDRESSING		0	0	0
3200	LIGHTING		0	0	5,000
3300	CAMERA		0	0	35,000
3400	PRODUCTION SOUND		0	0	32,000
3500	TRANSPORTATION		0	0	0
3600	LOCATION		0	0	0
3700	PRODUCTION FILM & LAB		0	0	0
3800	PROCESS PHOTOGRAPHY		0	0	0
3900	TESTS		0	0	0
4000	SECOND UNIT		0	0	0
4200	FACILITY PROD EXPENSE		0	0	0
4900	PRODUCTION - FRINGES & TAXES		0	0	16,800
	TOTAL - PRODUCTION PERIOD		**0**	**0**	**113,800**
	POST PRODUCTION				
4500	EDITING		0	0	33,000
4600	MUSIC		0	0	0
4700	POST PRODUCTION SOUND		0	0	0
4800	POST PROD. FILM & LAB		0	0	0
4900	MAIN & END TITLES		0	0	0
5100	PROJECTION		0	0	0
5200	POST PROD - FRINGES & TAXES		0	0	10,000
	TOTAL - POST PROD. PERIOD		**0**	**0**	**43,000**
	OTHER COSTS				
6500	PUBLICITY & PROMOTION		0	0	25,000
6600	LEGAL & ACCOUNTING		0	0	6,000
6700	INSURANCE		0	0	10,000
6800	OVERHEAD		0	0	0
6900	MISCELLANEOUS		0	0	10,000
	TOTAL - OTHER COSTS		**0**	**0**	**51,000**
	TOTAL ABOVE THE LINE		0	0	256,200
	TOTAL BELOW THE LINE		0	0	207,800
7000	FINANCE		0	0	0
7100	COMPLETION BOND		0	0	0
7200	CONTINGENCY		0	0	11,000
	GRAND TOTAL		**0**	**0**	**475,000**

Hoops Budget2/20/2011

APPENDIX

Resumes

Letters of Intent

Press Releases

News Clippings

Note: To conserve space the resumes, Letters of Intent, Press Releases and News Clippings will not be included.

∞∞∞∞∞∞∞∞∞∞∞∞

PHOTOGRAPHY CREDIT FOR CHAPTER 19
Chapter 19 Cover photo by Dr. Mel Caudle
Logo graphics for Hoops: Life off the Court by Dr. Mel Caudle
Basketball photo by Salvatore Vuono
"Lil Jumper" - AKA Jeremy L. Photo taken by Samuel Heist
"Ice" – AKA Malcolm C. photo taken by Graur Razvan Ionut
"JC" – AKA James C. photo taken by Emily Zahner
"T-Man" – AKA Sam J. photo taken by his best-friend Marcus Shelby
"Hooper" –AKA photo by Graur Razvan Ionut
"Bones" – AKA Tso T. photo taken by Graur Razvan Ionut
"Coach" – AKA Andy Coach photo taken by Andy Newson
Dr. Mel Photo by Robert Zaning Portrait Studio

APPENDIX A

Commonly Misspelled Words

The following is a list of frequently misspelled words. In some cases, a particularly common misspelling is given in parentheses.

accelerate	exhilarate	pharaoh *(pharoah)*
accidentally *(accidently)*	existence *(existance)*	pigeon *(pidgeon)*
accommodate accordion	Fahrenheit	plagiarize
(accordian) accumulate	fiery *(firey)*	playwright
acquaintance	flabbergast	plenitude *(plentitude)*
(acquaintence,	*(flabberghast)*	poinsettia *(pointsettia)*
aquaintance)	flotation *(floatation)*	precede
acquire *(aquire)*	frustum *(frustrum)*	presumptuous
acquit *(aquit)*	gauge	*(presumptious)*
aficionado	genius *(genious; see*	proceed
a lot *(alot)*	*"ingenious")*	pronunciation
amateur	grammar *(grammer)*	*(pronounciation)*
anoint	gross	propagate
apology	guttural	privilege *(priviledge)*
argument *(arguement)*	handkerchief	puerile
atheist	*(hankerchief)*	pursue *(persue)*
a while *(awhile)*	harass *(harrass)*	putrefy
axle *(axel)*	horrific	questionnaire
barbecue *(barbeque)*	hypocrisy	raspberry
believable *(believeable)*	imitate	receipt
believe	immediately	receive
broccoli *(brocolli)*	inadvertent	recommend
camouflage	*(inadvertant)*	refrigerator *(refridgerator)*
cantaloupe	incidentally *(incidently)*	renowned
carburetor	incredible	rhythm
Caribbean	independent	ridiculous
cartilage	indispensable	sacrilegious
cemetery *(cemetary)*	*(indispensible)*	sandal
chauvinism	ingenious *(ingenius;*	savvy
(chauvanism)	*see "genius")*	seize *(sieze)*
chili	inoculate *(innoculate)*	sensible *(sensable)*
chocolaty *(chocolatey)*	irascible	separate
coliseum, also	irresistible *(irresistable)*	septuagenarian
colosseum *(colliseum)*	its *(it's)*	*(septagenarian)*
collectible *(collectable)*	judgment *(judgement)*	sergeant
colonel	led *(lead)*	sheriff
commemorate	liaison	shish kebab
congratulations	lieutenant	siege
conscious	liquefy *(liquify)*	similar
consensus	lose *(loose)*	simile
coolly	maneuver, also	sorcerer *(sorceror)*
daiquiri	manoeuvre	subpoena
Dalmatian *(Dalmation)*	marshmallow	supersede *(supercede)*
deceive	*(marshmellow)*	tariff

defendant	medieval, also	their
definite *(definate)*	mediaeval	there
desiccate	memento *(momento)*	they're
desperate	millennium *(millenium)*	threshold
deterrence	minuscule *(miniscule)*	tongue
development	mischief *(mischeif)*	too *(to)*
(developement)	mischievous	tragedy
diorama	*(mischievious)*	tyranny
disappear	misogyny	ukulele *(ukelele)*
disappoint	missile	until *(untill)*
dissipate	misspell *(mispell)*	vacuum
drunkenness	nauseous	vicious
(drunkeness)	necessary	weird
dumbbell	no one *(noone)*	you're *(your)*
(dumbell)	occasion	
ecstasy	occurrence	
embarrass	octopus	
exercise *(excercise)*	onomatopoeia	
	parallel	
	parliament	
	pastime *(pasttime)*	
	peninsula	

Page | **391**

INDEX

ABOUT THE AUTHOR

Dr. Melissa Caudle earned a Ph.D. in statistical research and administration from the University of New Orleans. She is a retired award winning high school principal who came into the television and film production arena in 1986. Capitalizing on her educational training and background, she uses her experience to bring the reader a step-by-step guided teaching format so readers can learn how to write reality show business plans.

Dr. Melissa Caudle is an experienced reality show creator and producer and brings her expertise in the area of writing business plans for reality shows to you the reader. Dr. Mel has built a solid reputation as a reality show creator having started as a production coordinator in New Orleans, La on the reality show, *The Girls Next Door* featuring the three Playmates and Hugh Hefner. That was the beginning of transferring her knowledge from feature film production to reality shows. She discovered quickly that although there were vast similarities there were also substantial differences. Two significant differences were pitching a reality show and developing a business plan for one. Isolating the differences came as a direct result of applying her experience as an adjunct professor, teacher and researcher. "I never knew that a Ph.D. in Statistical Analysis would prove beneficial in creating reality shows and business plans, "she says. "But it did."

Since that time Dr. Mel has created five reality shows, produced four, and is currently in the process of developing two others at the time she wrote this book. Dr. Mel is the producer and director of the reality show featuring Darren Sharper, Super Bowl Champion with the New Orleans Saints, called *Darren: Sharper Than Ever, Lisa's House*, and is currently producing the reality Show *The Ace Mechanic* , Hoops: *Life off the Court*, and *The Baker Girls: Sealed with a Kiss* all of which she wrote each business plan. Lastly, she just pitched and optioned a new TV pilot series; *Does a Name Make a Difference?* This show will feature people with the same first and last names and investigate to determine if their name really does make a difference.

Producers and creators of reality shows worldwide consult with Dr. Mel on writing a business plans specifically for reality shows. "It's a tangled web that nobody wants to share how to develop," she says. "That is until now. I'm taking my 12 years of experience in production and tapping into my experience as a teacher and professor to bring knowledge to those who seek."

Dr. Mel is also a feature and documentary filmmaker. Her credits include producer on the feature film *Dark Blue* and associate producer

on the films *Varla Jean and the Mushroomheads* and *Girls Gone Gangsta*. She is in production of the feature film *Hunter*. She also produced and directed documentary films including *Mexico Missions*, *The Dolphins in Terry Cove*, *The Alabama Gulf Coast Zoo*, *Sean Kelly's Irish Pub*, *Beauvoir* and *Voices of the Innocent*. Dr. Mel has worked as a crew member on films two Sony films, *STRAWDOGS* starring Kate Bosworth, James Marsden, James Woods and Alexander Skarsgard, and *MARDI GRAS* starring Carmen Electra and Josh Gad.

Dr. Mel has written nine screenplays: *Never Stop Running* (Suspense/Thriller), *Auditing Richard Biggs*, *A.D.A.M.*, *MK-ULTRA*, *The Angelics* (SyFy); *Dreamweaver* (Drama), *Dragonfly Principal* (Drama), *The Lost Disciple* (Action/Drama) and *Secret Romance* (Romantic Comedy). She has placed in the *Scriptdig Screenplay Contest* as a

Quarter-finalist in both screenplay and TV pilot category and was a semi-finalist in *The Page International Screenwriting Contest*. She is also a frequent panelist at film festivals and pitching seminars. For more information on her books, screenplays or reality shows by Dr. Mel Caudle, visit her websites located at: www.drmelcaudle.com or www.onthelorproductions.com.   To contact Dr. Mel for a speaking engagement email her at drmelcaudle@google.com.

Screenplays

A.D.A.M written by Dr. Melissa Caudle

MK-Ultra written by Dr. Melissa Caudle

Auditing Richard Biggs written by Dr. Melissa Caudle and Dennis W. Martin

Secret Romance written by Dr. Melissa Caudle

Never Stop Running written by Dr. Melissa Caudle

The Angelics written by Dr. Melissa Caudle and David Repogle

Dreamweaver written by Dr. Melissa Caudle and Michael Ragsdale

Dragonfly Principal written by Dr. Melissa Caudle and Gabriel Dyan

Reality Shows

Films

Dark Blue – Produced by New Guy Films in association with On the Lot Productions, LLC

Varla Jean and the Mushroomheads – Assoicate Producer – filmed by Danny Girl Productions

Girls Gone Gangsta – Associate Producer – filmed by G3 Films

New Orleans, LA   **Gulf Shores, AL**

Dr. Melissa Caudle is available for consult on your reality show project by appoint on Skype or at her office. She is also available to travel to your city. She can help you develop your reality show, design or review your reality show business plan, field produce your show. She provides valuable assistance in many areas for your reality show.

Dr. Mel is available to speak at film festivals and seminars in your area. Reach her by E-mailing her at drmelcaudle@gmail.com or visit her production website, On the Lot Productions, LLC, located at www.onthelotproductions.com.

Made in the USA
Lexington, KY
10 September 2012